Clinical Intelligence for Attorneys

Reconstructing the Patient's Clinical Story Before Building the Legal Case

MICHELLE CARROLL

Founder & CEO, Lexcura Summit

First Revised Edition

Published by Lexcura Summit.

Clinical Intelligence for Better Litigation Decisions™

Preface

The most important decision in a healthcare case is often made before the attorney fully understands what happened to the patient. It is the decision to accept the case, invest in it, and begin building the theory that will guide everything that follows.

At intake, the attorney may have a compelling account from the patient or family, a devastating outcome, selected medical records, and an allegation that appears clinically reasonable. There may be evidence of a delayed diagnosis, a medication error, a failure to recognize deterioration, an unexpected surgical complication, or another event that seems difficult to explain. The concerns may be genuine, but the clinical story is rarely complete at that stage.

That creates an immediate problem. The first decision is also the decision most likely to shape every later one, yet it is often made when the attorney has the least reliable understanding of the case. Once the matter is accepted, records are pursued, experts are retained, costs begin accumulating, and the original allegation gradually develops into a formal litigation theory. The client's expectations also change. Even when everyone remains committed to objectivity, the case begins acquiring momentum, and momentum can make it increasingly difficult to step back when later evidence challenges the original understanding.

Traditional medical record review does not always protect the attorney from that risk. A chronology may accurately show what was documented. A narrative summary may explain the treatment. A reviewer may identify apparent deviations from care. Each of those products can be valuable, but they do not necessarily determine whether the evidence supports a sustainable case. They often organize the record without integrating the patient, physiology, progression, professional obligations, system conditions, and outcome into one clinical explanation.

That is the difference Clinical Intelligence was developed to address.

The Lexcura Clinical Intelligence Model™ does not begin by asking whether the allegation appears persuasive. It begins by asking whether the attorney has enough reliable clinical understanding to make the first decision safely. Are the records complete? Who was the patient before the event? What did the imaging and other objective evidence actually show? When did the patient's condition begin to change? At what point should a reasonably competent professional have responded differently? Did the healthcare system contribute to the failure? Most importantly, did any of those failures probably alter the patient's outcome?

Those questions change the intake process because they separate a serious outcome from a sustainable case. A devastating injury may exist without a supportable breach. An obvious error may have little causal significance. A delayed response may appear central until the timeline shows that the intervention window had already closed. Conversely, a matter that initially appears weak may become much stronger when missing records, prior imaging, or a reconstructed progression reveals a clinically meaningful opportunity that had not previously been recognized.

This is where Clinical Intelligence offers an advantage over traditional review. It gives the attorney more than an organized medical history. It provides an integrated clinical understanding that can be used to make decisions about acceptance, expert retention, discovery, valuation, settlement, and trial strategy. It identifies what is known, what remains uncertain, what evidence is missing, where the theory is strongest, and where it is likely to be challenged.

The purpose is not to replace attorneys or experts. It is to ensure that both begin from the strongest possible clinical foundation.

The attorney still makes the legal decision. The retained expert still provides the formal specialty opinion. Clinical Intelligence makes those decisions more informed because the patient's complete clinical journey has been reconstructed before the case is allowed to build momentum around an incomplete or misleading first impression.

That is why the first decision matters so much. Every later decision depends upon it.

And that is where this book begins.

Contents

PART I

BEGINNING WITH THE PATIENT

The clinical investigation that must precede the legal theory

CHAPTER 1

Why Traditional Medical Record Review Is No Longer Enough

For decades, medical record review has been one of the foundations of healthcare litigation. Attorneys have relied on experienced nurses, physicians, therapists, and other clinicians to organize medical records, summarize treatment, identify potential departures from accepted practice, and explain complex clinical issues in language that supports legal analysis. That work has been invaluable to the legal profession and continues to play an essential role in the investigation of healthcare cases.

This book is not an argument against traditional medical record review.

In fact, it begins by recognizing the enormous contribution that medical record reviewers have made to healthcare litigation over many years. Without their work, attorneys would be left trying to navigate thousands of pages of highly technical documentation without the benefit of clinical interpretation. Chronologies, narrative summaries, standard of care reviews, and expert consultations have helped attorneys understand complex medicine and have become established components of the litigation process.

The question, however, is no longer whether traditional medical record review has value.

The question is whether it is sufficient for the healthcare cases attorneys are handling today.

Healthcare has changed dramatically over the past several decades. Patients often receive treatment across multiple hospitals, physician groups, rehabilitation facilities, home health agencies, and outpatient clinics. A single hospitalization may generate several thousand pages of electronic health records, imaging studies, laboratory data, medication administration records, telemetry strips, consultation reports, operative notes, and regulatory documentation. At the same time, healthcare litigation has become increasingly sophisticated. Attorneys are expected to evaluate complex clinical decisions, organizational failures, regulatory compliance, competing expert opinions, and intricate questions of causation while developing litigation strategies that may ultimately determine the outcome of the case.

As healthcare became more complex, I began noticing something that I could not easily explain.

Two experienced clinicians could review exactly the same medical records and reach very different conclusions. Both reviewers could be knowledgeable. Both could be conscientious. Both could genuinely believe they had interpreted the records correctly. Yet one might conclude that the standard of care had clearly been breached, while the other believed the care was entirely appropriate. One might identify strong evidence of causation, while another found the relationship between the alleged breach and the patient's outcome far less convincing.

At first, I assumed that these differences reflected variations in clinical experience or specialty background. To some extent, they did. Different professionals naturally bring different perspectives to complex cases. The more cases I reviewed, however, the more I realized that something else was happening.

The reviewers were often answering different questions.

One reviewer might concentrate primarily on whether the documentation supported a departure from the standard of care. Another focused on the chronology of treatment. A third emphasized the patient's pre-existing medical conditions. A fourth examined the imaging. Each review was clinically sound within its own scope, yet no one was necessarily reconstructing the patient's complete clinical journey before reaching a conclusion.

That observation became increasingly important because litigation decisions are rarely based on one clinical issue in isolation.

An attorney deciding whether to accept a case is not simply asking whether a delay occurred. The attorney also needs to know whether the delay was clinically significant, whether meaningful intervention remained possible, whether the patient's baseline altered the likely outcome, whether the objective evidence supports the proposed mechanism of injury, whether the healthcare system influenced the decisions being made, and whether the available evidence is sufficient to support the litigation theory that is beginning to develop.

Those questions cannot be answered reliably by looking at one part of the case at a time.

They require the entire clinical picture to be reconstructed before the legal analysis begins.

That distinction became the turning point in my own thinking.

Traditional medical record review is exceptionally effective at organizing information. It tells us what was documented, when events occurred, what treatment was provided, and where potential concerns may exist. Those functions remain essential and should never be undervalued.

Clinical Intelligence asks a different question.

It asks what all of that information means once it has been tested, connected, and understood as a single clinical investigation.

That difference may appear subtle, but in practice it changes almost every stage of healthcare litigation.

A chronology may accurately document that antibiotics were administered six hours after a patient arrived in the emergency department. Clinical Intelligence asks whether the patient's physiological deterioration had already become recognizable before that point, when a reasonably competent clinician should have suspected sepsis, what objective evidence supported that suspicion, whether earlier intervention remained capable of altering the patient's outcome, and how those findings should influence liability, causation, expert selection, and litigation strategy.

A narrative summary may identify that a patient developed neurological deficits following surgery. Clinical Intelligence asks whether those deficits were consistent with the patient's baseline condition, when they first became objectively identifiable, whether imaging supported progressive deterioration, what intervention opportunities existed, and whether the evidence supports a clinically sustainable theory that the delay materially altered the patient's long-term outcome.

The difference is not that one review is accurate and the other is inaccurate.

The difference is that they serve different purposes. Traditional medical record review organizes and explains the medical evidence.

Clinical Intelligence integrates, tests, and interprets that evidence so the attorney understands not only what happened, but what the evidence means for the litigation.

That distinction became increasingly important to me because I began seeing cases that appeared very strong during the initial review but weakened considerably once the patient's baseline, imaging, chronology, and causation pathway were examined together. I also saw cases that appeared relatively weak at intake become substantially stronger after missing records were obtained, objective evidence was integrated into the chronology, and the patient's complete clinical journey was reconstructed.

Those experiences convinced me that the greatest risk in healthcare litigation often occurs at the very beginning of the case.

Not because attorneys lack judgment. Not because reviewers lack expertise.

But because the first litigation decisions are frequently made before anyone has reconstructed the complete clinical picture.

That realization became the foundation of Clinical Intelligence. It was never intended to replace traditional medical record review. It was developed to build upon it. Medical record review remains the foundation.

Clinical Intelligence becomes the structure built upon that foundation. One organizes the evidence.

The other transforms that evidence into disciplined clinical understanding that can guide every litigation decision that follows.

One of the misconceptions I occasionally hear is that Clinical Intelligence simply represents a more detailed medical record review. On the surface, that assumption is understandable because both begin with the same material. Both require medical records, both involve clinical analysis, and both seek to help attorneys understand complicated healthcare issues. It would be easy to conclude that Clinical Intelligence simply produces a longer report or a more comprehensive chronology.

That is not the difference. The difference lies in the objective of the investigation.

Traditional medical record review is generally designed to explain what is contained within the medical record. The reviewer organizes documentation, summarizes treatment, identifies significant events, and may comment on potential departures from accepted practice. It provides an organized understanding of the documentation itself.

Clinical Intelligence begins with a different premise.

It assumes that the documentation, while essential, is only one source of evidence. The patient's story must be reconstructed from every available source of reliable clinical information before meaningful litigation decisions can be made. Documentation is tested against physiology. Clinical observations are compared with objective findings. Imaging is examined alongside progress notes. The patient's baseline is reconstructed before deterioration is evaluated. Organizational factors are considered alongside individual clinical decisions. Every discipline is tested against the others until the entire clinical picture becomes internally consistent.

That process often produces findings that would never become apparent if each component were reviewed independently.

Consider the following example.

An attorney receives a potential sepsis case involving the death of a sixty-eight-year-old patient following admission through the emergency department. The family reports that the patient waited several hours before antibiotics were administered and believes the delay caused the patient's death. The medical records appear to support that account. The chronology shows a delay between presentation and treatment, and several nursing notes describe progressive deterioration during that period.

A traditional review would quite properly identify those events, summarize the sequence, and note that delayed antibiotic administration may warrant further evaluation by an appropriate expert.

Clinical Intelligence asks several additional questions before reaching that point.

Was sepsis clinically recognizable when the patient first arrived, or did the diagnostic criteria develop later? What objective evidence existed at each stage of the admission? Were abnormal laboratory findings available before the deterioration became obvious? Did the patient's pre-existing illnesses alter the interpretation of those findings? Was there still a realistic opportunity to change the outcome once the delay occurred? Did staffing levels, communication failures, or escalation processes contribute to the delayed recognition?

Those additional questions fundamentally change the investigation because they move beyond identifying an apparent delay and begin testing whether the delay is clinically meaningful.

In one case, the analysis may conclude that the patient's deterioration was already well advanced before arrival and that earlier antibiotics were unlikely to have altered the ultimate outcome. In another, the investigation may demonstrate that objective evidence supporting sepsis was present several hours before treatment began, that escalation opportunities were repeatedly missed, and that timely intervention would probably have prevented irreversible organ failure.

The chronology may appear similar in both cases. The litigation value is not.

That distinction is one of the reasons Clinical Intelligence places such emphasis on disciplined investigation rather than isolated findings. Attorneys do not simply need to know that an event occurred. They need to understand whether the event changes the strength of the case.

The same principle applies across virtually every area of healthcare litigation. A delayed stroke diagnosis is not automatically malpractice. A medication error does not automatically establish causation. An unexpected surgical complication is not necessarily evidence of negligence.

Likewise, documentation stating that care was appropriate does not automatically mean the care actually met the applicable standard.

Clinical Intelligence requires every conclusion to be tested against the complete clinical picture before it becomes part of the litigation strategy.

That disciplined approach also changes the way attorneys think about expert witnesses.

Many firms retain experts early in the process, often because they need guidance before deciding whether to invest further in the case. There is nothing inherently wrong with that approach, and expert involvement remains indispensable in healthcare litigation. The difficulty is that experts are frequently asked to evaluate a case before the underlying clinical investigation has been completed.

As a result, the expert may spend valuable time reconstructing the chronology, identifying missing records, establishing the patient's baseline, or resolving inconsistencies in the documentation before addressing the specialist questions they were actually retained to answer.

Clinical Intelligence changes that sequence.

Instead of asking the expert to begin the investigation, it asks the expert to build upon an investigation that has already been systematically performed. The chronology has been reconstructed. The patient's baseline has been established. The objective evidence has been integrated. Missing information has been identified. The likely breach points have been tested against the available evidence. The causation questions requiring specialist opinion have been clearly defined.

The expert is no longer trying to discover the clinical story.

The expert is applying specialized knowledge to a clinical story that has already been carefully reconstructed.

That distinction saves time, improves efficiency, reduces unnecessary cost, and often results in more focused expert opinions because the investigation has already answered many of the foundational questions that do not require specialty expertise.

One of the earliest questions you should ask when reviewing any healthcare case is not "Do I have negligence?" but rather:

"Do I understand the patient's complete clinical story well enough to decide whether negligence is clinically sustainable?"

Those are two very different questions. The first begins with the allegation. The second begins with the evidence. Clinical Intelligence always begins with the evidence.

One of the greatest strengths of traditional medical record review is that it brings order to what often appears to be overwhelming amounts of information. Anyone who has handled healthcare litigation understands how quickly medical records accumulate. A relatively straightforward hospital admission can generate thousands of pages of documentation. Add records from emergency medical services, primary care physicians, specialists, rehabilitation facilities, home health agencies, pharmacies, and prior hospitalizations, and the volume of information can become difficult to manage before any meaningful analysis has even begun.

Chronologies and narrative summaries solve an important part of that problem. They organize the information, place events into sequence, and allow attorneys to navigate the records far more efficiently than attempting to review them page by page. That alone saves considerable time and remains an essential component of every healthcare case.

Clinical Intelligence does not replace that process. It starts where that process naturally ends. Organizing records and understanding records are not the same thing.

Knowing that a patient's oxygen saturation fell from ninety-six percent to eighty-eight percent over several hours is important. Understanding why that deterioration occurred, whether it should have been recognized sooner, whether appropriate intervention remained available, whether the patient's underlying physiology altered the interpretation of those findings, and whether that progression ultimately influenced the outcome requires a completely different level of investigation.

That distinction may appear subtle when discussed in theory, but in practice it changes the entire direction of the case.

Consider another example.

A fifty-four-year-old patient undergoes routine abdominal surgery and is transferred to the surgical floor following an uncomplicated procedure. During the evening shift, nursing documentation records increasing pain, tachycardia, falling blood pressure, reduced urine output, and progressive abdominal distention. Overnight, those findings continue to worsen. Early the following morning the patient is returned to the operating room where significant internal bleeding is identified.

A traditional medical record review would likely produce an excellent chronology. The reviewer would identify the changing observations, summarize the nursing documentation, describe the physician assessments, outline the timing of the return to surgery, and note that delayed recognition of postoperative bleeding should be evaluated further.

All of that information is useful. Clinical Intelligence continues asking questions.

- When did the physiological evidence first suggest that the patient was no longer following an expected postoperative course?
- Which observations represented ordinary recovery, and which should have prompted immediate reassessment?
- Did the nursing staff recognize the significance of the changing observations but encounter barriers to escalation?
- Were the treating clinicians interpreting each observation independently rather than recognizing the pattern developing over time?
- Did existing hospital policies support timely escalation, or were there organizational failures that delayed intervention?
- Most importantly, at what point did meaningful opportunity still exist to alter the patient's outcome?

Notice how the investigation has changed. We are no longer reviewing documentation. We are reconstructing clinical decision-making.

That difference becomes enormously important during litigation because attorneys are not trying to prove that observations were documented. They are trying to establish whether reasonably competent healthcare professionals should have interpreted those observations differently, acted differently, and, if so, whether those actions would probably have changed the patient's outcome.

Those questions cannot be answered by chronology alone.

They require the chronology to be interpreted within the context of human physiology, clinical judgment, professional responsibility, healthcare systems, and causation.

That is the point at which Clinical Intelligence begins to distinguish itself from traditional review.

It is not adding more information.

It is increasing the quality of the understanding derived from the information already available.

I think this distinction is one of the easiest ways to understand the relationship between traditional medical record review and Clinical Intelligence.

Traditional review asks, "What happened?" Clinical Intelligence asks,

"Why did it happen, what should have happened instead, did the difference matter, and how should that influence the litigation?"

Those are fundamentally different investigations. One describes events. The other evaluates their significance. One organizes information. The other develops clinically defensible understanding. Neither is unnecessary. In fact, one depends upon the other.

Without an accurate medical record review, Clinical Intelligence has no reliable foundation upon which to build. Equally, without Clinical Intelligence, even an excellent medical record review may leave the attorney responsible for integrating the clinical findings into a litigation strategy that has not yet been fully tested.

That relationship is important because I do not see these approaches as competitors.

I see them as successive stages of the same investigation. The first stage establishes the facts. The second determines what those facts actually mean.

For the attorney, that distinction has practical consequences from the very beginning of the case. It influences whether additional records should be requested before experts are retained. It helps determine whether the apparent breach remains significant once the patient's baseline has been reconstructed. It identifies situations in which the chronology appears compelling but the objective evidence tells a different story. It highlights where organizational failures may be just as important as individual clinical decisions. It also allows the attorney to distinguish between a case that appears persuasive and one that is likely to remain persuasive after it has been challenged by experienced defense experts.

That last point deserves particular attention because every experienced litigator understands that healthcare cases rarely become easier as they progress.

The initial records may appear compelling. The family may present a convincing account of what happened. The alleged breach may seem obvious. Then additional records arrive. Prior imaging becomes available.

Another specialist offers an alternative interpretation. The patient's medical history proves more complicated than originally understood.

A defense expert introduces a physiological explanation that had not previously been considered.

It is at that stage that many litigation theories begin to weaken, not because anyone acted improperly, but because the original theory had never been tested against the complete clinical picture.

Clinical Intelligence attempts to perform that testing much earlier.

Rather than allowing the litigation theory to develop first and the clinical investigation to follow, it reverses the process. The clinical investigation is completed first. The litigation strategy is then built upon the strongest understanding the available evidence can support.

That difference, in my opinion, is not simply an improvement in medical record review.

It represents a different philosophy of healthcare litigation.

Instead of asking the evidence to support an existing theory, Clinical Intelligence requires the theory to emerge from the evidence itself.

One of the easiest ways to recognize the difference between traditional medical record review and Clinical Intelligence is to ask a simple question at the end of every review.

"Do I understand what happened?" or

"Do I understand why it happened, whether it should have happened, whether it could have been prevented, and how that should influence every legal decision that follows?"

The first question explains the case. The second prepares the attorney to litigate it.

One of the questions attorneys should ask themselves at the beginning of every healthcare case is surprisingly simple.

"What am I actually investigating?"

At first glance, that question appears to have an obvious answer. The attorney is investigating an allegation of negligence. A patient has suffered an injury, a serious complication, or perhaps a death, and someone believes that the healthcare provided fell below an acceptable standard. The purpose of the investigation, therefore, is to determine whether the allegation can be supported by the evidence.

In reality, that is not the first question that should be answered.

Before an attorney can determine whether negligence occurred, they must first understand what actually happened to the patient. Those two questions are related, but they are not the same.

This distinction is more important than it may first appear because allegations often begin with an outcome rather than with an investigation. A family experiences a devastating loss, a patient suffers a permanent injury, or an unexpected complication changes the course of someone's life. Understandably, they want to know why it happened. By the time the attorney becomes involved, the allegation has usually begun to take shape. Certain events are considered important, others are overlooked, and an initial theory of the case often starts to emerge before the clinical evidence has been examined in its entirety.

That process is entirely understandable. It is also where the first clinical risk begins.

Clinical Intelligence deliberately separates the allegation from the investigation. It does not begin by asking whether the allegation appears convincing. It begins by asking whether the evidence supports the allegation once the patient's entire clinical journey has been reconstructed. That distinction protects both the attorney and the client because it prevents the litigation strategy from becoming anchored to an early assumption that may later prove to be incomplete or incorrect.

To understand why this matters, consider the following example.

Case example: When the Allegation Is Not the Investigation

A sixty-two-year-old patient undergoes elective spinal surgery. During recovery, the patient develops progressive weakness in both legs. Several hours later, emergency imaging identifies a postoperative epidural hematoma requiring urgent decompression. Despite surgery, the patient is left with permanent neurological deficits.

The family believes the hospital failed to respond quickly enough when the patient first complained of increasing pain and weakness. They contact an attorney convinced that the delay in returning the patient to the operating room caused the permanent injury.

At intake, the allegation appears compelling.

The medical records confirm that neurological observations changed over several hours. There are documented delays in communication between nursing staff and the surgical team. The outcome is catastrophic. The chronology appears to support the family's concerns.

A traditional medical record review would likely identify each of those events accurately. The chronology would be organized, the documentation summarized, and the apparent delays highlighted for further consideration.

Clinical Intelligence asks the attorney to pause before drawing conclusions.

Before deciding whether the delay represents actionable negligence, the investigation asks several additional questions.

- When did the patient's neurological deterioration become objectively identifiable rather than simply suggestive of routine postoperative pain?
- Were there earlier clinical signs that should reasonably have prompted reassessment?

Did the treating team appreciate the significance of the changing neurological findings, or were those findings obscured by medications, expected postoperative symptoms, or incomplete assessments?

- How rapidly was the hematoma progressing?

Most importantly, if the patient had returned to surgery at the earliest clinically reasonable opportunity, is there objective evidence that the long-term neurological outcome would probably have been different?

Those questions may appear subtle, but they often determine whether the case succeeds or fails.

If the investigation demonstrates that meaningful neurological function could probably have been preserved through earlier intervention, the delay becomes clinically significant. If, however, the evidence shows that irreversible spinal cord injury had already occurred before the delay became clinically recognizable, the litigation theory changes considerably. The delay may still represent a departure from accepted practice, but the relationship between that departure and the patient's permanent injury becomes far more difficult to establish.

The allegation has not changed. The records have not changed. What has changed is the attorney's understanding of the evidence. That distinction lies at the heart of Clinical Intelligence. The purpose is not to prove or disprove negligence.

The purpose is to ensure that every allegation is tested against the complete clinical picture before the attorney commits the case to a litigation strategy.

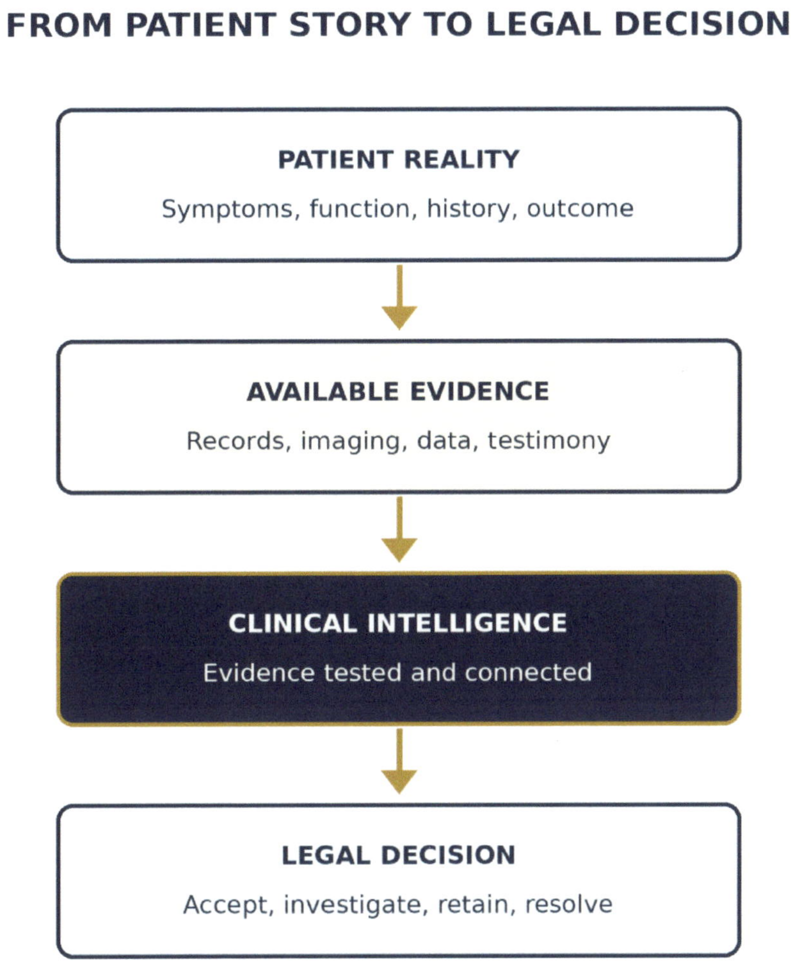

Figure 1 Clinical Intelligence reconstructs the patient first so the legal decision rests on tested clinical meaning.

CHAPTER 2

The Decision That Shapes the Entire Case

Why This Changes the Attorney's First Decision

This example illustrates why the first decision in a healthcare case deserves such careful attention. Once a case is accepted, it begins to acquire momentum. Experts are retained, litigation costs increase, discovery is planned, and the attorney naturally begins refining the legal theory. If that theory has developed before the clinical investigation is complete, later evidence may require significant changes to the strategy, sometimes after substantial time and expense have already been invested.

Clinical Intelligence is designed to reduce that risk.

It does so by ensuring that the investigation is driven by the evidence rather than by the allegation. Every subsequent discipline within the Lexcura Clinical Intelligence Model™ builds upon that same principle. The integrity of the records must first be established. The patient's baseline must then be understood. The chronology must be reconstructed, the standard of care evaluated, the organizational influences examined, and the causal relationship tested before the attorney can confidently determine the true strengths and weaknesses of the case.

Only then does the litigation strategy rest upon a clinically defensible foundation rather than an early impression.

One of the questions I encourage attorneys to ask at the beginning of every healthcare case is not whether the records appear complete, but whether they are clinically complete. Those two concepts are often confused, yet they can lead to very different investigations.

A file may contain every page that was requested from every healthcare provider involved in the patient's care. From an administrative perspective, the record set is complete. The attorney has received everything that was asked for, and the reviewer can begin organizing the documentation. Unfortunately, having every available record does not necessarily mean the attorney has every piece of evidence needed to understand the patient's clinical journey.

Clinical completeness is something very different.

Clinical completeness asks whether the available evidence is sufficient to explain the patient's progression, the clinical decisions that were made, and the outcome that followed. If any of those questions cannot be answered confidently, the investigation is not yet complete, regardless of how many thousands of pages have been collected.

This distinction becomes particularly important because healthcare litigation is built upon evidence, not documentation alone. Documentation records what clinicians observed, what they believed, and what they decided to record at a particular moment in time. Evidence is broader. It includes objective findings, diagnostic imaging, physiological progression, laboratory trends, medication response, monitor data, communication between clinicians, organizational processes, and sometimes even what is missing from the record itself.

One of the greatest misconceptions in healthcare litigation is that the medical record tells the whole story.

It rarely does. The medical record tells the documented story.

Clinical Intelligence attempts to determine whether the documented story accurately reflects the clinical story.

Those are not always the same. Consider another example.

Case example: When Complete Records Still Produce an Incomplete Investigation

A fifty-eight-year-old woman presents to the emergency department complaining of severe chest pain, shortness of breath, and nausea. She is evaluated, laboratory studies are obtained, and an electrocardiogram is performed. Several hours later she is discharged home with a diagnosis of musculoskeletal pain. The following morning she suffers a fatal myocardial infarction.

The attorney receives every available hospital record. Nothing appears to be missing. The emergency department documentation is complete, the physician notes are present, the nursing records are available, laboratory reports have been included, and the discharge instructions are documented appropriately.

From a traditional perspective, the investigation can begin immediately because the record set appears complete.

Clinical Intelligence asks a different question.

- Is the evidence complete?

The emergency department records document that an electrocardiogram was performed.

- Where is the actual tracing?

The physician documents that the electrocardiogram showed no acute abnormalities.

- Was it independently reviewed?
- Were serial electrocardiograms performed?
- How did the cardiac biomarkers change during the patient's stay?
- Were previous electrocardiograms available for comparison?
- What was the patient's cardiac history before arriving at the emergency department?
- Did the documented symptoms change while the patient remained under observation?
- Were there telephone calls after discharge?
- Did emergency medical services document findings the following morning that suggest deterioration had begun much earlier?

The investigation has moved beyond collecting records. It has begun identifying evidence. The attorney is no longer asking whether the hospital produced the chart.

The attorney is asking whether the available evidence is sufficient to support a reliable clinical opinion.

That difference frequently determines the strength of the litigation.

Suppose the original electrocardiogram demonstrates subtle ischemic changes that were not recognized at the time but become obvious when reviewed alongside previous studies. Suddenly, the chronology alone is no longer the defining issue. The investigation now raises questions regarding interpretation, clinical decision-making, diagnostic reasoning, and whether the patient should have remained under observation rather than being discharged.

On the other hand, suppose the electrocardiogram is genuinely unremarkable, serial biomarkers remain within expected limits, and subsequent expert review concludes that the patient's presentation was clinically atypical despite appropriate investigation. The allegation may still appear compelling because of the tragic outcome, but the objective evidence may not support the conclusion that earlier intervention would probably have changed the patient's prognosis.

Once again, the records have not changed. The difference lies in the investigation.

Clinical Intelligence requires the attorney to distinguish between documentation that appears complete and evidence that is sufficient to explain the clinical reality of the case.

That distinction becomes increasingly important as healthcare grows more technologically advanced. Modern litigation rarely depends upon narrative documentation alone. Physiological monitoring, imaging, laboratory analytics, electronic medication records, audit trails, and digital communication all contribute to the patient's story. When those sources are considered together, they often provide a level of understanding that cannot be obtained from progress notes alone.

This is one of the reasons the first stage of the Lexcura Clinical Intelligence Model™ is Record Integrity rather than record collection.

Record collection asks whether the file has been received. Record Integrity asks whether the evidence can be trusted. That is a fundamentally different investigation.

One of the most expensive assumptions in healthcare litigation is believing that a complete chart automatically represents a complete case.

Before accepting or declining any healthcare matter, ask yourself:

Do I have all of the records?

Do I have all of the evidence?

Can the patient's clinical progression be explained from the available evidence?

What objective findings support or contradict the documented narrative?

What additional information would I want before asking an expert to form an opinion?

Those questions often determine whether the investigation begins with confidence or with assumptions.

One of the reasons healthcare litigation presents such unique challenges is that attorneys are rarely investigating a single decision. They are investigating a sequence of clinical decisions made by different professionals, often working under different circumstances, at different times, and sometimes with very different information available to them.

That distinction is critical because litigation naturally encourages us to look backward. Once we know the outcome, every decision leading up to that outcome appears connected. It becomes very easy to identify the moment where something should have been done differently because we already know what happened next.

Clinical practice does not work that way.

Every healthcare professional makes decisions based upon the information available at that moment, not upon information that will only become apparent hours or days later. Understanding what was reasonably knowable at each stage of the patient's progression is one of the most important principles in Clinical Intelligence because it protects the investigation from one of the greatest risks in healthcare litigation-hindsight bias.

Hindsight bias is rarely intentional.

It affects experienced clinicians, attorneys, expert witnesses, investigators, and, in many respects, every person involved in reviewing a healthcare case. Once the outcome is known, the progression leading to that outcome appears more obvious than it actually was at the time care was being delivered.

Clinical Intelligence deliberately works against that tendency.

Rather than beginning with the outcome and working backward, the investigation reconstructs the patient's journey as it unfolded in real time. Every decision is evaluated according to the information that should reasonably have been available when that decision was made. New information is introduced only when it became clinically available, allowing the investigation to recreate the circumstances facing the treating professionals rather than the perspective of someone reviewing the case months or years later.

This distinction frequently changes the attorney's understanding of the case.

Case example: The Danger of Hindsight

A forty-three-year-old woman presents to an urgent care center complaining of a severe headache, nausea, and neck discomfort. She is diagnosed with a migraine, treated symptomatically, and discharged home. Twelve hours later she is admitted to the hospital with a subarachnoid hemorrhage.

Viewed from the end of the story, the diagnosis appears obvious. The patient complained of a severe headache. She later suffered a catastrophic intracranial bleed. The conclusion seems almost unavoidable.

Clinical Intelligence asks the attorney to remove the outcome temporarily from the investigation.

- What information was actually available during the urgent care assessment?
- Was the headache sudden or gradual?
- Did the patient describe it as the worst headache of her life?
- Were there objective neurological deficits?
- Was neck stiffness clinically significant or related to muscular discomfort?

- Were vital signs abnormal?
- Did the patient have risk factors suggesting aneurysmal disease?
- Were there findings that should reasonably have prompted immediate neuroimaging, or did those findings develop later?

Notice how different the investigation becomes. Instead of asking, "How could they have missed the hemorrhage?" the attorney begins asking,

"Based upon what was reasonably knowable at that time, should another diagnosis have been actively pursued?"

Those are very different questions. One begins with the outcome. The other begins with the evidence.

Clinical Intelligence always begins with the evidence because evidence is considerably more reliable than hindsight.

This principle has practical consequences throughout healthcare litigation. It influences how experts should be instructed. It influences which records become important.

It influences deposition strategy because witnesses should be questioned about the information available to them at the time rather than knowledge obtained later during the investigation.

It also influences settlement discussions because a case that appears compelling when viewed retrospectively may become substantially more complex once the clinical decision-making process is reconstructed accurately.

That is one of the reasons Clinical Intelligence insists upon reconstructing the patient's journey chronologically before evaluating whether the standard of care was met.

The chronology is not simply a list of events. It recreates the clinical environment within which every decision was made.

Without that reconstruction, it becomes remarkably easy to judge yesterday's decisions using today's knowledge.

Healthcare professionals never have that advantage.

Attorneys should be careful not to give it to themselves during the investigation.

Traditional Medical Record Review vs. Clinical Intelligence

This distinction also highlights another important difference between traditional medical record review and Clinical Intelligence.

A traditional review may correctly identify that a diagnosis was delayed by eight hours.

Clinical Intelligence asks an additional series of questions.

- When did the diagnosis first become clinically recognizable?
- What information was available before that point?
- Which objective findings supported the diagnosis?
- Which findings reasonably supported alternative explanations?
- When did the standard of care require a different course of action?
- Did meaningful opportunity still exist to alter the patient's outcome?

Those additional questions frequently determine whether an apparent delay represents actionable negligence or whether it reflects the natural progression of a clinically complex condition.

For the attorney, that distinction is invaluable because litigation depends not simply upon identifying an unfavorable outcome, but upon demonstrating that the available evidence supports a clinically sustainable theory explaining why that outcome occurred and how different decisions would probably have changed it.

A healthcare case should never be investigated from the outcome backward. It should be investigated from the evidence forward.

That single change in perspective protects the attorney from hindsight bias, strengthens expert analysis, improves deposition strategy, and produces a far more reliable understanding of the patient's clinical journey.

There is another important reason why traditional medical record review and Clinical Intelligence reach different conclusions, and it has very little to do with the quality of the reviewer. It has to do with the purpose of the investigation.

Traditional medical record review is generally retrospective. The reviewer receives the records after the events have occurred, organizes the documentation, identifies significant findings, and explains the medical care that was provided. The investigation is centered on the documentation because the documentation is the primary source of information available.

Clinical Intelligence is also retrospective, but its objective is fundamentally different.

Rather than asking, "What does the documentation tell us?" it asks, "Can the patient's clinical journey be reconstructed accurately enough to support litigation decisions?"

That difference may seem subtle, but it changes the entire investigation.

The medical record becomes one source of evidence rather than the only source of evidence. The investigation begins testing the documentation against physiology, objective findings, accepted clinical practice, and the sequence in which information became available to the treating clinicians. Every conclusion must be capable of surviving that process before it becomes part of the litigation strategy.

For the attorney, this distinction is significant because litigation is not won by proving that something was documented. It is won by demonstrating that the available evidence supports a clinically sustainable explanation of what happened, why it happened, whether it should have happened, and whether different clinical decisions would probably have changed the outcome.

That is a much higher standard than simply reviewing documentation.

Why This Matters at Intake

One of the most common questions attorneys ask during an initial consultation is, "Do I have a case?"

It is a perfectly reasonable question, but it is also one that can be misleading if it is asked too early.

At intake, the attorney rarely has a complete understanding of the patient's clinical journey. They may have selected medical records, a chronology of events from the client or family, and an allegation that appears both logical and compelling. Unfortunately, healthcare litigation has repeatedly demonstrated that first impressions can be remarkably unreliable.

Some cases that appear exceptionally strong during the first review become significantly weaker once additional evidence is obtained. Other cases that initially appear unlikely to succeed become much stronger after the patient's baseline, objective findings, or clinical progression have been properly reconstructed.

The attorney's first responsibility, therefore, is not to determine whether the case should succeed.

The attorney's first responsibility is to determine whether the available evidence is sufficient to understand what actually happened.

That is an important distinction because Clinical Intelligence recognizes two very different stages of case evaluation.

The first asks: "What do we think happened?" The second asks:

"What can we prove probably happened after the evidence has been clinically tested?"

Those questions are separated by investigation.

The quality of that investigation often determines the quality of every decision that follows.

Case example: The Case That Almost Shouldn't Have Been Accepted

An attorney is contacted by the family of a seventy-six-year-old man who died three days after being admitted to the hospital with pneumonia. The family believes that antibiotics were delayed and that the delay caused his death. They provide several hospital records, describe repeated requests for assistance that they believe were ignored, and explain that the patient appeared significantly worse long before treatment was escalated.

At first review, the allegation appears persuasive.

The documentation confirms a delay before broad-spectrum antibiotics were administered. Nursing notes describe increasing respiratory distress. Laboratory values demonstrate progressive infection, and the ultimate outcome is tragic.

The attorney is understandably concerned that an avoidable delay may have contributed to the patient's death.

A traditional review would likely identify the sequence accurately and recommend further expert evaluation.

Clinical Intelligence deliberately slows the investigation before that conclusion is reached.

Additional records reveal that the patient had advanced pulmonary fibrosis, severe chronic heart failure, and recurrent aspiration pneumonia requiring multiple hospital admissions during the previous year. Previous imaging demonstrates extensive irreversible lung disease. Discussions regarding palliative care had begun several months before the admission in question.

None of those findings excuse delayed treatment if a delay occurred. They do, however, change the investigation. The attorney must now ask additional questions.

- Would earlier antibiotics probably have altered the outcome?
- Did the patient's pre-existing disease substantially limit the likelihood of recovery regardless of treatment?
- Was the progression consistent with overwhelming infection despite appropriate therapy, or did the available evidence suggest that meaningful intervention opportunity remained?

The allegation has not disappeared. The investigation has become more sophisticated. Clinical Intelligence has not weakened the case. It has strengthened the attorney's understanding of the case.

If negligence exists, the attorney will now pursue it with a far more defensible clinical foundation.

If the investigation demonstrates that causation cannot be supported, the attorney has avoided investing significant resources in a theory that would likely fail during expert review or trial.

In both situations, the attorney has benefited. That is one of the most important principles in Clinical Intelligence. Its purpose is not to prove negligence. Its purpose is to improve the quality of litigation decisions.

The first question should never be: "Do I have a case?" The first question should be:

"Do I understand the patient's clinical journey well enough to know whether I have a case?"

That single change in thinking is where Clinical Intelligence begins.

The purpose of Clinical Intelligence is not to replace legal analysis. It is to strengthen it.

Every experienced healthcare attorney understands that successful litigation depends upon asking the right questions at the right time. The difficulty is that many of those questions are legal in nature. Was the standard of care breached? Is there sufficient evidence to establish causation? What experts will be required? What are the anticipated defenses? Is the case economically viable?

Those are all essential questions.

Clinical Intelligence simply recognizes that there are several clinical questions that must be answered first because the legal analysis depends upon the quality of the clinical investigation.

For example, before asking whether the standard of care was breached, the attorney should understand exactly what condition the patient was in before the alleged negligence occurred. Before evaluating whether a delay caused harm, the attorney should determine whether there was still a meaningful opportunity to change the patient's outcome. Before concluding that documentation supports the allegation, the attorney should determine whether the documentation accurately reflects the patient's physiological progression.

Those may appear to be clinical questions, but they directly influence legal decisions.

This is where the relationship between traditional medical record review and Clinical Intelligence becomes particularly important. Traditional review provides much of the information necessary to begin asking those questions. Clinical Intelligence provides the framework for answering them in a logical sequence so that each conclusion is built upon the one before it.

That sequence matters because healthcare litigation is rarely lost on one dramatic mistake. More often, cases become vulnerable because a series of smaller assumptions gradually develops into the accepted theory of the case without each assumption being independently tested against the available evidence.

Clinical Intelligence deliberately interrupts that process. It asks the attorney to slow down. Not because the investigation should take longer. Because the investigation should become more disciplined. That distinction is fundamental to the doctrine.

A disciplined investigation is not necessarily a slower investigation. In many cases, it is actually more efficient because the important clinical questions are identified early rather than emerging months later after experts have been retained, depositions have been completed, and significant litigation costs have already been incurred.

The objective, therefore, is not to create more work.

The objective is to perform the right work at the right stage of the investigation.

Case example: Asking the Wrong Question

A forty-nine-year-old patient presents to the emergency department with severe abdominal pain. Several hours later the patient is diagnosed with a perforated bowel requiring emergency surgery. The family alleges that the emergency physician failed to diagnose the condition quickly enough and that the delay resulted in overwhelming sepsis.

An attorney reviewing the case might naturally begin by asking: "Was there a delay in diagnosis?" That is an important question. It is not the first question. Clinical Intelligence begins somewhere else.

How did the patient present?

- What objective findings were available during the initial assessment?
- What symptoms were reported?
- Were the vital signs stable?
- What did the laboratory studies demonstrate?
- What did the physical examination reveal?
- What alternative diagnoses were clinically reasonable at that time?
- What information became available later that was not available during the initial assessment?

Already, the investigation is moving in a different direction.

Rather than assuming that a delay automatically represents negligence, the attorney is reconstructing the clinical environment in which the emergency physician made each decision.

Only after that reconstruction has been completed does Clinical Intelligence begin asking whether the standard of care required a different course of action.

That sequence protects the investigation from reaching conclusions before the evidence has been fully understood.

It also strengthens the attorney's position regardless of the outcome.

If the investigation ultimately supports negligence, the attorney can explain exactly why the standard of care required different action at a specific point in time and how that failure probably influenced the patient's outcome.

If the investigation demonstrates that the presentation was genuinely atypical and that earlier diagnosis was not reasonably achievable, the attorney has avoided developing a litigation theory that would likely have failed under expert scrutiny.

In both situations, the attorney has benefited because the investigation has produced greater certainty before significant litigation resources were committed.

That illustrates one of the central principles of Clinical Intelligence. It does not exist to make every case stronger. It exists to make every decision better.

One of the most valuable habits an attorney can develop is learning to recognize when they are asking a legal question before the underlying clinical question has been answered.

When reviewing a healthcare case, pause before reaching conclusions and ask:

What clinical question must be answered before I can answer the legal question?

Am I relying on an allegation, or has the evidence been clinically tested?

What assumption am I making that still needs to be verified?

If I retained an expert tomorrow, what foundational questions would I want answered first?

Those questions shift the investigation from building a legal theory to building a clinically sustainable legal theory.

One of the recurring themes throughout this book is that attorneys and clinicians naturally think differently.

That difference is not a weakness. It is precisely why Clinical Intelligence exists. The attorney brings legal reasoning. The clinician brings clinical reasoning.

Clinical Intelligence integrates both so that legal decisions are built upon the strongest possible clinical foundation.

There is another assumption that quietly influences almost every healthcare case, and because it is rarely recognized, it has the potential to affect every decision that follows.

The assumption is that once the medical records have been obtained, the investigation has begun.

In reality, obtaining the records is simply the point at which the investigation becomes possible.

Those two ideas are often treated as though they are the same, but they are fundamentally different.

Every experienced attorney has received what appeared to be a complete record set, only to discover later that additional records changed the direction of the case. A prior admission reveals an underlying condition that was never mentioned during intake. An earlier CT scan demonstrates that the abnormality existed before the alleged negligence. A specialist consultation contradicts the working diagnosis. An EMS report describes a very different clinical presentation from the one documented in the emergency department. None of those records changes history. They change our understanding of history.

That distinction is critical because Clinical Intelligence is not built upon documentation alone. It is built upon the continual testing of every developing conclusion against all available evidence.

This requires a different investigative mindset.

Instead of asking, "What have I been given?" the attorney begins asking, "What else would I expect to find if this clinical story is accurate?"

That single question often transforms the investigation.

Suppose a patient is alleged to have suffered an avoidable hypoxic brain injury during hospitalization. The nursing records describe progressive respiratory deterioration over several hours. Oxygen saturations are documented. Physician notes record increasing concern. The chronology appears complete.

Clinical Intelligence asks whether the chronology is sufficient to explain the physiology.

- Where are the arterial blood gas results?
- Was continuous telemetry being used?
- What do the respiratory therapy records show?
- Were there ventilator changes?
- Was there a rapid response activation?
- What was happening during the periods between the nursing observations?
- Were there bedside assessments that never became formal progress notes?
- Did the monitor data support the documented deterioration, or does it suggest something different?

The investigation is no longer limited by the structure of the chart. Instead, it is being guided by the patient's physiology.

That is one of the most significant differences between traditional medical record review and Clinical Intelligence.

Traditional review follows the documentation. Clinical Intelligence follows the patient. Sometimes those two journeys are identical. Sometimes they are not. When they are not, the attorney needs to understand why.

At this point in the investigation, resist the temptation to ask whether the records support the allegation.

Instead ask yourself:

- Does the documentation explain the patient's physiological progression?
- If I removed the diagnosis from the chart, would the objective evidence still lead me to the same conclusion?
- What evidence should exist if the documented clinical story is accurate?
- Is there anything in this record that appears inconsistent with the patient's progression?
- What information would I expect a defense expert to identify that I have not yet considered?

Those questions do not make the investigation longer. They make it stronger.

They force the attorney to move beyond accepting the documentation at face value and begin evaluating whether the documentation withstands clinical scrutiny.

That is where Clinical Intelligence begins. Not with answers. With disciplined questions.

One of the habits that distinguishes experienced healthcare litigators is that they learn to become comfortable delaying conclusions.

There is understandable pressure to determine whether a case has merit as early as possible. Clients want answers. Firms must decide whether to invest resources. Deadlines begin immediately. Yet the strongest attorneys recognize that premature certainty is often more dangerous than temporary uncertainty.

Clinical Intelligence encourages a different mindset. The objective is not to reach a conclusion quickly.

The objective is to reach the right conclusion by ensuring that every important clinical question has been asked before the litigation strategy begins to take shape.

That may be the most valuable investment you make in the life of the case.

Traditional Medical Record Review follows the documentation. Clinical Intelligence follows the patient.

CHAPTER 3

Reading a Chart and Conducting an Investigation

The Difference Between Reading a Chart and Conducting an Investigation

One of the reasons healthcare litigation is so challenging is that medical records are not written for attorneys. They are not even written to explain the patient's entire clinical journey. They are created by individual healthcare professionals documenting their own observations, decisions, treatments, and communications at specific points in time. Each entry represents a small part of a much larger story.

That distinction is important because attorneys often receive the records as a finished document. The chart appears complete. It has a beginning, a middle, and an end. It is natural to assume that reading the chart means understanding the patient's journey.

In reality, a medical record is much like the witness statements collected after a motor vehicle collision.

Every witness describes the same event. No witness describes the entire event. One driver remembers the traffic light. Another remembers the speed. A pedestrian notices the weather. Someone else hears the impact but never sees the collision.

None of those witnesses is necessarily wrong. Each simply observed one part of a much larger event. Healthcare documentation works in much the same way. The emergency physician documents the initial assessment.

The nurse records observations during the shift. The radiologist interprets imaging. The pharmacist verifies medications. The respiratory therapist documents ventilator management. The intensivist records decisions made in the intensive care unit.

Each professional is documenting the patient's care from their own clinical perspective, during their own period of involvement, and for their own professional responsibilities.

No individual clinician is documenting the patient's complete journey. That responsibility falls to the investigator.

This is one of the first major differences between traditional medical record review and Clinical Intelligence.

Traditional review organizes the documentation so the attorney can locate information efficiently.

Clinical Intelligence reconstructs the patient's entire clinical journey by integrating every piece of evidence into one coherent investigation.

That distinction changes the attorney's role. The attorney is no longer reviewing a collection of records. The attorney is overseeing the reconstruction of a clinical event.

Case example: The Story Hidden Between the Notes

A patient is admitted following a fall resulting in multiple rib fractures.

During the first twenty-four hours, nursing documentation notes increasing pain, reduced mobility, and intermittent confusion. Respiratory therapy documents declining inspiratory effort. The physician records that the patient is clinically stable. Laboratory values show a gradual rise in inflammatory markers. Overnight, oxygen requirements increase, and by the following afternoon the patient is transferred to the intensive care unit with respiratory failure.

If each note is read independently, nothing appears particularly unusual. Every clinician documented their own observations appropriately. The investigation changes, however, when those observations are integrated. The increasing pain reduced the patient's ability to breathe deeply.

Reduced ventilation contributed to atelectasis. Atelectasis increased the risk of pneumonia. Progressive hypoxia contributed to confusion. Confusion reduced participation in respiratory therapy. The deterioration was not caused by one dramatic event.

It resulted from a sequence of interconnected physiological changes that became visible only when the patient's journey was reconstructed as a whole.

The documentation never explicitly states that story. The investigation does. That is the difference. Clinical Intelligence is not looking for isolated events. It is looking for relationships between events.

Those relationships frequently determine liability, causation, damages, and ultimately the strength of the litigation.

When reviewing a healthcare case, avoid asking: "What happened next?" Instead ask: "How did one clinical event influence the next?" That single question transforms a chronology into an investigation. Healthcare cases are rarely won because one document contains the answer.

They are won because the attorney understands how dozens of seemingly unrelated clinical events combined to produce the patient's outcome.

When those relationships are understood, depositions become more focused, expert instructions become more precise, and the litigation strategy becomes significantly more difficult to undermine.

Clinical Intelligence therefore teaches attorneys to investigate connections rather than simply collecting facts.

Medical records document episodes of care. Clinical Intelligence reconstructs the patient's journey.

No individual healthcare professional is responsible for documenting the patient's complete story. Each clinician records the portion of care they delivered, based on the information available to them at that time. The attorney's challenge is that liability, causation, and damages often depend on understanding how those individual episodes connect.

Clinical Intelligence bridges those individual records into a single, evidence-based reconstruction of the patient's journey. Only then can the attorney evaluate whether the clinical progression supports the developing litigation theory.

The chart is a collection of clinical observations. The investigation is the process of turning those observations into clinical understanding.

Clinical Investigation Begins With Questions, Not Conclusions

One of the greatest strengths an attorney can develop in healthcare litigation is the discipline of delaying conclusions until the investigation has earned them.

That may seem obvious, yet it is surprisingly difficult in practice.

By the time a healthcare case reaches an attorney's office, it already has a story. The patient has lived it. The family has interpreted it. The referring attorney may have discussed it. The medical records contain their own version of events, and sometimes the healthcare providers have already explained why they believe the outcome occurred. Before the investigation has even begun, multiple narratives are competing for acceptance.

Clinical Intelligence deliberately resists choosing one of those narratives too early. Instead, it begins with questions. Not because questions delay progress.

Because questions prevent assumptions from becoming conclusions before the evidence has been fully examined.

That approach changes the attorney's role. Rather than looking for evidence that supports an existing theory, the attorney begins looking for evidence that explains the patient's journey as accurately as possible. Only when that journey has been reconstructed does the legal theory begin to emerge.

This is one of the most important differences between advocacy and investigation. Advocacy seeks to persuade. Investigation seeks to understand. Healthcare litigation requires both, but they should occur in that order.

An attorney who begins advocating before understanding the patient's clinical journey risks building a persuasive legal argument on an incomplete clinical foundation. An attorney who begins with disciplined investigation enters every later stage of the case with greater confidence because the strategy has developed from the evidence rather than the other way around.

Case example: The Missing Piece That Changed Everything

A thirty-nine-year-old woman arrives at the emergency department complaining of sudden shortness of breath and chest discomfort. She is assessed, treated for anxiety, and discharged home. Later that evening she suffers a fatal pulmonary embolism.

The allegation appears straightforward.

The family believes the emergency physician failed to recognize the warning signs of a pulmonary embolism and discharged the patient when she should have been admitted for further investigation.

An attorney reviewing the emergency department records could reasonably conclude that the case deserves serious consideration.

Clinical Intelligence agrees. But it does not stop there. The investigation asks additional questions.

- Was this the patient's first presentation?
- Had she recently undergone surgery?
- Was she taking hormone therapy?
- Had she traveled long distances?
- Was there a history of previous thromboembolic disease?
- Were there telephone consultations before her arrival?
- Did emergency medical services document findings that were not repeated in the emergency department?
- Was there previous imaging performed at another facility?

One additional record obtained during the investigation reveals that the patient had undergone major orthopedic surgery eight days earlier at another hospital. That single piece of information significantly changes the clinical assessment because it alters the patient's risk profile from the moment she arrived in the emergency department.

The emergency department documentation has not changed. The patient's physiology has not changed.

What has changed is the attorney's understanding of the clinical context in which every decision was made.

That is why Clinical Intelligence insists upon building the clinical picture before building the litigation strategy.

The strongest cases are rarely strengthened by assumptions. They are strengthened by context. Experienced investigators become comfortable asking one question repeatedly: "What am I still missing?" Not because they expect every case to contain hidden evidence.

Because they understand that every unanswered question represents a potential weakness in the investigation.

Sometimes the missing information strengthens the case. Sometimes it weakens it. Either outcome benefits the attorney because uncertainty has been replaced by understanding. Before developing a litigation strategy, ask yourself:

- What facts do I know with confidence?
- Which conclusions are supported by objective evidence?
- Which conclusions are based upon assumptions?
- What additional information could completely change my understanding of this case?
- Have I reconstructed the patient's journey or merely reviewed the documentation?

Those questions are not designed to create doubt. They are designed to create confidence.

Confidence built upon disciplined investigation is far more durable than confidence built upon first impressions.

The investigation should shape the litigation strategy. The litigation strategy should never shape the investigation.

Healthcare litigation is most vulnerable when attorneys become committed to a theory before the clinical investigation has been completed. Once that happens, every new piece of evidence is unconsciously measured against the existing theory rather than evaluated on its own merits.

Clinical Intelligence deliberately reverses that sequence. The investigation comes first. The litigation strategy emerges afterward. This protects the attorney from confirmation bias, strengthens expert instruction, and produces a case that is built upon evidence rather than assumption.

A good attorney builds a persuasive case. A great healthcare attorney first builds a trustworthy investigation.

The Attorney as Clinical Investigator

One of the misconceptions surrounding healthcare litigation is that success depends primarily upon understanding medicine. While medical knowledge is undoubtedly important, the most successful healthcare attorneys are not necessarily those who know the most medicine.

They are the ones who ask the best questions.

That distinction deserves careful consideration because medicine is constantly evolving. New treatments emerge, technology advances, standards of care develop, and clinical practice continues to change. No attorney can reasonably be expected to master every medical specialty, every disease process, and every diagnostic challenge they will encounter throughout their career.

Fortunately, they do not have to.

What they must master is the ability to investigate clinical problems with discipline.

Clinical Intelligence was never intended to transform attorneys into clinicians.

It was developed to help attorneys think like investigators who understand how clinicians think.

Those are two very different objectives.

An experienced clinician approaches a deteriorating patient by asking a series of disciplined questions. What has changed? Why has it changed? What evidence supports that conclusion? What alternative explanations remain possible? What information is still missing? What intervention remains available?

Clinical Intelligence teaches attorneys to approach litigation in much the same way. Not because attorneys should practice medicine. But because clinical reasoning frequently determines whether the legal theory ultimately succeeds.

The attorney's responsibility is not to diagnose the patient.

The attorney's responsibility is to determine whether the clinical investigation has been sufficiently thorough to support the legal decisions that will follow.

That may be one of the most important distinctions in this entire book.

Clinical Intelligence does not ask attorneys to become medical experts. It asks them to become better consumers of clinical reasoning.

That change in perspective has practical consequences throughout the life of the case.

The attorney becomes more effective at identifying missing evidence before expert review begins.

Expert instructions become more focused because the important clinical questions have already been identified.

Depositions become more productive because witnesses are questioned about their clinical reasoning rather than simply their recollection of events.

Settlement discussions become more informed because the attorney understands not only where the case appears strong, but why it is strong and where it remains vulnerable.

Even trial preparation changes because the attorney is presenting a clinically coherent story rather than a collection of isolated facts.

Ultimately, Clinical Intelligence is not about knowing more medicine than the opposing attorney.

It is about understanding the patient's clinical journey more accurately than anyone else in the courtroom.

That is a profound difference.

Winning healthcare litigation is rarely about discovering one dramatic piece of evidence that everyone else missed.

More often, it is about recognizing the significance of evidence that was already there but had never been connected into a coherent clinical narrative.

That is where disciplined investigation becomes one of the attorney's greatest advantages.

Case example: The Evidence Was Always There

A sixty-year-old patient is admitted following elective knee replacement surgery. During the second postoperative day, nursing documentation records increasing shortness of breath, mild tachycardia, and intermittent oxygen desaturation. The physician attributes the symptoms to postoperative atelectasis and encourages aggressive pulmonary exercises. The following morning the patient suffers a cardiac arrest caused by a massive pulmonary embolism.

When the case first arrives, the attorney's attention naturally focuses on the cardiac arrest.

That is the outcome. Clinical Intelligence deliberately redirects the investigation. Not to the cardiac arrest. Not even to the pulmonary embolism. Instead, it asks a different question.

When did the patient's clinical story begin to change?

That question changes the direction of the investigation.

Rather than concentrating on the catastrophic event itself, the investigation begins examining the subtle physiological changes that occurred during the previous twenty-four hours.

The increasing heart rate. The gradual reduction in oxygen saturation. The patient's reluctance to mobilize because of worsening calf pain.

The nursing observations that, individually, appeared relatively insignificant but collectively suggested a developing pattern.

None of those observations, viewed in isolation, proves that a pulmonary embolism was present.

Together, however, they describe a patient whose clinical trajectory was changing. That trajectory is often where the most important answers are found.

Clinical Intelligence teaches attorneys to recognize that healthcare cases rarely fail because one obvious warning sign was ignored.

More commonly, they fail because multiple smaller warning signs were never connected into one clinically meaningful picture.

Once that picture is reconstructed, the investigation changes from asking, "Why wasn't the pulmonary embolism diagnosed?" to asking, "At what point should a reasonably competent clinician have recognized that this patient was no longer following the expected postoperative course?"

Those are very different investigations. One searches for an event. The other reconstructs a process.

Clinical Intelligence always investigates the process because understanding the process often explains the event.

When reviewing any healthcare case, ask yourself one simple question:

- Am I investigating the outcome, or am I investigating the process that produced the outcome?

The answer to that question will often determine the quality of every conclusion that follows.

Outcomes rarely explain themselves. Processes do.

Every healthcare outcome is the product of a clinical process. Sometimes that process reflects excellent care. Sometimes it reveals missed opportunities, delayed recognition, communication failures, or departures from accepted practice. The outcome tells you what happened. The process explains why it happened.

Clinical Intelligence therefore investigates the process before evaluating the outcome.

Attorneys who understand the clinical process ask better questions during discovery, provide clearer instructions to experts, identify stronger evidence, and develop litigation strategies that are grounded in clinical reality rather than hindsight.

The outcome may begin the investigation. The process determines where the investigation leads.

The Danger of the First Theory

Every healthcare case begins with a theory. Sometimes it comes from the patient. Sometimes it comes from the family. Sometimes it develops during the first attorney interview.

Occasionally, it begins with a referring attorney who has already identified what they believe to be the central issue. By the time the records are requested, everyone involved often believes they already know what happened.

That is entirely understandable. It is also one of the greatest risks in healthcare litigation.

The first theory is rarely built upon the complete clinical picture. It is built upon the information available at the time. Unfortunately, the information available during intake is often incomplete, selective, emotionally influenced, or viewed through the lens of hindsight. It may identify an important concern, but it rarely explains the patient's entire clinical journey.

Clinical Intelligence recognizes that every early theory should be treated as a working hypothesis rather than an established conclusion.

There is an important reason for this.

Once a theory begins to develop, it naturally influences the investigation that follows. Questions become directed toward supporting the existing explanation. Records that appear consistent with the theory receive greater attention. Information that challenges the theory may be overlooked, not because anyone intends to ignore it, but because the human mind naturally looks for patterns that confirm what it already believes.

This is not a weakness unique to attorneys. It affects clinicians. It affects investigators. It affects expert witnesses. It affects every profession that must interpret complex information. Clinical Intelligence therefore establishes a simple rule.

No theory should become the foundation of a healthcare case until it has survived a disciplined clinical investigation.

That principle protects everyone involved in the litigation.

It protects the attorney from investing significant time and resources in a theory that cannot ultimately be supported.

It protects the client from unrealistic expectations based upon incomplete information.

It protects retained experts by ensuring that they begin their work with the strongest possible clinical foundation rather than being asked to validate assumptions that have never been fully investigated.

Most importantly, it protects the integrity of the litigation itself. The purpose of Clinical Intelligence is not to prove the first theory. It is to determine whether the first theory survives the evidence.

That distinction may be one of the most important concepts in this entire book.

Case example: The Wrong Theory

A fifty-seven-year-old patient undergoes elective colon surgery. Forty-eight hours later, the patient develops septic shock following an anastomotic leak and requires multiple additional procedures. The family believes the surgeon made a technical error during the original operation and contacts an attorney alleging negligent surgery.

At intake, the theory appears logical. An anastomotic leak occurred. The patient became septic. The complication followed surgery. The conclusion seems obvious. Clinical Intelligence deliberately resists that conclusion until the investigation has been completed.

The investigation begins asking different questions.

- Were there recognized risk factors for an anastomotic leak before surgery?
- What was the condition of the bowel?
- Was there impaired blood supply to the anastomosis?
- Did the patient have poorly controlled diabetes?
- Was the patient receiving steroids or immunosuppressive therapy?
- Were there signs of leakage that should have been recognized earlier during postoperative care?
- Did the delay in recognizing the leak contribute more to the patient's outcome than the leak itself?

As additional evidence is gathered, the clinical picture changes.

The operative report is reviewed alongside pathology findings. Imaging studies are correlated with the patient's postoperative physiology. Nursing documentation demonstrates that the patient's deterioration became apparent several hours before the surgical team was notified. Escalation pathways were not followed promptly, and opportunities for earlier intervention appear to have been missed.

By the conclusion of the investigation, the attorney reaches a very different understanding.

The strongest theory may no longer involve negligent surgical technique. The stronger case may involve delayed recognition and delayed intervention after surgery. The patient has not changed. The records have not changed.

The investigation changed. And because the investigation changed, the litigation strategy changed with it. That is exactly what Clinical Intelligence is designed to accomplish. It does not seek to confirm the first explanation.

It seeks to discover the strongest explanation supported by the evidence.

One of the most valuable questions you can ask during the early stages of any healthcare case is remarkably simple:

"If my current theory is wrong, what evidence would prove it?" That question forces the investigation to remain objective.

It reminds the attorney that every developing theory should be challenged before it is trusted.

Strong cases become stronger by surviving that challenge. Weak cases often reveal themselves before substantial litigation costs have been incurred.

The first theory is the beginning of the investigation. It should never become the conclusion of the investigation.

Every healthcare case arrives with a story, but stories are not evidence. They are starting points. Clinical Intelligence requires every theory to earn its place through disciplined investigation rather than early acceptance.

Attorneys who remain willing to challenge their own theory frequently discover stronger, more clinically sustainable explanations than the ones they first considered. They also avoid becoming committed to litigation strategies that cannot withstand expert review or cross-examination.

The attorney who tests their own theory before the opposing expert does gains a significant strategic advantage. Weaknesses are identified earlier. Better questions are asked. Better experts are retained. Stronger cases emerge.

Never ask whether your theory explains the evidence. Ask whether the evidence explains your theory.

Facts Require Clinical Context

One of the first lessons every attorney learns is the importance of gathering facts. Medical records are requested. Witnesses are interviewed. Policies are obtained. Imaging is reviewed. Laboratory reports are analyzed. Every new piece of information helps build the factual foundation of the case.

Facts are essential. Without them, there can be no investigation.

However, healthcare litigation presents a challenge that is different from many other areas of law.

Facts rarely explain themselves. A blood pressure of 82/48 is a fact. A heart rate of 128 beats per minute is a fact. An elevated lactate level is a fact.

A CT scan demonstrating intracranial bleeding is a fact. A nursing note documenting increasing confusion is a fact. Individually, each fact is important. Collectively, they may tell an entirely different story.

Clinical Intelligence is concerned with that story.

The attorney's responsibility is not simply to identify important facts. It is to understand how those facts interact, whether they support one another, whether they contradict one another, and whether they explain the patient's clinical progression in a logical and medically defensible way.

This is where many investigations begin to separate themselves. One investigation collects facts. Another investigation explains why those facts matter. Only one of them prepares the attorney to make confident litigation decisions.

Case example: Every Fact Was Correct

A seventy-two-year-old patient is admitted following elective hip replacement surgery. Over the next eighteen hours the following events are documented. The patient develops mild tachycardia. Blood pressure gradually declines. Urine output decreases.

The white blood cell count rises. Temperature increases from 98.7°F to 101.4°F. Respiratory rate increases. The patient becomes increasingly confused. Every one of those observations is documented accurately. Every individual fact is correct.

Yet nowhere in the medical record does anyone explicitly document that the patient is developing septic shock.

Clinical Intelligence asks a different question.

- If all of these documented facts are viewed together rather than individually, what clinical story do they tell?

Suddenly the investigation changes. The elevated heart rate is no longer simply an abnormal vital sign. It becomes part of a developing physiological response. The falling blood pressure is no longer an isolated observation.

It becomes evidence of worsening circulatory compromise. The increasing confusion is no longer viewed as postoperative disorientation. It becomes another indicator of deteriorating perfusion. The facts themselves have not changed.

Their meaning has. That distinction is one of the defining characteristics of Clinical Intelligence. Medicine is rarely understood by looking at individual findings in isolation. Patients deteriorate through patterns. Healthcare professionals recognize patterns.

Clinical Intelligence teaches attorneys to investigate those patterns before reaching legal conclusions.

Why Patterns Matter More Than Isolated Events

Healthcare litigation often focuses attention on one moment. The missed diagnosis. The delayed operation. The medication error. The unexpected cardiac arrest. Those moments are important. They are rarely where the story begins.

Clinical deterioration is usually progressive. Communication failures are often cumulative.

System failures frequently develop over hours, days, or even months before they become visible.

When attorneys concentrate exclusively on the event that ultimately caused the injury, they risk overlooking the sequence of smaller events that made the injury possible.

Clinical Intelligence therefore asks attorneys to investigate the pattern before investigating the event.

The event explains where the patient's journey ended. The pattern explains how the patient arrived there.

Understanding that pattern frequently determines whether negligence can be established, whether causation can be demonstrated, and whether the litigation strategy can withstand expert scrutiny.

When reviewing a healthcare case, pause whenever you identify an important clinical event.

Then ask yourself: Is this the beginning of the story...

...or simply the point where everyone finally noticed the story?

Those are rarely the same moment.

Some of the strongest healthcare cases are built not upon the event itself, but upon recognizing that the warning signs had been developing long before anyone appreciated their significance.

Facts become evidence only when they are understood in context.

Healthcare litigation is built upon facts, but facts alone rarely explain why a patient deteriorated, why clinicians acted as they did, or whether different decisions would probably have changed the outcome.

Clinical Intelligence transforms facts into evidence by placing every observation within its proper clinical, physiological, and chronological context. Only then can the attorney understand not merely what happened, but why it happened and how it should influence the litigation.

Attorneys who understand relationships between facts ask better deposition questions, challenge expert opinions more effectively, identify stronger theories of liability, and recognize weaknesses before they become problems at trial.

Facts tell you what happened. Context tells you what those facts mean.

Clinical Intelligence Is About Reducing Uncertainty

One of the realities of healthcare litigation is that uncertainty can never be eliminated completely.

Medicine is not mathematics.

Patients do not always present with textbook symptoms. Diseases do not always progress predictably. Experienced clinicians can make appropriate decisions based on the information available to them and still encounter unexpected outcomes. Likewise, two highly qualified experts may reasonably disagree about whether a particular intervention would probably have changed the patient's prognosis.

Clinical Intelligence does not claim to eliminate that uncertainty. It does something more practical.

It reduces unnecessary uncertainty by ensuring that every conclusion is built upon the strongest clinical foundation the available evidence can provide.

That distinction is important.

Attorneys are often asked to make significant decisions long before every answer is available. They must decide whether to accept the case, retain experts, invest substantial financial resources, begin discovery, or recommend settlement. Every one of those decisions carries risk because it is made before absolute certainty is possible.

Clinical Intelligence recognizes that uncertainty is part of litigation. Assumptions should not be.

The purpose of a disciplined clinical investigation is to replace assumptions with evidence wherever possible. It identifies which questions have been answered, which questions remain unresolved, and which questions may never be answered with complete confidence.

Understanding those differences allows the attorney to evaluate the case realistically rather than optimistically.

That alone represents a significant advantage.

Case example: Knowing What You Don't Know

A fifty-five-year-old patient presents to the emergency department with dizziness, nausea, and intermittent slurred speech. A CT scan is interpreted as normal, and the patient is discharged with a diagnosis of vertigo. Two days later the patient is admitted with a cerebellar infarction.

The attorney receives the records and immediately recognizes the possibility of a missed stroke.

The temptation is understandable. The symptoms appear consistent. The diagnosis was delayed. The outcome is significant. Clinical Intelligence begins by asking a different question.

What do we know with confidence?

We know the symptoms documented during the initial presentation. We know the timing of the CT scan. We know the interpretation recorded by the radiologist. We know the patient's neurological condition at discharge.

Those are facts. Now comes the more important question.

What do we not know?

- Was advanced vascular imaging clinically indicated?
- Were subtle neurological deficits present but undocumented?
- Did the symptoms fluctuate during observation?
- Did the patient receive appropriate discharge instructions if symptoms worsened?
- Would earlier diagnosis probably have prevented the eventual infarction?

The investigation has not become weaker because uncertainty exists. It has become stronger because uncertainty has been identified. Clinical Intelligence does not ignore unanswered questions.

It identifies them, investigates them where possible, and clearly distinguishes between what is supported by evidence and what remains uncertain.

That distinction gives the attorney something extremely valuable. Honest confidence.

The Value of Honest Confidence

Jurors understand uncertainty. Judges understand uncertainty. Experienced attorneys certainly understand uncertainty. What they do not accept is unsupported certainty.

One of the quickest ways to weaken a healthcare case is to express greater confidence than the available evidence can reasonably support. Opposing experts will identify those weaknesses quickly, and credibility becomes difficult to recover.

Clinical Intelligence therefore encourages attorneys to become comfortable with carefully defined uncertainty. There is nothing wrong with saying, "Based upon the available evidence, the most probable explanation is..." There is nothing wrong with acknowledging,

"This conclusion depends upon whether additional records confirm..." Those statements do not weaken the case. They strengthen credibility because they demonstrate disciplined reasoning rather than advocacy.

Ironically, attorneys who acknowledge uncertainty early often develop stronger litigation strategies because they investigate the uncertainty before the opposing side has the opportunity to exploit it.

One of the most powerful questions in healthcare litigation is not: "What do I know?" It is:

"What would have to be true for my current understanding to be wrong?"

That question keeps the investigation intellectually honest.

It also protects the attorney from becoming committed to a theory before the evidence has fully earned that confidence.

Clinical Intelligence does not eliminate uncertainty. It eliminates avoidable uncertainty.

Healthcare cases will always contain elements that remain uncertain. Medicine is complex, and every patient is different. The objective is not to create false certainty but to reduce uncertainty by systematically investigating every question that can reasonably be answered through disciplined clinical analysis.

The attorney who understands the difference between unavoidable uncertainty and avoidable uncertainty makes better litigation decisions, retains experts more strategically, and presents more credible arguments throughout the life of the case.

Cases built upon disciplined investigation are more resilient because their strengths and weaknesses are understood before litigation strategy becomes fixed. That allows attorneys to adapt confidently as new evidence emerges rather than being surprised by it.

Confidence should come from the investigation... ...never from the assumption.

Seeing the Case Before Seeing the Claim

One of the habits that distinguishes exceptional healthcare attorneys is their ability to separate the patient's clinical story from the legal claim being made.

At first, those two concepts appear inseparable. A patient suffers harm. A claim is made. The attorney investigates. In reality, they are two entirely different things. The patient's clinical story exists whether litigation ever occurs.

The legal claim is one interpretation of that story.

Clinical Intelligence teaches attorneys to understand the patient's journey before deciding whether the legal claim accurately reflects it.

That distinction may seem subtle, but it fundamentally changes the order of the investigation.

Too often, the claim becomes the lens through which every record is reviewed. If the allegation is delayed diagnosis, the investigation naturally begins looking for evidence of delay. If the allegation concerns a medication error, attention immediately shifts toward prescribing decisions. If informed consent is questioned, documentation surrounding the consent process becomes the primary focus.

Each of those investigations may uncover important evidence. Each also carries a risk. The attorney may begin investigating the allegation before understanding the patient. Clinical Intelligence deliberately reverses that sequence.

It asks a different question.

- Who was this patient, and what happened to them, before we decide why we believe it happened?

That simple change in perspective frequently alters the entire direction of the case.

Case example: Two Attorneys, Two Different Investigations

Imagine two attorneys receiving the same referral.

A fifty-nine-year-old man presents to the emergency department complaining of chest discomfort, fatigue, and mild shortness of breath. He is discharged with a diagnosis of acid reflux. Twelve hours later he suffers a fatal myocardial infarction.

Attorney A begins exactly where most investigations begin. "Did the emergency physician miss the heart attack?"

The investigation immediately focuses on electrocardiograms, cardiac enzymes, emergency department documentation, and discharge decisions.

Attorney B begins somewhere different. "Who was this patient before he entered the emergency department?"

The investigation explores his baseline cardiac history, previous episodes of chest pain, cardiovascular risk factors, recent symptoms, medications, family history, prior investigations, and functional status. Only after understanding the patient's clinical background does the investigation move into the events occurring during the emergency department visit.

Neither attorney is acting improperly. Both are conducting legitimate investigations. The difference is that one investigation begins with the allegation. The other begins with the patient.

As additional records become available, Attorney B discovers that the patient had reported worsening exertional chest discomfort to his primary care physician three weeks earlier. An outpatient stress test had been recommended but never completed. Pharmacy records reveal that prescribed cardiac medication had not been collected for several months. Previous electrocardiograms provide an important comparison that changes the interpretation of the emergency department tracing.

Suddenly, the investigation has acquired depth.

The emergency department encounter is no longer viewed as an isolated event. It has become one chapter in a much longer clinical story.

That broader understanding benefits the attorney regardless of the eventual conclusion. If the emergency physician failed to recognize evolving myocardial infarction despite available evidence, the attorney can explain that failure within the context of the patient's overall clinical progression. If the investigation instead demonstrates that the presentation was genuinely atypical despite appropriate evaluation, the attorney has reached that conclusion through disciplined analysis rather than assumption.

In either situation, the attorney understands the case more completely. That is the objective.

Clinical Intelligence is not designed to produce more plaintiff cases or more defense cases.

It is designed to produce better-founded cases.

Why the Patient Must Come First

When attorneys begin with the patient rather than the allegation, several things happen naturally.

The investigation becomes more objective because it is no longer trying to prove a predetermined theory.

The chronology develops more accurately because it begins before the alleged negligence rather than at the moment the allegation arises.

Baseline function becomes easier to understand because the patient's life before the event is reconstructed rather than assumed.

Alternative explanations receive appropriate consideration because they are explored before they are dismissed.

Most importantly, causation becomes clearer because the patient's journey is viewed as a continuous process rather than a series of isolated incidents.

This approach often changes the questions attorneys ask during depositions.

Instead of immediately asking a physician why they failed to diagnose a condition, the attorney is able to ask how the physician interpreted the patient's presentation at that moment, what differential diagnoses were considered, what evidence supported each possibility, and what additional information influenced subsequent decisions.

Those are more clinically informed questions. They also tend to produce more meaningful answers. Before identifying the alleged negligence, ask yourself:

- Could I explain this patient's clinical journey to someone who has never seen the records?

If the answer is no, you are probably not ready to decide whether negligence occurred.

Understanding the patient must always come before evaluating the claim. The patient is the investigation. The claim is the hypothesis.

Every healthcare claim begins with an allegation. Every Clinical Intelligence investigation begins with the patient. That distinction prevents attorneys from allowing the allegation to dictate the direction of the investigation before the patient's clinical journey has been fully understood.

Clinical Intelligence therefore treats the legal claim as a hypothesis that must be tested-not as a conclusion that must be defended.

Attorneys who understand the patient before evaluating the claim build stronger cases because their litigation strategy grows out of the clinical evidence rather than being constrained by the original allegation.

The patient creates the story. The evidence explains the story. The law determines the consequences of the story. You've just spent an entire chapter learning to investigate healthcare cases differently.

Now I want you to pause before reading another page. Think about the last healthcare case you handled. Not the verdict. Not the settlement. Not the expert opinions. Think about the investigation.

Ask yourself honestly...

- Did I begin with the allegation or with the patient?
- Did I investigate the documentation or the patient's clinical journey?
- Did I accept my first theory too quickly?
- Did I ask enough clinical questions before asking legal questions?
- Did I know which evidence was missing?
- Did I understand the patient's baseline before evaluating the outcome?
- Did I investigate the process that produced the injury, or did I focus primarily on the injury itself?
- If I handled that same case today, after reading this chapter, what would I do differently?

If your answer is, "I would investigate differently," then Chapter One has already changed the way you practice healthcare litigation.

That is the purpose of Clinical Intelligence. Not to replace your legal judgment. To strengthen it.

Now let's learn how to determine whether the evidence itself deserves your trust.

The patient creates the story. The evidence explains the story. The law determines the consequences of the story.

PART II

THE LEXCURA CLINICAL INTELLIGENCE MODEL

Seven analytical pillars leading to Litigation-Ready Output

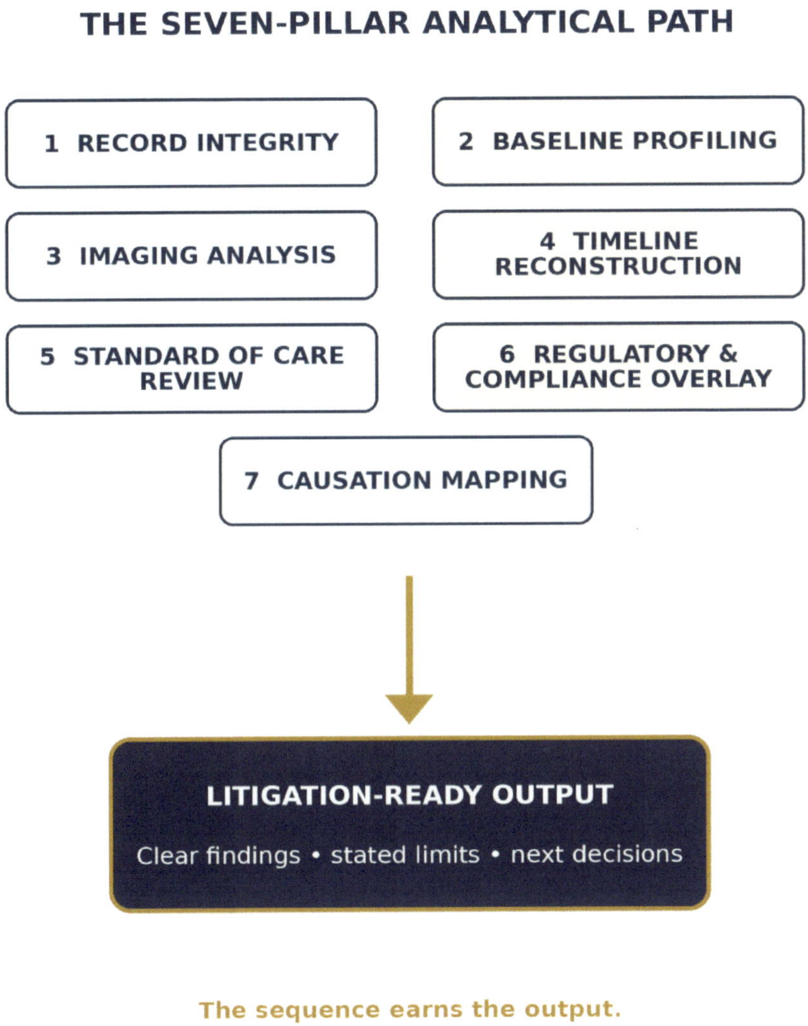

Figure 2 The seven pillars operate in sequence and together produce Litigation-Ready Output.

CHAPTER 4

Record Integrity

Imagine asking a room full of experienced healthcare attorneys a simple question. "When does a healthcare investigation actually begin?" Many would reasonably answer: "When the medical records arrive." Others might say:

"When I receive the first expert opinion."

Some would argue that it begins during the initial client interview, when the patient's story is first heard and the allegations are outlined.

Each answer contains some truth. None of them identifies where a Clinical Intelligence investigation begins. Clinical Intelligence begins one step earlier. It begins by asking a question that is surprisingly easy to overlook.

Can I trust the evidence upon which every future decision will depend?

That question may appear obvious, yet it is one of the most neglected aspects of healthcare litigation.

Attorneys understandably devote enormous effort to understanding the contents of the medical record. They analyze timelines, identify potential departures from the standard of care, retain respected experts, and develop carefully considered litigation strategies.

Far less attention is often given to a more fundamental issue. Whether the evidence itself deserves to become the foundation of those decisions.

That distinction lies at the heart of the first discipline of Clinical Intelligence.

Before we ask whether negligence occurred... Before we evaluate causation... Before we estimate damages... Before we retain experts...

We must first determine whether the evidence accurately reflects the patient's clinical journey.

Because if the foundation is unreliable, every conclusion built upon it becomes vulnerable.

The Medical Record Is Not The Patient

This is one of the most important concepts in Clinical Intelligence. A medical record is an extraordinarily valuable document. It records observations. Clinical decisions. Treatments. Communications. Investigations. Responses. Plans.

Without it, modern healthcare could not function, and healthcare litigation would be almost impossible.

Yet the medical record has never claimed to be a complete reconstruction of the patient's clinical journey.

It is a professional record created by multiple individuals, documenting different aspects of care, at different times, for different purposes.

Every clinician documents from their own perspective. Every entry reflects the information available at that particular moment. Every record therefore represents one part of a much larger clinical story. Clinical Intelligence asks attorneys to remember something that can easily be forgotten.

The chart is not the patient. The chart is one representation of the patient's journey. Sometimes it is remarkably complete. Sometimes it contains gaps. Sometimes it contains inconsistencies. Sometimes it contains assumptions that later prove incorrect.

Occasionally, it contains errors. None of those possibilities automatically weakens the case.

They simply remind us that evidence should always be evaluated before it is accepted.

That is not skepticism. It is disciplined investigation.

Case example: The Complete Record That Wasn't

An attorney receives more than four thousand pages of records involving a patient who developed permanent neurological injury following cervical spine surgery.

Every requested provider has responded. The hospital records are complete. Office records are available. Radiology reports are included. Operative notes are present. From an administrative standpoint, nothing appears to be missing.

Many investigations would begin immediately. Clinical Intelligence pauses. Not because additional records have necessarily been overlooked. Because completeness and reliability are different questions.

As the investigation progresses, one member of the Clinical Intelligence team notices that the operative report describes stable neurological monitoring throughout the procedure.

Later nursing documentation records immediate postoperative weakness. The anesthesia record documents several periods of significant hypotension. The intraoperative neuromonitoring report, however, has not been included. The attorney requests it. When it arrives, the investigation changes.

The report demonstrates sustained deterioration in motor evoked potentials nearly forty minutes before the conclusion of surgery.

The issue is no longer whether records were missing.

The issue is whether the available evidence was sufficient to explain what actually happened.

Nothing about the original chart suggested that the investigation was incomplete.

Only disciplined questioning revealed that an essential piece of the patient's story had not yet been examined.

That single document changed the direction of the case. Not because anyone intentionally concealed it.

Because no one had yet asked whether the evidence itself was complete enough to explain the patient's clinical journey.

That is Record Integrity.

Whenever you believe you have received a complete medical record, pause and ask one additional question.

- If this patient's clinical story is accurate, what evidence should I reasonably expect to exist?

Sometimes the answer will be: "Nothing else." Sometimes it will identify the one document that changes the entire investigation.

The discipline lies in asking the question before deciding that the investigation is complete.

Evidence should never be accepted simply because it exists. It should be trusted because it has been tested.

Healthcare litigation depends upon evidence, but not all evidence carries equal weight. Before conclusions are reached, Clinical Intelligence asks whether the evidence is complete, internally consistent, objectively supported, and capable of explaining the patient's clinical journey.

Only after that process has been completed should the attorney begin building the litigation strategy.

Attorneys who test their evidence before testing their legal theories identify weaknesses earlier, instruct experts more effectively, avoid unnecessary litigation costs, and develop cases that are significantly more resilient under scrutiny.

Never confuse having the records with understanding the evidence.

Record Integrity Begins Before the First Opinion

One of the most common mistakes in healthcare litigation is assuming that record review begins when someone starts reading the chart.

Clinical Intelligence disagrees. Record review begins much earlier.

It begins with determining whether the evidence deserves to be reviewed in the first place.

That statement may sound unusual at first, but consider how every other profession approaches an investigation.

A structural engineer does not evaluate a bridge until they are confident they are examining the correct structure and that the available inspection data are reliable.

An accident investigator does not reconstruct a collision before confirming that the measurements, photographs, and witness statements accurately represent the scene.

A forensic accountant does not calculate financial loss before determining whether the underlying records are complete and authentic.

Healthcare litigation should be no different.

Before asking an expert to explain the patient's outcome, before identifying potential departures from the standard of care, and before developing a litigation strategy, the attorney should have confidence that the evidence accurately reflects the patient's clinical journey.

That confidence does not come from simply possessing thousands of pages of records.

It comes from testing the integrity of those records.

This first discipline within the Lexcura Clinical Intelligence Model™ is called Record Integrity because the objective extends far beyond confirming that documents have been received.

The objective is to determine whether the available evidence can be trusted to support every important decision that follows.

That is a very different investigation.

What Does Record Integrity Actually Mean?

When attorneys first hear the term Record Integrity, they often assume it refers to verifying that records have not been altered or that pages are not missing.

Those issues are certainly important. They represent only a small part of the investigation. Record Integrity asks a much broader question.

Does the available evidence accurately and sufficiently explain the patient's clinical journey?

Answering that question requires much more than checking whether every page has been produced.

It requires the investigator to examine the quality of the evidence itself.

- Are the records internally consistent?
- Do the documented observations agree with the objective findings?
- Does the chronology make clinical sense?
- Are there unexplained gaps in treatment or documentation?
- Do laboratory trends support the documented assessment?
- Does diagnostic imaging confirm the working diagnosis?
- Do medication records align with physician orders and nursing documentation?
- Are there inconsistencies between different members of the healthcare team?

Most importantly...

- Does the evidence tell one coherent clinical story?

If the answer is no, the investigation is not yet ready to move forward.

Not because negligence has been ruled out. Not because negligence has been established. Because the foundation has not yet been tested. Clinical Intelligence deliberately refuses to build conclusions upon an unstable foundation.

Case example: When the Documentation Conflicted With the Evidence

A sixty-eight-year-old patient was admitted with increasing shortness of breath following major abdominal surgery.

Progress notes repeatedly described the patient as "clinically stable." The nursing documentation, however, painted a different picture. Respiratory rate continued to increase. Oxygen requirements steadily rose. Heart rate remained persistently elevated.

The patient became progressively less responsive. Arterial blood gases demonstrated worsening respiratory failure. Individually, none of these observations appeared remarkable. Collectively, they described a patient whose condition was steadily deteriorating.

Clinical Intelligence did not ask which document was correct.

It asked why two different clinical stories were emerging from the same admission.

The investigation revealed that the progress notes reflected intermittent physician assessments performed several hours apart, while the nursing documentation captured the patient's gradual deterioration throughout each shift. The objective physiological data consistently supported the nursing observations.

The issue was not that one clinician had documented incorrectly.

The issue was that no one had yet integrated all of the available evidence into one continuous clinical picture.

That integration fundamentally changed the investigation.

Instead of debating isolated documentation, the attorney now understood the patient's actual physiological progression.

Only then could meaningful questions regarding recognition, escalation, intervention, and causation be answered.

That is the purpose of Record Integrity. Not simply to verify documents. To verify the clinical story.

Whenever two parts of the medical record appear to tell different stories, resist the temptation to decide which one is correct.

Instead ask: "What clinical explanation could account for both?"

That question frequently reveals whether the apparent inconsistency represents a documentation issue, a communication failure, a difference in clinical perspective, or an important clue that the patient's deterioration was not being recognized consistently across the healthcare team.

Clinical Intelligence does not investigate inconsistencies to criticize documentation.

It investigates them because inconsistencies often identify the precise points where the patient's clinical journey became misunderstood.

This principle has enormous practical value during litigation. Opposing counsel will almost certainly identify inconsistencies within the medical record. Expert witnesses will interpret those inconsistencies. Jurors will hear competing explanations.

If the attorney has already investigated those issues through Record Integrity, very little comes as a surprise.

The inconsistencies have already been examined. The competing explanations have already been tested. The strengths and weaknesses have already been identified. The attorney enters litigation prepared rather than reactive. That is one of the greatest advantages of disciplined clinical investigation.

It reduces surprises.

The purpose of Record Integrity is not to prove that the records are complete. It is to determine whether the patient's clinical story can be trusted.

A healthcare chart is a collection of documents. A Clinical Intelligence investigation asks whether those documents, when viewed together, produce a coherent, evidence-based explanation of the patient's clinical journey. If they do not, the investigation is incomplete regardless of how many pages have been collected.

Attorneys who establish Record Integrity before evaluating liability, causation, or damages begin every later stage of litigation from a position of greater confidence. Expert opinions become more focused, depositions become more precise, and litigation strategy rests on evidence that has already been critically examined.

The investigation does not begin when you read the chart. It begins when you decide whether the chart deserves your trust.

Evidence Is Not Created Equal

One of the assumptions that can quietly undermine a healthcare case is the belief that every piece of evidence carries the same weight.

It does not.

Experienced attorneys understand that eyewitness testimony may be more persuasive than hearsay, contemporaneous documentation may carry greater weight than recollection years later, and objective evidence often becomes the anchor around which competing opinions are evaluated.

Healthcare litigation is no different. Not every piece of clinical evidence deserves the same level of confidence. Some evidence is highly objective. Some evidence is interpretive. Some evidence reflects observation.

Some evidence reflects opinion. Some evidence records what happened. Some evidence records what someone believed was happening. Clinical Intelligence teaches attorneys to recognize those differences before drawing conclusions.

That distinction becomes critically important because litigation often depends upon determining not simply what evidence exists, but which evidence should carry the greatest influence when conflicts arise.

Understanding the Hierarchy of Clinical Evidence

One of the most valuable habits an attorney can develop is learning to ask not only what the evidence says, but how the evidence was created.

For example, continuous cardiac monitoring provides a direct physiological record of the patient's heart rhythm. Laboratory values measure objective biological changes. Diagnostic imaging captures anatomical findings that can often be independently reviewed by multiple specialists.

These forms of evidence are fundamentally different from a retrospective progress note explaining why a decision was made several hours earlier.

Both are important. Both deserve careful consideration. Neither should automatically override the other. Clinical Intelligence teaches attorneys to understand the relationship between them. Objective findings frequently explain why clinicians should have become concerned.

Clinical documentation explains how clinicians interpreted those findings at the time. The investigation is strongest when both tell the same story.

When they do not, the attorney should not immediately decide which one is correct.

The attorney should investigate why the difference exists. Sometimes the explanation is entirely reasonable. Sometimes it identifies one of the most important issues in the case.

Case example: The Silent Monitor

A sixty-three-year-old patient was admitted following major vascular surgery.

Throughout the evening, nursing documentation described the patient as comfortable and recovering appropriately.

Several hours later the patient suffered an unexpected cardiac arrest. During discovery, the attorney obtained the bedside telemetry strips.

When reviewed alongside the nursing documentation, the monitor demonstrated repeated episodes of significant cardiac rhythm disturbance beginning almost two hours before the arrest.

The telemetry was accurate. The nursing documentation was also accurate. The nurse had documented what she observed during intermittent bedside assessments. The monitor recorded what occurred continuously between those assessments.

Neither source of evidence was incorrect. Neither source told the entire story.

Only when both were integrated did the patient's clinical deterioration become fully visible.

That discovery fundamentally altered the investigation. The issue was no longer whether appropriate observations had been documented.

The issue became whether the available physiological evidence should have prompted earlier recognition and intervention.

The difference is profound. One investigation evaluates documentation. The other evaluates the patient's actual clinical progression. That is the purpose of Record Integrity. Whenever two sources of evidence appear to disagree, ask yourself:

Are they actually inconsistent...

...or are they describing different parts of the same clinical story?

Healthcare is dynamic. Patients change from minute to minute. Documentation captures moments. Physiology continues between those moments. Clinical Intelligence teaches attorneys to investigate both.

Why Record Integrity Is About Trust

By now, you may have noticed that very little in this chapter has focused on missing pages, incomplete production, or clerical errors.

Those issues certainly matter. They are not the heart of Record Integrity. The real question is much simpler.

- Can I trust this evidence enough to allow it to influence every important decision that follows?

Trust does not require perfection. No healthcare record is perfect. Trust requires understanding. It requires knowing where the evidence is strong. Where it is weak. Where it is incomplete. Where it is objective.

Where it is interpretive. Where it answers questions. And where it raises entirely new ones. Only then can the attorney confidently move from investigation to legal analysis.

Clinical Intelligence therefore treats Record Integrity as the quality control process for the entire case.

Every later discipline depends upon it.

If the evidence cannot be trusted, neither can the conclusions drawn from it.

That is why Record Integrity is not simply the first discipline of the Lexcura Clinical Intelligence Model™.

It is the discipline that protects every other discipline.

Attorney's Evidence Checklist

Before you move beyond Record Integrity, ask yourself:

- □ Have I identified all sources of clinical evidence?

- □ Do the objective findings support the documented narrative?
- □ Are there unexplained inconsistencies within the record?
- □ Have I distinguished observation from interpretation?
- □ Are important records, images, monitoring data, or diagnostic studies still missing?
- □ Can I explain the patient's clinical journey without making assumptions?
- □ Would I feel confident presenting this evidence to my own expert without further investigation?

If any answer is no, the Record Integrity investigation is not yet complete.

Evidence earns trust through investigation, not assumption.

Healthcare litigation is built upon evidence, but confidence should never come simply from possessing records. Confidence comes from understanding the quality, consistency, completeness, and reliability of the evidence before it becomes the foundation for expert opinions and legal strategy.

Record Integrity is therefore not a preliminary administrative task. It is the first act of disciplined clinical investigation.

Attorneys who establish confidence in their evidence before developing liability theories enter every subsequent stage of litigation from a position of strength. Their experts work from a reliable foundation. Their depositions are more focused. Their case strategy is grounded in tested evidence rather than unexamined assumptions.

Evidence does not become trustworthy because it is documented. It becomes trustworthy because it has survived disciplined investigation.

Record Integrity Is an Investigation, Not a Checklist

One of the greatest mistakes an attorney can make is believing that Record Integrity is completed once every requested document has been received.

That is an administrative milestone. It is not an investigative milestone.

Clinical Intelligence views Record Integrity as an active process rather than a passive review. Every document, every observation, every laboratory result, every image, and every communication must be evaluated within the context of the patient's entire clinical journey. The purpose is not to collect information. The purpose is to determine whether the available evidence tells a complete, accurate, and clinically defensible story.

That distinction changes the attorney's role. Instead of asking, "Do I have everything?" the attorney begins asking, "Can I explain what happened without making assumptions?" If the answer is no, the investigation continues.

This approach requires discipline because healthcare records often create the illusion of completeness. Thousands of pages can create a false sense of confidence. The volume of documentation should never be confused with the quality of the evidence.

In Clinical Intelligence, confidence comes from understanding-not from page count.

Looking Beyond What Is Written

One of the habits developed by experienced Clinical Intelligence investigators is learning to pay as much attention to what is not documented as to what is.

That statement should not be misunderstood. Clinical Intelligence does not assume that every omission represents negligence.

Healthcare is practiced by human beings in busy, complex environments. Documentation will never capture every conversation, every observation, or every clinical thought.

The absence of documentation is not automatically evidence of poor care. It is, however, often the beginning of an important question.

- If a patient's condition was clearly deteriorating, was there evidence that escalation occurred?
- If a consultant was contacted, where is that communication documented?
- If medication was administered, where is the documented response?

- If the patient's family raised concerns repeatedly, how were those concerns addressed?
- If a clinician believed the patient was stable despite objective deterioration, what evidence supported that conclusion?

Clinical Intelligence does not treat these questions as accusations. It treats them as opportunities to understand the clinical story more completely. Sometimes the answers strengthen the case. Sometimes they weaken it.

In both situations, the attorney benefits because decisions are being made on understanding rather than assumption.

Case example: The Conversation That Was Never Documented

An eighty-year-old patient is admitted from a nursing facility with fever, confusion, and increasing lethargy.

The nursing documentation reflects repeated concerns regarding the patient's declining condition throughout the evening. Several entries indicate that the physician was notified.

The physician's progress note the following morning simply states, "Patient reviewed overnight. Continue current management." The patient deteriorates rapidly and dies later that afternoon from overwhelming sepsis. The family believes repeated requests for medical review were ignored.

The physician maintains that he was contacted several times, received appropriate information, and gave reasonable clinical instructions based upon what he had been told.

The documentation alone cannot resolve the disagreement. Clinical Intelligence therefore asks additional questions.

- What information was communicated during each telephone call?
- Did the nurse accurately describe the patient's physiological deterioration?
- Did the physician appreciate the significance of the information provided?
- Were escalation policies followed?

- Were there objective findings that should have prompted immediate bedside assessment regardless of the telephone discussion?

Notice that the investigation has moved beyond the absence of documentation. It is now examining the quality of the clinical communication itself.

Whether the conversations were documented perfectly becomes only one part of the investigation.

The larger question is whether the communication accurately reflected the patient's clinical condition and whether that communication supported appropriate decision-making.

That distinction frequently determines where responsibility ultimately lies.

Whenever you encounter limited or conflicting documentation, resist the temptation to immediately conclude that someone failed to document appropriately.

Instead ask:

"What clinical event should have occurred here, and what evidence would I expect to find if it did?"

That question changes the investigation.

Rather than searching for missing words, you begin searching for missing clinical understanding.

That is the purpose of Record Integrity.

As your investigation progresses, continually test the clinical story against four fundamental questions:

Does the documentation make clinical sense?

Does the physiology support the documentation?

Does the chronology support the physiology?

Does the combined evidence explain the patient's outcome?

If any one of those questions cannot be answered confidently, the investigation is not complete.

Do not move forward simply because the next stage of litigation is waiting.

A weak foundation does not become stronger because the case progresses. It simply becomes more expensive.

That is why Record Integrity is the first discipline within the Lexcura Clinical Intelligence Model™.

Every later conclusion depends upon the confidence established here.

Clinical Intelligence does not assume the record is wrong. It asks whether the record is sufficient to explain the patient's story.

Healthcare records are invaluable, but they are only one representation of a patient's clinical journey. Record Integrity is not an exercise in finding documentation errors. It is a disciplined process of determining whether the available evidence is sufficient, consistent, and clinically coherent before it becomes the basis of litigation strategy.

The attorney who asks whether the record is sufficient, rather than merely complete, begins the investigation from a fundamentally stronger position.

When Record Integrity is performed thoroughly, expert opinions become more reliable because they are based on a tested clinical foundation. Depositions become more focused because inconsistencies have already been investigated. Most importantly, attorneys develop litigation strategies based upon evidence that has been challenged before the opposing side has an opportunity to challenge it.

A complete file answers administrative questions. Record Integrity answers investigative questions.

Figure 3 Record Integrity tests source, time, consistency, completeness, and reliability before an opinion is allowed to rest on the evidence.

CHAPTER 5

Evidence Experts and Earned Conclusions

The Expert Should Not Be Your Investigation

One of the most common practices in healthcare litigation is to obtain the medical records, perform an initial review, and then send everything to an expert with a simple question.

"Do I have a case?" That approach is understandable.

Experts possess specialized medical knowledge. They understand disease processes, standards of care, and clinical decision-making in ways that most attorneys cannot reasonably be expected to.

Clinical Intelligence does not diminish the importance of expert review. It strengthens it. The purpose of Clinical Intelligence is not to replace the expert.

The purpose is to ensure that the expert begins their work with the strongest possible clinical foundation.

Those are two very different objectives. Consider the position of the expert.

If they receive incomplete records, an untested chronology, unresolved inconsistencies, unidentified missing evidence, and a litigation theory that has never been critically examined, they are forced to spend valuable time performing work that should already have been completed.

Instead of applying their expertise to answering sophisticated clinical questions, they are reconstructing the basic investigation.

That is not the highest and best use of an expert's time. Clinical Intelligence prepares the case before the expert becomes involved. The investigation identifies missing evidence. The chronology has been tested.

The patient's baseline has begun to emerge. Documentation inconsistencies have been investigated. Alternative explanations have been considered.

The expert is then asked to address the questions that truly require expert opinion rather than spending time discovering problems that could have been identified much earlier.

That approach benefits everyone. The attorney receives a more focused opinion. The expert works from a stronger investigative foundation.

The client benefits from a more efficient and disciplined evaluation of the case.

Most importantly, the litigation strategy develops from evidence that has already survived careful clinical scrutiny.

Case example: Two Different Expert Referrals

Two attorneys retain the same critical care physician to review separate sepsis cases.

Attorney A sends 6,000 pages of medical records with one instruction.

"Please review these records and let me know whether the standard of care was breached."

Attorney B sends the same records. The accompanying instruction is different. It includes: A verified chronology. A summary of the patient's baseline. Identified documentation inconsistencies. Outstanding questions requiring expert clarification.

Objective laboratory trends. Evidence that remains incomplete. Alternative clinical explanations already considered. Specific questions regarding recognition, escalation, intervention, and causation. The physician reviews both cases. The medicine is identical. The records are identical.

The physician's expertise is identical. The quality of the investigation is not.

- Which attorney is more likely to receive a focused, efficient, and clinically meaningful expert opinion?

The answer is obvious. Clinical Intelligence did not replace the expert.

It allowed the expert to practice at the highest level of their expertise.

That is precisely what the discipline is intended to accomplish. Before retaining your first expert, ask yourself:

"Am I asking this expert to apply their expertise...or to perform my investigation?"

Experts should answer expert questions. Clinical Intelligence ensures the investigation has already identified what those questions are.

Why This Changes Litigation

Many attorneys believe the expert begins the clinical investigation. Clinical Intelligence teaches something different. The expert should begin where the investigation ends. That distinction has profound consequences. Experts become more efficient.

Reports become more focused. Weaknesses are identified earlier. Costs are reduced. Discovery becomes more targeted. Depositions become more productive. Settlement discussions become more informed. Most importantly...

The attorney enters every stage of litigation with greater confidence because the expert opinion has been built upon a disciplined investigative foundation rather than an incomplete review of the records.

Clinical Intelligence therefore changes the relationship between the attorney and the expert. The attorney is no longer asking, "Please tell me what happened." The attorney is asking,

"Here is the clinical investigation. Help me understand whether these conclusions withstand expert scrutiny."

That is a far more sophisticated conversation.

It is also one that experienced experts generally appreciate because it allows them to concentrate on applying their professional judgment rather than reconstructing the case from the beginning.

Experts should strengthen the investigation-not begin it.

Expert witnesses are among the most valuable resources in healthcare litigation. Their role is to provide independent professional opinions on issues that require specialized medical knowledge. Their expertise should not be consumed by reconstructing an investigation that could have been substantially completed before the records ever reached their desk.

Clinical Intelligence prepares the investigation so that expert time is devoted to answering the questions that truly require expert judgment.

Attorneys who present experts with disciplined, clinically investigated cases receive more focused opinions, identify weaknesses earlier, reduce unnecessary costs, and develop litigation strategies that are grounded in both evidence and expert reasoning.

Clinical Intelligence prepares the case. The expert validates the medicine.

Record Integrity Changes Every Decision That Follows

One of the easiest ways to understand the importance of Record Integrity is to imagine building a house.

No experienced builder begins constructing the walls before confirming that the foundation is stable. It makes little difference how carefully the remainder of the house is designed if the structure beneath it cannot support the weight above.

Healthcare litigation is remarkably similar.

Every important decision rests upon the quality of the investigation that came before it.

The decision to accept or decline the case. The experts you retain. The questions you ask during depositions. The documents you request during discovery. The value you assign to the claim.

The settlement recommendations you make to your client. The strategy you ultimately present at trial. Each of those decisions depends upon one fundamental assumption. That the evidence supporting them is reliable.

Clinical Intelligence asks attorneys not to assume reliability. It asks them to establish it.

That is why Record Integrity is not simply the first discipline within the Lexcura Clinical Intelligence Model™.

It is the discipline that protects every decision that follows. If Record Integrity is weak, every later conclusion becomes vulnerable. If

Record Integrity is strong, every later conclusion becomes more defensible.

The attorney may still lose the case. The expert may still disagree. The jury may still reach an unexpected verdict. Those realities can never be eliminated.

What Clinical Intelligence does eliminate is the avoidable weakness that develops when important decisions are made before the evidence has been thoroughly investigated.

That distinction is one of the defining characteristics of disciplined healthcare litigation.

Case example: The Expensive Assumption

A forty-seven-year-old patient suffers permanent neurological injury following cervical spine surgery. The initial allegation is straightforward.

The surgeon is accused of negligently positioning the patient during the operation, resulting in spinal cord injury.

The attorney retains a neurosurgical expert shortly after receiving the hospital records. The expert raises an unexpected question. "Where are the intraoperative neuromonitoring records?" The attorney is surprised.

The operative report had stated that neurological monitoring remained satisfactory throughout the procedure.

No one realized that the actual monitoring records had never been requested. Several weeks later they are obtained. The findings dramatically change the investigation.

The monitoring demonstrates a gradual decline in neurological signals beginning shortly after prolonged hypotension develops during anesthesia.

The surgical positioning now appears considerably less significant than the patient's sustained reduction in spinal cord perfusion.

The litigation strategy changes. A new anesthesia expert is retained. Additional discovery is required. Several depositions must be repeated.

Months of work are redirected because one critical assumption was made before Record Integrity had been established.

The issue was never the expert. The issue was never the attorney. The issue was the investigation.

Had Record Integrity been completed before the first expert was retained, the missing evidence would almost certainly have been identified much earlier.

The litigation strategy would have developed upon a much stronger foundation. That is not simply a more efficient investigation. It is a more reliable investigation.

The Cost of Getting It Wrong

When Record Integrity is incomplete, the consequences extend far beyond missing documents. Attorneys may retain the wrong specialty of expert. Experts may be asked to answer the wrong questions. Depositions may focus on issues that later prove to be secondary.

Discovery requests may overlook evidence that ultimately becomes central to the case.

Settlement decisions may be made before the true strengths and weaknesses of the evidence are understood.

Each of these problems shares the same origin. The litigation strategy moved ahead of the investigation. Clinical Intelligence deliberately reverses that sequence. The investigation must always move ahead of the litigation strategy.

That principle protects every subsequent stage of the case.

It also explains why Record Integrity cannot be treated as an administrative task delegated entirely to support staff.

It is an investigative discipline. It requires clinical reasoning. It requires legal judgment.

Most importantly, it requires the willingness to delay important conclusions until the evidence has earned them.

That discipline often determines whether the attorney spends the remainder of the case confirming strong decisions or correcting avoidable ones.

Before making any significant litigation decision, ask yourself:

What assumption am I making that depends upon evidence I have not yet tested?

If you cannot answer that question confidently, pause. The next stage of the investigation may depend upon it. Clinical Intelligence is not about slowing the case.

It is about preventing avoidable mistakes that become progressively more difficult-and more expensive-to correct later.

Experienced healthcare attorneys often say that cases become more expensive as they become more complicated.

Clinical Intelligence offers a different perspective. Cases become more expensive when uncertainty is discovered late rather than early.

Record Integrity moves uncertainty to the beginning of the investigation, where it is least costly to address.

That single change improves almost every decision that follows. Experts receive stronger instructions. Discovery becomes more purposeful. Depositions become more focused. Settlement evaluations become more realistic. Trial preparation becomes more disciplined.

The attorney gains something that cannot easily be purchased later in the life of the case.

Confidence built upon tested evidence.

Every litigation strategy inherits the strengths and weaknesses of the investigation that created it.

A litigation strategy cannot become stronger than the evidence upon which it is built. Record Integrity ensures that the evidence has been critically examined before it begins influencing expert opinions, discovery, settlement, or trial preparation.

Strong investigations produce strong strategies. Weak investigations eventually expose weak strategies. Clinical Intelligence exists to identify those weaknesses before they become expensive.

Attorneys who complete Record Integrity before committing to a litigation strategy reduce avoidable surprises, improve expert collaboration, strengthen discovery, and make more confident decisions throughout the life of the case.

The quality of your strategy will never exceed the quality of your investigation.

Strategy Depends on the Investigation

"Every litigation strategy inherits the strengths and weaknesses of the investigation that created it."

Healthcare litigation does not become stronger because more experts are retained, more depositions are taken, or more motions are filed. It becomes stronger when every legal decision is supported by a disciplined clinical investigation.

A weak investigation produces uncertain conclusions. Uncertain conclusions produce vulnerable strategies.

Strong investigations produce strategies that remain stable as new evidence emerges because they were built upon evidence that had already been challenged before the litigation began.

Clinical Intelligence therefore places investigation before advocacy. Not because advocacy is less important. Because advocacy is only as persuasive as the investigation supporting it. Before accepting a case... Investigate. Before retaining experts...

Investigate. Before alleging negligence... Investigate. Before valuing damages... Investigate. Before preparing for trial... Investigate. Every stage of litigation becomes stronger when the investigation comes first. The investigation earns the right to build the strategy.

Evidence Is Dynamic, Not Static

One of the easiest mistakes to make in healthcare litigation is to think of medical evidence as something fixed.

The records are produced. The chart is assembled. The pages are numbered. The investigation begins.

From that point forward, it is tempting to believe that the evidence simply waits to be analyzed.

Clinical practice tells a different story. Evidence evolves. Not because the events themselves change. The patient's journey has already occurred. What changes is our understanding of that journey.

A laboratory result that appears insignificant during an initial review may become critically important once later events are understood.

A nursing observation that seems routine may suddenly acquire new meaning when viewed alongside telemetry data.

A brief consultation note may become the turning point in the investigation after the patient's baseline has been reconstructed.

The evidence has not changed. The attorney's understanding has. Clinical Intelligence recognizes that distinction. Evidence is not static. It develops as the investigation develops.

That is why experienced investigators repeatedly return to the same records throughout the life of a case.

Not because they overlooked something.

Because each stage of the investigation allows them to ask better questions than they were capable of asking before.

That is an important principle. Clinical Intelligence is not a single review of the records. It is an evolving investigation.

Case example: The Laboratory Result No One Noticed

A sixty-nine-year-old patient was admitted with abdominal pain, vomiting, and increasing confusion. Initial laboratory studies demonstrated a mildly elevated lactate level. Nothing in the emergency department documentation suggested immediate concern.

The patient was admitted for observation.

Over the next twelve hours, the lactate level increased significantly, blood pressure gradually declined, urine output decreased, and the patient ultimately required emergency surgery for bowel ischemia.

When the attorney first reviewed the case, the elevated lactate appeared to be one laboratory result among many.

Months later, after reconstructing the patient's timeline, reviewing the physiological progression, and understanding the patient's baseline vascular disease, that same laboratory value became one of the earliest objective indicators that tissue perfusion was already deteriorating.

The laboratory result had not changed. Its significance had.

Clinical Intelligence therefore teaches attorneys never to assume that the first interpretation of the evidence will necessarily be the most accurate one.

As the investigation becomes stronger, the evidence often becomes clearer.

The Investigation Should Mature

One of the characteristics of an effective Clinical Intelligence investigation is that it matures over time.

Early in the investigation, the attorney is identifying questions. Later, those questions begin to acquire answers. Still later, relationships between seemingly unrelated pieces of evidence become visible. Finally, a clinically coherent explanation emerges that can withstand expert scrutiny.

That progression should be expected. Attorneys should not become concerned because their understanding of the case changes. They should become concerned if it does not.

A healthcare case involving thousands of pages of records, multiple specialties, and complex physiology should produce a deeper understanding as the investigation progresses.

If the attorney's understanding remains unchanged despite significant additional evidence, an important opportunity may have been missed.

Clinical Intelligence therefore encourages intellectual flexibility. The strongest investigators are not those who defend their first opinion. They are those who continuously refine their understanding as the evidence develops. That is not uncertainty.

That is disciplined investigation. Ask yourself throughout the life of every case:

"If I reviewed these same records again today, what would I notice now that I couldn't have recognized three months ago?"

That question reminds the attorney that investigations mature. So should the investigator. This principle has practical consequences throughout healthcare litigation.

Expert reports become stronger because they are informed by an investigation that has evolved rather than remained fixed.

Depositions become more productive because earlier assumptions have already been tested.

Settlement discussions become more realistic because the attorney's understanding reflects the entire investigation rather than the first review of the records.

Trial preparation becomes more confident because every important conclusion has matured alongside the evidence itself.

Clinical Intelligence therefore rejects the idea that record review is a single event.

It is a continuous process of refinement. The evidence does not change. Your understanding of the evidence should.

Every healthcare investigation begins with incomplete understanding. That is not a weakness; it is the nature of complex litigation. As additional evidence is gathered, relationships are recognized, and clinical questions are answered, the attorney's understanding should mature. Clinical Intelligence expects that progression and encourages attorneys to revisit their conclusions as the investigation develops.

Attorneys who continually refine their understanding identify stronger theories, recognize weaknesses earlier, provide better expert instructions, and enter trial with conclusions that have been tested repeatedly rather than accepted prematurely.

An investigation that never changes its thinking usually stops asking better questions.

Record Integrity and Intellectual Honesty

Every attorney enters a healthcare case hoping to find answers. That is entirely appropriate. Clients expect answers. Courts expect answers. Experts are retained to provide answers. Ultimately, juries are asked to reach answers.

Clinical Intelligence agrees that answers are important.

It simply insists that the quality of those answers depends upon the quality of the questions that came first.

That may sound philosophical. It is actually intensely practical.

The strongest healthcare investigations are rarely distinguished by having more information than everyone else.

They are distinguished by asking better questions about the information already available. Record Integrity is built upon that principle. It requires the attorney to become intellectually honest before becoming legally persuasive.

That means resisting the temptation to overlook inconvenient evidence simply because it complicates the theory of the case.

It means acknowledging when two pieces of evidence genuinely appear inconsistent rather than forcing them into premature agreement.

It means recognizing when an important question has not yet been answered instead of assuming that an answer must already exist.

Most importantly, it means remaining willing to change your understanding of the case when the evidence justifies doing so.

That last point deserves particular attention. Some attorneys worry that changing their understanding demonstrates uncertainty. Clinical Intelligence views it differently. Changing your understanding in response to better evidence demonstrates discipline.

The investigation is doing exactly what it should do. Healthcare is complex. Patients are complex. The strongest investigations are not those that never change direction. They are those that become progressively more accurate as understanding develops.

That is not inconsistency. That is professional maturity.

Case example: The Investigation That Changed Course

A sixty-two-year-old woman underwent elective carotid endarterectomy.

Several hours after surgery she developed weakness affecting her left arm and leg.

The family's immediate concern was that the surgeon had caused an intraoperative stroke.

The attorney's initial review focused almost entirely on the operation itself. The operative report. The anesthesia record. The surgical technique. Everything appeared to point toward an intraoperative event. Record Integrity required the investigation to continue.

As additional evidence was reviewed, postoperative blood pressure recordings demonstrated prolonged hypotension during recovery.

Neurological observations showed a gradual progression of symptoms rather than an immediate deficit.

Vascular imaging suggested postoperative thrombosis rather than technical injury during surgery. The investigation changed. Not because the original theory was unreasonable. Because the evidence supported a different explanation. The attorney had two choices.

Defend the original theory. Or follow the evidence. Clinical Intelligence requires only one answer. Follow the evidence.

The investigation became stronger because the attorney was willing to let the evidence lead the case rather than allowing the case to lead the evidence.

That is intellectual honesty. That is Record Integrity.

One of the most difficult questions you will ever ask yourself is also one of the most important.

"If the evidence takes me somewhere I wasn't expecting to go...am I willing to follow it?"

Every healthcare attorney believes the answer is yes. Clinical Intelligence asks you to prove it. Not to anyone else. To yourself. Because the integrity of the investigation depends upon it.

Why This Matters to the Client

Clients come to attorneys seeking certainty. They want someone to explain what happened. They want accountability. They want justice. Those are entirely reasonable expectations. The greatest service an attorney can provide is not simply confidence.

It is confidence that has been earned. A client is better served by hearing, "Our investigation changed because we discovered additional evidence,"

than by discovering months later that an important assumption should have been questioned much earlier.

Clinical Intelligence therefore protects more than the litigation. It protects the attorney's credibility. It protects the expert's credibility. Most importantly, it protects the client's trust. That trust is built upon one principle.

The investigation followed the evidence wherever it led. The investigation owes its loyalty to the evidence-not to the theory.

Clinical Intelligence is founded on intellectual honesty. Every theory is provisional until it has been tested against the available evidence. Attorneys who remain willing to refine, modify, or even abandon an early theory when the evidence demands it build stronger, more credible cases than those who become committed to defending their first impression.

The discipline is not measured by how confidently conclusions are reached.

It is measured by how rigorously those conclusions have been challenged before they are accepted.

Attorneys who allow evidence to direct the investigation identify stronger theories of liability, recognize viable defenses earlier, work more effectively with experts, and develop litigation strategies that withstand scrutiny because they were never built upon convenience or assumption.

The strongest investigator is not the one who proves a theory.

It is the one who is willing to change the theory when the evidence requires it.

The Discipline of Suspending Judgment

One of the greatest challenges in healthcare litigation is that attorneys are expected to make decisions long before every answer is available.

- Should the case be accepted?
- Should additional records be requested?

- Should experts be retained?
- Should significant financial resources be committed?
- Should settlement discussions begin?

Every one of these decisions requires professional judgment.

The difficulty is that judgment often develops before the investigation has been completed.

Clinical Intelligence asks attorneys to develop a habit that may initially feel uncomfortable.

Suspend judgment until the investigation has earned it. This does not mean delaying every decision indefinitely. Healthcare litigation cannot function that way.

It means recognizing the difference between a working conclusion and a final conclusion.

A working conclusion allows the investigation to move forward while remaining open to change.

A final conclusion closes the investigation before every important question has been answered.

Record Integrity deliberately encourages attorneys to work with provisional conclusions rather than permanent ones.

That distinction protects the investigation from becoming anchored to assumptions that later prove inaccurate.

Professional investigators in many disciplines understand this principle.

Aviation investigators rarely announce the cause of an aircraft accident before every piece of evidence has been examined.

Fire investigators do not identify the origin of a fire before eliminating alternative explanations.

Homicide investigators do not build a prosecution around the first suspect without continually testing the evidence as the investigation develops.

Healthcare litigation deserves the same discipline. The objective is not to delay decisions.

The objective is to ensure that important decisions mature as the investigation matures.

That discipline often separates exceptional investigators from merely experienced ones.

Case example: The Diagnosis That Was Too Obvious

A forty-five-year-old woman presented repeatedly to her primary care physician complaining of fatigue, weight loss, and intermittent abdominal discomfort.

Over several months she was treated for stress, irritable bowel syndrome, and depression.

Eventually she was diagnosed with advanced colorectal cancer. The family believed the diagnosis had been missed. The attorney understandably focused on delayed cancer diagnosis. Clinical Intelligence began with a different question.

Was cancer the first diagnosis that should reasonably have been suspected?

The investigation reconstructed each consultation individually. At the first visit the symptoms were nonspecific. At the second visit laboratory studies were only mildly abnormal. By the third visit additional warning signs had emerged.

By the fourth visit the pattern had changed significantly. The investigation demonstrated something important.

The issue was not whether cancer should have been diagnosed at the first consultation.

The issue was identifying the point at which the accumulating clinical evidence required a different diagnostic pathway.

That distinction changed the entire litigation strategy.

Instead of arguing that every consultation represented negligence, the attorney could identify the specific consultation at which the standard of care changed and explain precisely why.

The argument became more focused. More credible. More persuasive. Clinical Intelligence had not strengthened the allegation. It had strengthened the reasoning supporting the allegation. That is a much more powerful position.

Why Precision Matters

One of the characteristics shared by outstanding healthcare litigators is precision. They do not make broader allegations than the evidence can support. They identify the precise clinical decision that changed the patient's course.

They identify the precise physiological evidence supporting that conclusion.

They identify the precise opportunity where different action would probably have altered the patient's outcome.

Precision builds credibility. Broad allegations often weaken it.

Record Integrity exists to create that precision before the attorney ever reaches questions of negligence, causation, or damages.

That is why it is impossible to separate disciplined investigation from effective advocacy.

One depends upon the other.

Whenever you believe you have identified the central issue in a healthcare case, ask yourself one more question.

"Exactly when did the evidence become sufficient to support this conclusion?" Not when the outcome became obvious. Not when the family became concerned. Not when litigation began.

- When did the evidence itself justify the conclusion?

That question frequently transforms a reasonable opinion into a compelling one. The investigation earns the conclusion. The conclusion should never outrun the investigation.

One of the greatest threats to any healthcare investigation is premature certainty. Attorneys naturally want answers, but the strongest answers are those that emerge only after the evidence has been thoroughly examined, alternative explanations have been considered, and the patient's clinical journey has been accurately reconstructed.

Clinical Intelligence therefore encourages disciplined patience. Conclusions are not delayed because the attorney lacks confidence. They are delayed because confidence should be earned.

Attorneys who allow conclusions to mature alongside the investigation build stronger cases, instruct experts more effectively, ask more precise deposition questions, and present arguments that are grounded in disciplined reasoning rather than early assumption.

Never allow your conclusion to arrive before your investigation does.

Record Integrity Is About Reconstructing Clinical Reality

One of the most important lessons in Clinical Intelligence is that the medical record and the patient's clinical reality are not always identical.

That statement is not intended to criticize healthcare documentation. It is intended to recognize its purpose.

Medical records are created to support patient care. They document assessments, treatments, observations, communications, and clinical decision-making as care is being delivered. They are not written to explain every aspect of a patient's journey to future attorneys, expert witnesses, or juries.

Clinical Intelligence respects that distinction. It also recognizes that litigation requires something different.

Healthcare litigation requires the attorney to reconstruct, as accurately as possible, what actually happened to the patient.

Sometimes the documentation and the patient's clinical reality align almost perfectly. Sometimes they do not. Understanding the difference is one of the primary responsibilities of Record Integrity. The objective is never to criticize the documentation.

The objective is to determine whether the documentation accurately reflects the patient's physiological progression, the clinical decisions that were made, and the sequence in which those decisions influenced the patient's outcome.

That investigation requires more than reading the chart. It requires reconstructing reality.

Case example: The Stable Patient

A seventy-four-year-old patient is admitted with community-acquired pneumonia.

Throughout the first hospital day, several physician progress notes describe the patient as "stable."

When those notes are read in isolation, they create the impression of a patient who is responding appropriately to treatment.

The objective evidence tells a different story. The respiratory rate rises steadily. Oxygen requirements increase. Blood pressure gradually falls. Serum lactate doubles. Urine output declines. Family members repeatedly express concern that the patient appears significantly worse.

By the following morning, the patient requires transfer to the intensive care unit with septic shock.

Clinical Intelligence does not ask whether the physician documented incorrectly. Instead, it asks a more important question.

- How could a patient be described as stable while objective physiological evidence demonstrates progressive deterioration?

Several explanations are possible. The physician may have assessed the patient before the deterioration became obvious. The significance of the physiological changes may not yet have been appreciated. Communication between members of the healthcare team may have been incomplete.

The term stable may have been used differently than the attorney initially understood.

Notice what Record Integrity is doing. It is not looking for blame. It is looking for understanding.

Only after the clinical reality has been reconstructed can the attorney fairly evaluate whether the patient's deterioration should reasonably have been recognized sooner.

That distinction protects the investigation from reaching conclusions before the evidence has been fully integrated.

Clinical Reality Is Built From Relationships

One laboratory value rarely explains a case. One nursing note rarely explains a case. One imaging study rarely explains a case. Patients are not collections of isolated events. They are dynamic physiological systems.

Every observation influences another. Heart rate influences perfusion. Perfusion influences organ function. Organ function influences laboratory results. Laboratory results influence clinical decision-making. Clinical decisions influence outcome. Clinical Intelligence therefore investigates relationships before reaching conclusions.

The attorney should become comfortable asking questions such as:

- How does this observation relate to everything else I already know?
- Does this finding strengthen the current explanation?
- Does it weaken it?
- Does it suggest an entirely different explanation?
- Is this the beginning of deterioration or merely the point where deterioration became visible?

Those are Clinical Intelligence questions.

They are also the questions that separate an investigation from a record review.

When you review a healthcare record, remember this: You are not reading pages. You are reconstructing a human experience. Every entry represents a moment in that patient's journey.

Your responsibility is to understand how those moments connect into one clinically coherent story.

Why This Matters Before Discovery

One of the greatest advantages of completing Record Integrity before formal discovery begins is that the attorney enters discovery already understanding the clinical landscape of the case.

Discovery is no longer an exercise in searching for problems. It becomes an opportunity to answer specific clinical questions that remain unresolved. Depositions become more focused because the attorney understands where inconsistencies exist.

Experts receive clearer instructions because the important investigative issues have already been identified.

Additional document requests become more precise because the attorney knows exactly which gaps remain in the clinical story.

This changes the entire direction of litigation.

Rather than allowing discovery to define the investigation, the investigation begins defining discovery.

That is a significant strategic advantage.

Record Integrity is the discipline of reconstructing clinical reality before constructing legal strategy.

Attorneys do not litigate documentation. They litigate what happened to a patient.

Record Integrity ensures that the available evidence has been integrated into an accurate reconstruction of the patient's clinical reality before liability theories, causation opinions, or litigation strategies begin to develop.

That process protects the integrity of every later decision.

When attorneys understand the patient's clinical reality before entering discovery, they ask better questions, identify stronger evidence, prepare experts more effectively, and develop litigation strategies that are substantially more difficult to undermine.

Clinical reality should shape legal strategy-not the other way around.

How Investigations Begin to Fail

Contrary to popular belief, healthcare investigations rarely fail because someone overlooks one dramatic piece of evidence.

More often, they fail quietly. A small assumption goes unchallenged. A laboratory trend is accepted without considering its significance. A progress note is read without comparing it to the objective physiology.

A chronology is accepted without questioning whether the patient's deterioration actually began earlier.

None of these mistakes appears particularly significant in isolation.

Together, they gradually shape an investigation that begins moving away from the patient's clinical reality.

That is how weak investigations develop. Not through incompetence. Through accumulation. Every unchallenged assumption becomes part of the next conclusion. Every conclusion influences the next decision.

Eventually, the litigation strategy begins resting upon foundations that were never deliberately tested.

Clinical Intelligence was developed to interrupt that process.

It asks attorneys to stop periodically throughout the investigation and ask one very simple question.

"How do I know this is true?" That question sounds almost childlike.

It is one of the most powerful investigative tools an attorney can possess.

Every important conclusion should survive that question. If it cannot, the investigation has identified an opportunity to become stronger.

Case example: The Assumption That Followed the Entire Case

A fifty-eight-year-old man underwent elective coronary artery bypass surgery.

Several hours after surgery he became increasingly confused and developed weakness affecting his right side.

The initial progress note documented, "Likely postoperative delirium." That phrase appeared repeatedly throughout the following day. Subsequent clinicians continued documenting postoperative delirium as the working diagnosis. The attorney naturally accepted that explanation during the first review.

Clinical Intelligence did something different. It asked a single question. "How do we know this was postoperative delirium?" The investigation returned to the evidence. The patient's neurological examination. Blood pressure trends.

Telemetry recordings. Medication administration. Family observations. Repeat neurological assessments. Brain imaging. As each piece of evidence was examined, another possibility emerged.

The patient's symptoms were more consistent with an evolving ischemic stroke than uncomplicated postoperative delirium.

The original documentation had not been unreasonable. It reflected the working diagnosis at that moment.

The problem was that the working diagnosis gradually became accepted as though it had been proven.

Clinical Intelligence deliberately separates a working diagnosis from an established conclusion. The attorney's investigation therefore followed the evidence rather than the documentation. The result was a fundamentally different understanding of the patient's postoperative course.

One question changed the investigation. "How do we know?"

Conclusions Must Be Earned

Clinical Intelligence teaches attorneys never to inherit conclusions without understanding how those conclusions were reached.

Every diagnosis. Every opinion. Every interpretation. Every allegation. Every expert conclusion. Should be capable of answering the same question.

What evidence supports this conclusion?

That principle applies equally to plaintiff experts, defense experts, treating physicians, consultants, and Clinical Intelligence investigators themselves.

No opinion receives special protection. Every opinion earns credibility through evidence. That discipline protects the attorney from becoming dependent upon authority alone. Instead, authority is evaluated alongside reasoning. That is a far stronger position from which to litigate.

Whenever you encounter an important conclusion in the medical record, pause before accepting it.

Ask yourself:

What objective evidence supports this conclusion?

What evidence contradicts it?

Could another reasonable explanation exist?

Has this conclusion been tested...or simply repeated?

Remember... Repeated conclusions do not become stronger because they appear more often. They become stronger only when they are supported by stronger evidence.

One of the most effective ways to prepare for expert review, deposition, or trial is to challenge your own conclusions before anyone else has the opportunity.

Clinical Intelligence encourages attorneys to become the first and most demanding critic of their own investigation.

If your reasoning survives your own scrutiny, it is far more likely to survive the scrutiny of opposing experts, opposing counsel, and ultimately the court.

That is not pessimism. It is preparation. Every important conclusion should be capable of answering one question. "How do we know?"

Healthcare litigation often involves conclusions that gradually become accepted simply because they are repeated throughout the medical record. Clinical Intelligence requires every significant conclusion to be tested against the objective evidence supporting it.

The question is not whether a conclusion appears reasonable. The question is whether the evidence justifies confidence in that conclusion.

Attorneys who routinely ask "How do we know?" identify unsupported assumptions earlier, instruct experts more effectively, prepare stronger depositions, and build litigation strategies that are considerably more resistant to challenge.

Clinical Intelligence does not inherit conclusions. It investigates them.

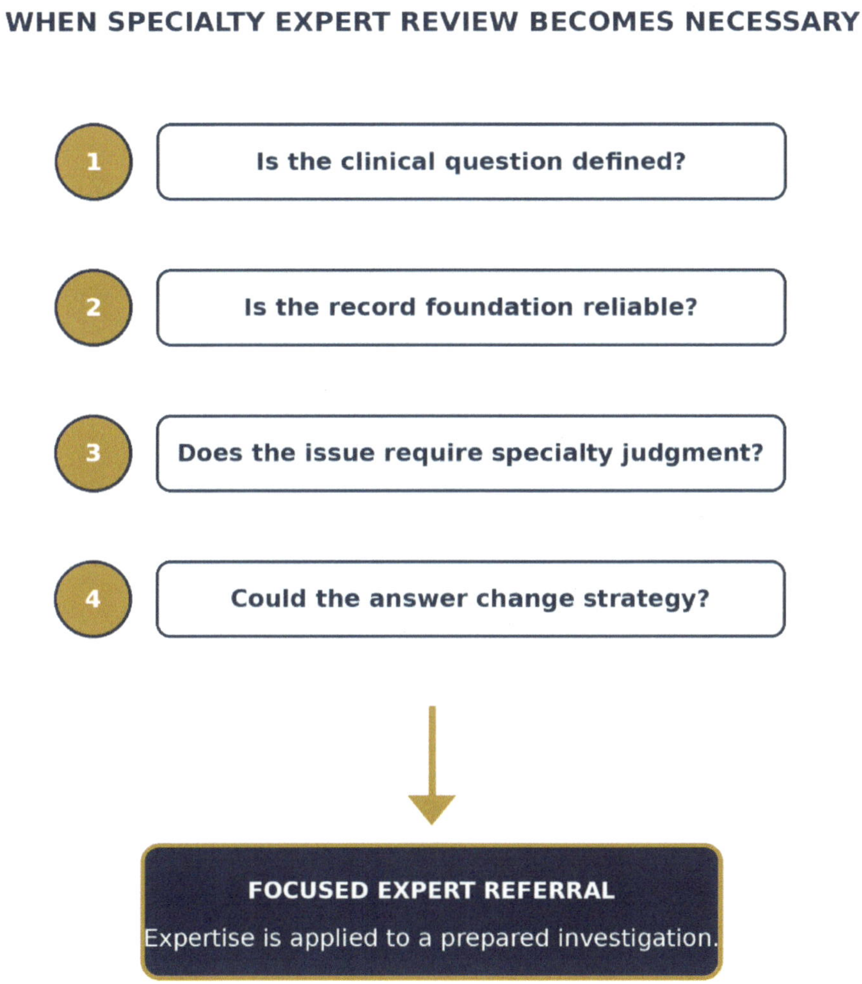

Figure 4 Specialty review becomes useful after the foundational clinical question and evidentiary limits have been defined.

CHAPTER 6

From Information to Clinical Intelligence

The Difference Between Information and Intelligence

Throughout this chapter we have discussed evidence, documentation, physiology, investigation, and disciplined reasoning.

All of these concepts point toward one fundamental distinction. There is a significant difference between possessing information and possessing intelligence. Although these terms are often used interchangeably, they are not the same.

Information is data. Intelligence is understanding. Healthcare generates extraordinary amounts of information. Every blood pressure measurement. Every laboratory result. Every medication administration. Every nursing assessment. Every physician note. Every radiology report.

Every operative record. Every monitor alarm. Every consultation. Every policy. Every protocol. Every communication. Each of these represents valuable information. None of them, individually, explains the patient's story. Clinical Intelligence begins when information is transformed into understanding.

That transformation does not occur because more documents are collected. It occurs because relationships are identified. Patterns are recognized. Assumptions are tested. Contradictions are investigated. Alternative explanations are considered.

The patient's clinical journey is reconstructed until the evidence produces a coherent explanation that can support legal decision-making.

That process is what transforms information into intelligence. This distinction may appear semantic. It is not. It is the reason Clinical Intelligence exists.

Case example: Six Thousand Pages of Information

A law firm receives approximately six thousand pages of records involving a catastrophic birth injury.

Everything appears to be there. Prenatal records. Fetal monitoring strips. Labor and delivery documentation. Operative reports. Neonatal intensive care records. Radiology. Laboratory studies. Specialist consultations. The attorney comments, "We have all the information."

From an administrative perspective, that statement is correct. From a Clinical Intelligence perspective, it is only partially true. The investigation has information. It does not yet have intelligence. The fetal heart rate tracing has not been correlated with nursing interventions.

The timing of physician notification has not been reconstructed. The relationship between uterine activity and fetal oxygenation has not been analyzed.

The mother's baseline risk factors have not yet been integrated into the investigation.

The sequence of clinical decisions has not been compared with the applicable standard of care.

No one has yet determined whether earlier intervention would probably have changed the child's neurological outcome.

The information exists. The intelligence does not. Not yet. Only through disciplined investigation does the information become clinically meaningful. That distinction materially changes the analysis. The attorney is no longer asking,

"What records do I have?" The attorney is asking, "What do these records actually tell me?" That is a fundamentally different investigation.

Why Clinical Intelligence Matters

Experienced attorneys rarely lose healthcare cases because they lack information.

They lose cases because critical information was never transformed into reliable understanding before important decisions were made.

The records existed. The evidence existed. The opportunity existed. The understanding did not. Clinical Intelligence closes that gap. It does not create new evidence. It allows attorneys to understand existing evidence more completely.

That is why Clinical Intelligence should never be viewed as another layer of paperwork.

It is a discipline of interpretation. A discipline of integration. A discipline of reasoning. Ultimately, a discipline of better decision-making.

The next time you receive thousands of pages of medical records, resist the temptation to ask,

"How quickly can we review this?" Instead ask, "How do we transform all of this information into reliable Clinical Intelligence?" That single question changes the purpose of the investigation. The objective is no longer speed.

The objective is understanding. Healthcare litigation rewards understanding. Jurors respond to coherent explanations. Experts defend opinions that are supported by disciplined reasoning. Judges evaluate arguments built upon reliable evidence.

Clients place their trust in attorneys who understand not only what happened, but why it happened.

Clinical Intelligence exists because understanding-not information-is what ultimately supports every important litigation decision.

Information tells you what was recorded. Clinical Intelligence tells you what it means.

Modern healthcare generates enormous amounts of information. Attorneys are rarely limited by the quantity of records they receive. The challenge is determining which information is significant, how individual facts relate to one another, and what those relationships reveal about the patient's clinical journey.

Clinical Intelligence transforms information into disciplined understanding by integrating evidence rather than merely collecting it.

Attorneys who understand the difference between information and intelligence are better equipped to evaluate cases, instruct experts, identify causation issues, prepare depositions, negotiate settlements, and present persuasive arguments at trial.

Information fills the file. Clinical Intelligence fills the gaps in understanding.

Clinical Intelligence Is Learned Through Discipline, Not Instinct

One of the misconceptions surrounding healthcare litigation is that experienced attorneys simply develop an instinct for strong cases.

There is certainly some truth in that observation. Experience matters. Judgment improves with time. Pattern recognition becomes more refined.

Experienced litigators often recognize issues far more quickly than attorneys who are new to healthcare cases.

Clinical Intelligence does not dismiss that experience. It explains where it comes from. Experienced attorneys do not develop judgment by chance.

They develop it because, over hundreds of cases, they unconsciously begin asking better questions.

They learn which records deserve closer attention. They recognize patterns of deterioration more quickly. They anticipate where documentation is likely to become inconsistent. They understand which physiological changes often precede catastrophic outcomes.

Eventually, much of that reasoning feels intuitive. It is not intuition. It is disciplined thinking repeated so often that it becomes second nature. That distinction matters because it means judgment can be taught.

Clinical Intelligence was developed to make that process deliberate rather than accidental.

Instead of waiting twenty years to develop investigative instincts through experience alone, attorneys can learn the habits that experienced investigators have gradually acquired throughout their careers.

That is one of the true purposes of this discipline. Not to replace experience. To accelerate it.

Case example: Two Attorneys Reviewing the Same Record

Imagine two attorneys reviewing the same emergency department record. The first attorney notices the diagnosis. The discharge instructions. The laboratory results. The imaging. The consultation. The second attorney notices all of those things.

But then asks additional questions.

- Why was the respiratory rate increasing while oxygen saturation remained relatively unchanged?
- Why did the physician order a repeat lactate if sepsis was not considered?
- Why was the patient's family describing confusion that was not reflected elsewhere in the documentation?
- Why was the nursing documentation becoming progressively more frequent during the final hour before admission?

Neither attorney is more intelligent. Neither attorney is working harder.

One attorney has simply learned to ask questions that reveal relationships hidden within the record.

That is Clinical Intelligence. Not because the second attorney knows more medicine. Because the second attorney has learned to investigate differently. That is exactly what this book is intended to teach.

Experience Should Become a Method

One of the challenges facing every profession is that experts often struggle to explain how they think.

Ask an experienced pilot how they recognized an approaching emergency. Ask an experienced surgeon how they knew something was wrong. Ask an experienced detective why one witness immediately attracted their attention.

Very often the answer begins with the same phrase. "It just didn't seem right." That answer reflects years of accumulated experience. It is helpful for the expert. It is far less helpful for someone trying to learn.

Clinical Intelligence attempts to bridge that gap. Rather than accepting instinct as something mysterious, it asks a different question.

What sequence of disciplined observations created that instinct?

If we can answer that question, experience becomes teachable.

That is exactly what the Lexcura Clinical Intelligence Model™ was designed to accomplish.

Every discipline within the model represents a thinking habit that experienced investigators gradually develop over time.

Record Integrity is not merely the first step. It is the first habit. Learn the habit... ...and better judgment begins to follow.

The next time you admire the judgment of an experienced healthcare attorney, remember this:

You are not seeing instinct. You are seeing thousands of disciplined investigations compressed into one professional decision. Clinical Intelligence simply makes those investigative habits visible. Once they become visible... They can be learned.

Implications for Practice

For decades, attorneys have improved through experience. Clinical Intelligence introduces another possibility. Attorneys can improve through a disciplined method. That distinction is significant.

Instead of waiting years to recognize recurring investigative patterns, attorneys begin developing those habits deliberately from the very first case.

Every investigation becomes a learning opportunity. Every inconsistency becomes a lesson. Every expert discussion strengthens the attorney's own clinical reasoning. Over time, something remarkable begins to happen. The attorney no longer depends entirely upon experience.

The attorney develops a disciplined way of thinking that makes every future investigation stronger than the last.

That is how professions evolve. Not because people become more intelligent. Because they become more disciplined.

Great investigators are not born with better instincts. They develop better investigative habits.

Experience is invaluable, but experience alone is difficult to teach. Clinical Intelligence identifies the habits of disciplined healthcare investigators and organizes them into a repeatable methodology. What once required decades of experience can now be learned intentionally through disciplined practice.

Clinical Intelligence therefore transforms instinct into method.

Attorneys who develop disciplined investigative habits identify stronger evidence, ask better questions, collaborate more effectively with experts, and make more confident litigation decisions throughout their careers.

Instinct is often nothing more than disciplined thinking repeated thousands of times.

Every Medical Record Tells Two Stories

One of the most important discoveries I made during the development of Clinical Intelligence was realizing that every healthcare record contains two different stories.

The first story is the one everyone reads. It is the documented story.

It consists of physician notes, nursing assessments, laboratory reports, imaging studies, medication records, consultation notes, operative reports, discharge summaries, and every other piece of documentation created during the patient's care.

This is the story contained within the chart. It is the story most investigations begin with. The second story is much harder to recognize. It is the patient's physiological story.

Unlike the documented story, it is rarely written in one place. It must be reconstructed. It exists within the relationships between the observations.

It is reflected in changing vital signs, evolving laboratory values, deteriorating organ function, increasing oxygen requirements, altered neurological status, medication responses, escalating interventions, and the countless physiological changes that occur as a patient's condition evolves.

The patient's body is telling a story long before anyone writes it down.

Sometimes those two stories move together. The documentation accurately reflects the patient's physiological progression. Clinical decisions evolve appropriately as the patient's condition changes. The medical record and the patient's clinical reality remain closely aligned.

Those are often the strongest records a clinician can produce. Sometimes, however, the two stories begin to separate. The patient's physiology changes before the documentation recognizes it. Communication breaks down.

Clinical deterioration becomes visible in objective findings before it becomes visible in clinical decision-making.

Opportunities for intervention begin to appear. This is often where the most important questions in healthcare litigation begin. Notice something important. Clinical Intelligence is not looking for errors in documentation.

It is looking for the point where the documented story and the physiological story begin to diverge.

That distinction changes the entire investigation.

Case example: Two Stories Developing at the Same Time

A sixty-five-year-old patient is admitted with severe community-acquired pneumonia.

At 8:00 a.m., the physician documents that the patient is responding appropriately to intravenous antibiotics.

At first glance, nothing appears unusual. The note is clear. The treatment plan is reasonable. The documentation is complete. Clinical Intelligence continues reading. Between 8:00 a.m. and noon, the nursing documentation records increasing respiratory distress.

Oxygen requirements increase from two liters to six liters. The respiratory rate rises steadily. The patient's heart rate increases. Urine output begins to fall. A repeat lactate level increases significantly.

By early afternoon, the patient requires transfer to the intensive care unit. Now read the record again. Not as documentation. As physiology. The patient's body began telling one story. The documentation was still describing another.

That observation does not automatically establish negligence. It establishes something far more important. It identifies the precise point where the investigation should become more focused.

- Why were the two stories no longer moving together?
- Was the deterioration too subtle to appreciate?
- Was information not communicated effectively?
- Did multiple clinicians each observe only one part of the patient's decline?
- Did system pressures delay reassessment?

Those questions matter because they move the investigation away from hindsight and toward understanding the clinical reality that existed at the time.

That is the purpose of Clinical Intelligence.

The Investigation Begins Where the Stories Separate

One of the habits you will develop throughout this book is learning to recognize the point where the documented story and the physiological story no longer appear to match.

Sometimes there is an entirely reasonable explanation. Sometimes the apparent discrepancy disappears once additional evidence is reviewed.

Sometimes it identifies one of the most important issues in the entire case.

The purpose is not to assume wrongdoing. The purpose is to recognize that divergence deserves investigation. That is why Record Integrity always comes first. Before asking whether the standard of care was breached...

Before evaluating causation... Before estimating damages... The attorney must first determine whether both stories have been accurately reconstructed.

Only then is it possible to understand what actually happened to the patient.

As you review the records, continually ask yourself: "Am I reading the documentation...or am I listening to the patient's physiology?" The best Clinical Intelligence investigators learn to do both simultaneously.

That is where understanding begins. Every healthcare case contains two stories. The documented story. The patient's physiological story. Clinical Intelligence begins when those two stories are investigated together.

The medical record describes what clinicians documented. The patient's physiology reveals what the body was experiencing. In many cases, those stories closely align. In others, the patient's physiological deterioration begins before it is fully recognized, documented, or acted upon. Clinical Intelligence teaches attorneys to investigate both stories-not to create conflict between them, but to determine whether they accurately reflect one another.

Attorneys who learn to recognize where these two stories diverge are better equipped to identify communication failures, delayed recognition, evolving clinical deterioration, and the points at which litigation-critical decisions may have changed the patient's outcome. More importantly, they develop investigations that are rooted in clinical reality rather than documentation alone.

The chart tells you what was documented. The patient tells you what was happening. Clinical Intelligence teaches you to understand both.

From the Clinical Story to the Legal Story

The purpose of Clinical Intelligence is to reconstruct the patient's clinical story before anyone attempts to construct a legal story.

That distinction changes the order of the entire investigation. The attorney arrives with a legal question: "Do I have a case?" Clinical Intelligence answers: "Not yet. First, let us reconstruct the patient's clinical story."

Only after that story has been understood can the legal questions be answered with confidence. That is why the disciplines within the Lexcura Clinical Intelligence Model™ follow the sequence they do. They are not separate reports or independent exercises. They are the connected stages of one investigation.

Record Integrity

- Can the evidence be trusted sufficiently to reconstruct the patient's clinical story?

Baseline Profiling

- Who was this patient before the clinical story began to change?

Timeline Reconstruction

- How did the clinical story unfold, and when did clinically meaningful change become recognizable?

Standard of Care Review

- At what point should reasonably competent care have changed the direction of that story?

Regulatory & Compliance Overlay

- What systems, policies, communication pathways, staffing conditions, or organizational failures influenced the clinical story?

Causation Mapping

- Which departures or system failures probably changed the patient's outcome, and to what extent?

Litigation-Ready Output

- Now that the patient's clinical story has been reconstructed, how should that understanding be translated into clear, objective, and defensible litigation intelligence?

The sequence is important because each discipline answers the question created by the one before it. The evidence cannot be interpreted confidently until its integrity has been tested. The outcome cannot be understood without the patient's baseline. The standard of care cannot be evaluated fairly until the progression has been reconstructed. Causation cannot be determined merely because a departure occurred. The attorney cannot make reliable strategic decisions until all of those findings have been integrated.

Clinical Intelligence therefore does not ask the attorney to memorize seven disciplines. It asks the attorney to follow one patient through one connected investigation.

That investigation begins with the evidence and ends with a litigation-ready understanding of what the patient's clinical story can honestly support.

Before an attorney can reconstruct the patient's clinical story, the evidence supporting that reconstruction must first deserve trust. That is why Record Integrity is not simply the first discipline in the Model. It is the foundation on which every later stage depends.

The First Decision Every Attorney Makes

Most attorneys believe the first decision in a healthcare case is whether to accept or decline representation.

Clinical Intelligence suggests that another decision comes first.

- Can this patient's clinical story be reconstructed with sufficient confidence to support reliable legal decision-making?

That question changes the direction of the analysis. Notice that Clinical Intelligence has not yet asked whether negligence occurred. It has not asked whether the standard of care was breached.

It has not asked whether the damages justify litigation. Those questions are important. They simply come later.

The first responsibility of the attorney is to determine whether the available evidence is capable of accurately reconstructing the patient's clinical story.

Without that understanding, every legal decision becomes progressively more uncertain.

This is one of the reasons experienced healthcare attorneys occasionally reach very different conclusions about the same case.

They are not necessarily interpreting the law differently. They are often beginning from different understandings of the patient's clinical story.

Clinical Intelligence attempts to remove as much of that uncertainty as possible before legal analysis begins.

That is why Record Integrity always comes first.

The Investigation Must Earn the Right to Move Forward

One of the principles that guides every Clinical Intelligence investigation is remarkably simple.

Every stage of the investigation must earn the right to move to the next stage.

That sentence deserves careful consideration. Record Integrity earns the right to begin Baseline Profiling. Baseline Profiling earns the right to begin Timeline Reconstruction. Timeline Reconstruction earns the right to evaluate the Standard of Care.

The Standard of Care Review earns the right to evaluate Causation. Causation earns the right to support litigation strategy. Nothing is assumed. Nothing is skipped. Nothing is accepted simply because it appears logical.

Each discipline produces the foundation required for the next discipline. That sequence is deliberate.

It protects the attorney from asking the wrong question before the previous question has been answered.

Healthcare investigations often become complicated because the order of thinking becomes confused. Attorneys begin discussing causation before the patient's baseline has been established.

Experts debate the standard of care before the timeline has been accurately reconstructed.

Settlement discussions begin before the strengths and weaknesses of the evidence have been fully understood.

Clinical Intelligence restores discipline to that process. It asks only one question at a time. When that question has been answered, it moves to the next. That is how complex investigations become manageable.

Case example: When the Sequence Was Ignored

A fifty-four-year-old woman underwent laparoscopic gallbladder surgery and subsequently developed bile peritonitis requiring multiple additional operations.

The referring attorney believed the central issue was surgical negligence. The first expert retained was a hepatobiliary surgeon.

The expert identified several technical questions but requested additional records before reaching an opinion.

As the investigation continued, it became apparent that postoperative nursing documentation demonstrated repeated complaints of increasing abdominal pain, tachycardia, and fever over the following thirty-six hours.

Imaging had been delayed. Escalation pathways had not been followed consistently.

The investigation gradually shifted away from the operation itself and toward delayed recognition of a postoperative complication.

Looking back, the sequence had been reversed.

The litigation strategy had begun before the patient's clinical story had been fully reconstructed.

Had Record Integrity, Baseline Profiling, and Timeline Reconstruction been completed first, the attorney would have recognized that the most significant issue might not have been the surgery at all.

The investigation did not fail. It simply began in the wrong place. Clinical Intelligence exists to prevent exactly that situation.

Whenever you find yourself asking questions about negligence, pause and ask one more.

"Have I earned the right to ask this question yet?"

If the patient's clinical story has not yet been reconstructed, the answer is often not yet.

That is not a delay. It is discipline. This sequential approach changes the rhythm of healthcare litigation.

Experts receive better instructions because the investigation has already established the patient's clinical story.

Discovery becomes more focused because unanswered questions have already been identified.

Depositions become more productive because they are directed toward specific clinical issues rather than broad allegations.

Settlement discussions become more realistic because they are based upon an investigation that has matured through disciplined analysis rather than early assumption.

Most importantly, attorneys become more confident because each conclusion has earned its place within the investigation.

That confidence is difficult to achieve through experience alone. Clinical Intelligence makes it repeatable.

Every stage of the investigation must earn the right to move to the next.

Healthcare investigations become vulnerable when attorneys begin answering later questions before earlier questions have been resolved. Clinical Intelligence restores order by requiring each discipline to establish the foundation for the next. This prevents premature conclusions, strengthens expert collaboration, and produces litigation strategies that are built upon progressively tested evidence.

Attorneys who follow this disciplined sequence are less likely to overlook critical evidence, retain the wrong experts, pursue unsupported theories, or commit substantial resources before the investigation has earned sufficient confidence.

Good investigations move forward. Great investigations earn the right to move forward.

Clinical Confidence Must Be Earned

One of the realities of healthcare litigation is that attorneys are constantly required to make decisions with incomplete information.

- Should the case be accepted?
- Should additional records be requested?
- Should another expert be retained?
- Should mediation be recommended?
- Should settlement be pursued?

None of these decisions can wait until every question has been answered. The challenge, therefore, is not eliminating uncertainty.

The challenge is understanding how much confidence the investigation has earned at each stage.

Clinical Intelligence approaches this differently from traditional medical record review. Traditional review often asks, "What have we learned?" Clinical Intelligence asks, "How confident should we be in what we have learned?"

That distinction changes every decision. Knowledge without confidence creates hesitation. Confidence without investigation creates risk. Clinical Intelligence seeks the balance between the two.

Every discipline contributes additional confidence because every discipline answers questions that previously remained uncertain.

Record Integrity establishes confidence in the evidence. Baseline Profiling establishes confidence in the patient's starting point. Timeline Reconstruction establishes confidence in the sequence of events. Standard of Care Review establishes confidence in the clinical decisions.

Regulatory & Compliance Overlay establishes confidence in understanding the system in which those decisions occurred.

Causation Mapping establishes confidence that the identified departures probably influenced the patient's outcome.

By the time the attorney reaches Litigation-Ready Output, confidence has not been assumed.

It has been earned. That is a profoundly different way of thinking.

Case example: Confidence Changed the Recommendation

A regional law firm was evaluating a potential failure-to-rescue case involving an elderly patient who deteriorated following bowel surgery.

During the initial intake, the attorney believed the case appeared strong. The patient deteriorated. Recognition seemed delayed. The outcome was catastrophic.

After completing Record Integrity, several important ICU records were obtained that had not been included in the original production.

Baseline Profiling demonstrated significant pre-existing vascular disease and severe frailty that substantially influenced the patient's ability to recover.

Timeline Reconstruction revealed that nursing staff recognized the deterioration much earlier than originally believed and had escalated concerns appropriately.

The Standard of Care Review identified several management decisions that deserved closer examination but also demonstrated that many interventions occurred within accepted clinical timeframes.

By the conclusion of Causation Mapping, the investigation had reached a different understanding.

There were still legitimate questions. There were still issues requiring expert opinion. But the confidence supporting the original allegation had changed. The attorney ultimately recommended against proceeding with litigation. That decision was not a failure.

It was the result of a disciplined investigation. Clinical Intelligence had done exactly what it was designed to do.

It prevented a major litigation decision from being based upon an incomplete understanding of the patient's clinical story.

That outcome served everyone. The client received an honest evaluation. The attorney avoided pursuing a weak case. The discipline maintained its integrity. That is success.

Confidence Is Not Certainty

One of the most important distinctions attorneys should understand is that confidence and certainty are not the same thing.

Medicine rarely provides absolute certainty. Healthcare litigation certainly does not. Clinical Intelligence does not promise certainty. It promises something far more valuable.

It provides the highest degree of confidence that can reasonably be achieved through disciplined clinical investigation.

That is the standard attorneys should seek. Not perfection. Not certainty. Earned confidence. Before making any major litigation decision, ask yourself:

"Has my confidence been earned by the investigation...or is it being borrowed from my assumptions?"

That question may be uncomfortable.

It is also one of the most valuable safeguards you will ever develop.

Confidence should never move ahead of the investigation.

Attorneys make important decisions every day based on the confidence they have in their understanding of a case. Clinical Intelligence teaches that confidence is not something you begin with-it is something you earn through disciplined investigation. Every discipline within the Lexcura Clinical Intelligence Model™ exists to reduce uncertainty and increase justified confidence before the next decision is made.

Attorneys who base their confidence on disciplined investigation make stronger strategic decisions, collaborate more effectively with experts, communicate more honestly with clients, and avoid committing significant resources before the evidence justifies doing so.

Confidence is strongest when it has been earned-not assumed.

The Attorney's Responsibility for the Investigation

One of the greatest misconceptions in healthcare litigation is that responsibility for the clinical investigation belongs primarily to the medical expert.

Clinical Intelligence views that relationship differently. The expert is responsible for applying specialized medical knowledge.

The attorney is responsible for ensuring that the investigation upon which that opinion is based is worthy of the expert's time and worthy of the court's confidence.

That distinction is important because experts answer questions. Attorneys decide which questions are asked.

If the investigation begins with incomplete evidence, poorly defined issues, or unsupported assumptions, even the most respected expert can only respond to the investigation they have been given.

Clinical Intelligence therefore places an important responsibility upon the attorney. The attorney becomes the guardian of the investigation. Not because the attorney knows more medicine than the expert. Not because the attorney replaces the expert.

Because someone must protect the integrity of the investigation before opinions begin to shape litigation strategy.

That responsibility belongs to the attorney.

Managing the Case and Leading the Investigation

Healthcare attorneys are exceptional case managers. They coordinate experts. Manage discovery. Monitor deadlines. Negotiate settlements. Prepare witnesses. Present evidence. Those responsibilities are essential. Clinical Intelligence introduces another responsibility. Leading the investigation.

Managing a case and leading an investigation are not the same thing. A case manager ensures the litigation progresses. An investigation leader ensures the understanding progresses. Those two responsibilities should occur together.

Throughout this book, I want you to think of yourself not simply as counsel.

Think of yourself as the leader of a multidisciplinary investigation. Every participant contributes something unique. The treating clinicians contribute documentation. Experts contribute specialized medical opinion. Nurses contribute clinical interpretation. Policies contribute organizational expectations.

Regulations contribute legal and professional obligations. The attorney brings them together. That integration is not administrative. It is intellectual.

Someone must ensure that every piece contributes to one coherent understanding of the patient's clinical story.

Clinical Intelligence teaches the attorney how to lead that process.

Case example: Two Different Law Firms

Two firms receive nearly identical cases involving delayed recognition of postoperative hemorrhage. Both firms retain experienced experts. Both request the complete medical record. Both conduct discovery. Yet the investigations develop very differently.

The first firm treats each stage of litigation as an independent task. Records are reviewed. Experts are instructed. Depositions are scheduled. Reports are exchanged. Each step is completed competently. The second firm approaches the case through Clinical Intelligence.

Before experts are instructed, Record Integrity is completed. Before liability is discussed, the patient's baseline is established. Before expert opinions are sought, the timeline has been reconstructed. When the experts receive the case, they are not beginning the investigation.

They are refining it.

By the time discovery begins, the attorney already understands the patient's clinical story.

Every deposition is directed toward unresolved questions rather than general exploration. Every expert instruction becomes more precise.

Every strategic decision is supported by a progressively stronger investigation. Neither firm worked harder.

One firm investigated more deliberately. That is the difference.

Leadership Through Questions

One of the observations I have made throughout my career is that outstanding investigators are rarely distinguished by having all the answers.

They are distinguished by consistently asking the questions that everyone else overlooked. Clinical Intelligence encourages attorneys to develop that habit. Not because every unanswered question changes the case.

Because every unanswered question deserves to be examined before important decisions are made.

The attorney who leads the investigation creates an environment where experts, clinicians, consultants, and support staff all contribute toward one shared objective.

Understanding the patient's clinical story as accurately as possible. That is leadership. Not directing people. Directing understanding. As your investigation progresses, ask yourself: "Am I simply managing this case...or am I leading the investigation?"

Those are two very different responsibilities. Clinical Intelligence asks you to do both.

The attorney is not merely the manager of the case. The attorney is the guardian of the investigation.

Healthcare litigation depends upon the quality of the investigation long before it depends upon the quality of advocacy. The attorney has a unique responsibility to ensure that every later opinion, expert conclusion, and litigation decision is built upon an investigation that has earned confidence through disciplined clinical analysis.

Clinical Intelligence therefore expands the attorney's role. It transforms the attorney from coordinator to investigative leader.

Attorneys who lead investigations rather than simply manage cases identify stronger evidence, collaborate more effectively with experts, improve the quality of discovery, and develop litigation strategies that remain stable because they are grounded in a disciplined reconstruction of the patient's clinical story.

Cases are managed. Investigations are led.

CHAPTER 7

Baseline Profiling

Who Was the Patient Before Everything Changed?

Imagine that I hand you two medical records.

Both involve a seventy-year-old man who suffered a stroke after carotid artery surgery.

Both patients experienced the same complication. Both required prolonged rehabilitation. Both ultimately retained legal counsel. At first glance, the cases appear remarkably similar.

But before I allow you to read another page of either record, I ask you one question.

Who were these patients before the surgery?

One attorney might answer, "I don't know yet. I haven't reached that part of the chart." Another might say, "Does it really matter? Both patients had the same outcome." Clinical Intelligence gives a very different answer.

It matters because the patient existed before the injury. That statement sounds obvious. Yet healthcare litigation often forgets it.

Once litigation begins, patients are frequently described by the event that brought them into the legal system.

"The stroke patient." "The birth injury." "The sepsis case." "The missed cancer diagnosis." Those descriptions are understandable. They are also incomplete. Before the stroke...

...there was a man who still worked three days a week, walked two miles every morning, cared for his grandchildren, and managed his hypertension with a single medication.

Before the birth injury...

...there was a healthy young woman experiencing an uncomplicated pregnancy, making plans for the arrival of her first child.

Before the sepsis...

...there was an elderly gentleman whose diabetes, kidney disease, and heart failure had already reduced his physiological reserve long before he entered the emergency department.

The event did not create these patients. The event interrupted lives that were already unfolding. That distinction is where Clinical Intelligence begins.

Why Traditional Investigations Often Miss the Most Important Part of the Story

Healthcare litigation naturally focuses on what happened. That is entirely appropriate. The attorney has been retained because something allegedly went wrong. The records documenting that event demand attention. Experts are asked to evaluate the care.

The investigation moves quickly toward liability.

The difficulty is that every one of those questions assumes we already understand the person to whom the event happened.

Very often, we do not. A diagnosis tells us what disease the patient had. It does not tell us how that patient lived with the disease. A medication list tells us what treatment was prescribed.

It does not tell us how well the patient functioned before the event.

A problem list identifies chronic illness. It does not explain resilience, independence, frailty, or physiological reserve.

Clinical Intelligence therefore asks attorneys to resist the temptation to begin with the allegation.

Instead, begin with the person. Only then can the significance of the allegation be understood.

The Baseline Is More Than Medical History

This is where I think Clinical Intelligence begins to separate itself from traditional approaches.

Many people assume that establishing a baseline simply means reviewing the patient's past medical history.

It is much more than that. A patient's baseline is not merely a list of diagnoses.

It is a picture of who that person was immediately before the clinical story began to change.

It includes their health. Their function. Their cognition. Their mobility. Their independence. Their chronic illnesses. Their physiological reserve. Their previous treatments. Their response to illness. Their social circumstances. Their support systems.

Even their goals of care.

Together, these elements answer a question that every attorney should understand before moving another step in the investigation.

What was normal for this patient?

Without that answer, words such as decline, injury, recovery, and damages lose much of their meaning.

You cannot measure change unless you understand where the patient started. That is why Baseline Profiling follows Record Integrity. Once we trust the evidence... We use that evidence to understand the patient.

Only then are we prepared to investigate how that patient's clinical story changed.

A Medical History Tells You What the Patient Had

A Baseline Profile Tells You Who the Patient Was

There is an important distinction between these two statements. A medical history tells you that a patient had hypertension.

A baseline profile tells you whether that hypertension limited the patient's daily life, influenced clinical decision-making, increased procedural risk, or contributed to the outcome being investigated.

A medical history tells you that the patient had diabetes.

A baseline profile tells you whether that diabetes was well controlled or poorly controlled, whether complications had already developed, how it affected healing, infection risk, vascular disease, kidney function, and ultimately how it influenced the patient's ability to recover.

A medical history tells you that the patient suffered a previous stroke.

A baseline profile tells you whether the patient returned to independent living, required assistance with activities of daily living, remained cognitively intact, continued working, drove independently, or had already experienced permanent neurological impairment before the event now being litigated.

Those differences are profound. One describes diagnoses. The other describes the person living with those diagnoses. Clinical Intelligence is interested in the person. Because medicine treats people. Not diagnoses. Courts compensate people.

Not diagnoses. Experts evaluate people. Not diagnoses.

The attorney therefore has an obligation to understand the patient as a person before evaluating the legal significance of what happened to them.

That is the purpose of Baseline Profiling.

Baseline Explains More Than Damages

One of the common misconceptions in healthcare litigation is that a patient's baseline becomes important only when damages are being evaluated.

Clinical Intelligence views baseline very differently. Baseline influences almost every important question in the investigation. It influences recognition. A frail ninety-year-old patient may deteriorate differently from a healthy forty-year-old. It influences diagnosis.

Symptoms that are alarming in one patient may be expected in another with advanced chronic disease.

It influences treatment decisions.

The risks and benefits of surgery, medication, intensive care, or aggressive intervention are often inseparable from the patient's pre-existing health.

It influences prognosis.

The likelihood of recovery depends not only on what happened during the event, but on the patient's physiological reserve before the event occurred.

And ultimately... It influences causation. Because one of the central questions in healthcare litigation is not simply: "What happened?" It is: "What changed?"

That question cannot be answered unless we first understand where the patient started.

Case example: The Marathon Runner and the Retired Carpenter

Two sixty-five-year-old men undergo identical knee replacement surgery. Both develop postoperative pulmonary emboli. Both require admission to intensive care. At first glance, the cases appear almost identical. Their baseline profiles reveal a very different picture.

The first patient is an active marathon runner.

He exercises daily, takes no regular medication, and has no significant chronic illness.

The second patient is a retired carpenter with severe chronic obstructive pulmonary disease, coronary artery disease, obesity, insulin-dependent diabetes, and limited mobility. He becomes short of breath walking from his living room to the kitchen.

The complication is the same. The patients are not. Their physiological reserve is different. Their expected recovery is different. Their vulnerability to complications is different. Their long-term prognosis is different.

Their future losses may also be very different.

Clinical Intelligence therefore never evaluates the complication without first understanding the patient who experienced it.

The event gains meaning only when viewed in the context of the person's baseline.

When reviewing the first fifty pages of a medical record, don't ask: "What diagnosis brought this patient to the hospital?" Ask:

"If I had met this person the week before this event, how would I have described their life, their health, and their abilities?"

That answer is often more valuable than any diagnosis listed in the chart.

Because it tells you what was at stake before the clinical story changed.

Why Baseline Is the Anchor for the Entire Investigation

As the investigation progresses, you will find yourself continually returning to the patient's baseline.

When reviewing imaging... You will compare it to what previously existed. When reconstructing the timeline... You will compare every change against the patient's normal state. When evaluating the standard of care...

You will consider how the patient's baseline should reasonably have influenced clinical decisions.

When analyzing causation...

You will ask whether the identified failures changed the patient's trajectory from the path that would otherwise have been expected.

Notice what happened. The baseline is no longer simply the beginning of the story. It becomes the reference point for every chapter that follows.

That is why Baseline Profiling occupies such a central position within the Lexcura Clinical Intelligence Model™.

It does not merely introduce the patient. It anchors the entire investigation.

The patient's baseline is not background information. It is the reference point against which every later opinion must be measured.

Every conclusion in healthcare litigation depends upon comparison. Improvement, deterioration, disability, recovery, causation, prognosis, and damages all require an understanding of what existed before the clinical story changed. A patient's baseline is therefore not preliminary information gathered for completeness. It is the benchmark that gives meaning to every subsequent finding.

Attorneys who establish a comprehensive baseline profile develop more accurate theories of liability, provide better instructions to experts, evaluate causation more realistically, and present damages within the context of the patient's actual life rather than the event alone.

You cannot understand what changed until you understand what existed before the change.

Why Clinicians Cannot Treat Diagnoses Alone

One of the greatest misconceptions about healthcare is the belief that clinicians simply diagnose disease and apply treatment.

Medicine is far more complex than that. Every clinical decision is individualized.

The same diagnosis can produce different treatment decisions depending upon the patient sitting in front of the clinician.

Age matters. Physiological reserve matters. Previous illnesses matter. Functional independence matters. Frailty matters. Medications matter. Cognitive status matters. Patient wishes matter. Family support matters.

Every one of these factors influences how clinicians assess risk, choose treatments, communicate with families, and respond to deterioration.

Healthcare has never treated diagnoses in isolation. Healthcare treats people.

That is why attorneys cannot fairly evaluate clinical decisions without first understanding the patient for whom those decisions were made.

Clinical Intelligence therefore begins exactly where medicine begins. With the patient.

The Baseline Explains Clinical Decisions

One of the questions attorneys frequently ask is, "Why didn't the physician order that test sooner?" Or... "Why wasn't surgery performed immediately?" Or... "Why wasn't the patient admitted to intensive care?"

Those are reasonable legal questions. Clinical Intelligence asks an earlier question.

What did the patient's baseline tell the clinician at that moment?

That question is incredibly important. Because clinicians do not make decisions based solely on a diagnosis. They make decisions based upon the patient who has the diagnosis.

A healthy thirty-year-old and a frail ninety-year-old with exactly the same laboratory result may require entirely different clinical management.

Neither decision is automatically right or wrong. It depends upon the patient. That is why Baseline Profiling is not simply about understanding the patient.

It is about understanding why the clinical team made the decisions they made.

Without that understanding, attorneys risk judging yesterday's decisions using today's knowledge.

Clinical Intelligence insists that we judge those decisions within the context that existed at the time.

That is both clinically fair and legally stronger.

Case example: The Blood Pressure That Meant Two Different Things

Two patients arrive in the emergency department with a blood pressure of 94/58 mmHg.

On paper, the numbers are identical.

The first patient is a healthy twenty-eight-year-old marathon runner who normally maintains a resting blood pressure of 100/60.

The second patient is an eighty-three-year-old woman with chronic hypertension whose usual blood pressure is approximately 165/90.

The same reading carries very different clinical significance. For the younger patient, it may represent normal physiology.

For the older patient, it may indicate significant circulatory compromise requiring urgent investigation.

If an attorney evaluates those numbers without understanding each patient's baseline, the investigation begins with an incomplete understanding of the clinical reality.

The blood pressure itself has not changed. Its meaning has. That meaning comes from the patient. Not from the number. Clinical Intelligence therefore teaches attorneys to ask not simply, "What was the value?"

But, "What did that value mean for this patient?" That is a very different investigation. When you review any clinical finding, ask yourself:

"Would this finding have the same meaning if it occurred in a different patient?"

If the answer is no... You have just discovered why Baseline Profiling matters.

Clinical findings acquire meaning only when interpreted within the context of the individual patient.

The Investigation Begins to Think Like Medicine

This is one of the most important transitions in the entire Lexcura Clinical Intelligence Model™.

Until now, the investigation has focused on establishing confidence in the evidence. Now the investigation begins thinking the way experienced clinicians think. Not to practice medicine. Not to replace medical experts.

But to understand how medicine was being practiced for this particular patient at this particular moment.

That shift is profound. Attorneys are no longer asking, "What happened?" They are beginning to ask, "Why did this happen to this patient?" The answer to that question cannot be found in a diagnosis alone.

It can only be found by understanding the patient's baseline.

That is why Baseline Profiling is not merely the second discipline of Clinical Intelligence.

It is the bridge between evidence and clinical reasoning. Clinical decisions are made for patients, not diagnoses.

Medicine is individualized. Two patients with the same disease may appropriately receive different investigations, different treatments, and different clinical decisions because they are different people. Attorneys who evaluate medical care without first understanding the patient's baseline risk misunderstanding why those decisions were made.

Clinical Intelligence therefore requires the attorney to understand the patient before evaluating the clinician.

Attorneys who understand the patient's baseline evaluate medical decision-making more fairly, instruct experts more effectively, identify stronger liability theories, and avoid hindsight bias by interpreting decisions within the clinical context that existed at the time.

A diagnosis explains the disease. A baseline explains the patient.

A Baseline Is Not a Snapshot

When attorneys hear the word baseline, they often imagine a fixed point in time.

A single office visit. A hospital discharge. A list of diagnoses. A medication list. A physical examination. Those things contribute to understanding the patient's baseline. None of them, by themselves, define it.

A patient's baseline is a living picture of who that individual was immediately before the clinical story began to change.

It is the culmination of everything that shaped that person's health before the event under investigation.

Some patients improve over time. Others gradually decline. Some live independently despite multiple chronic illnesses. Others require increasing assistance while remaining medically stable. Understanding the patient's baseline therefore requires more than identifying what illnesses existed.

It requires understanding how those illnesses affected that person's life immediately before the event.

Clinical Intelligence is interested in the patient's functional baseline, clinical baseline, and physiological baseline, because together they explain what "normal" meant for that individual.

Without that understanding, every later conclusion rests upon an assumption rather than a comparison.

The Difference Between Disease and Function

One of the mistakes I have seen throughout healthcare litigation is assuming that disease automatically predicts function.

It does not.

Two patients may carry exactly the same diagnosis and live entirely different lives.

One patient with congestive heart failure may continue gardening, traveling, and living independently.

Another with the same diagnosis may become breathless walking across the room. Both have heart failure. Their baselines are completely different. The same is true for chronic kidney disease. Cancer.

Chronic obstructive pulmonary disease. Multiple sclerosis. Parkinson's disease. Dementia. Even advanced age. A diagnosis tells you what condition the patient had. It does not tell you how that patient functioned.

Clinical Intelligence therefore asks attorneys to look beyond the diagnosis.

- How independent was the patient?
- What could they do without assistance?
- How did they recover from previous illnesses?
- What was their normal level of activity?
- What limitations had already become part of daily life?

Those questions provide context that a diagnosis alone can never provide. That context is what gives meaning to every later event.

Case example: Two Patients With Dementia

Two eighty-four-year-old patients are admitted to hospital with urinary tract infections. Both have documented dementia. On paper, they appear remarkably similar. The baseline profiles tell a different story.

The first patient has mild cognitive impairment. She lives alone, manages her own finances, cooks daily, and drives short distances. Her family notices occasional forgetfulness, but she remains highly independent.

The second patient has advanced dementia. He lives in a skilled nursing facility, requires assistance with all activities of daily living, is unable to recognize family members consistently, and is non-verbal for much of the day.

The diagnosis is the same. The patients are not.

If both experience postoperative confusion, the investigation cannot assume that the clinical significance is identical.

Nor can it assume that the expected outcome, rehabilitation potential, or long-term consequences will be the same.

The diagnosis provides one piece of the story. The baseline explains the person living with that diagnosis. That is why Clinical Intelligence investigates people before conditions.

When you identify an important diagnosis in the medical record, ask yourself one additional question.

"How did this diagnosis affect this patient's life before the event?"

If you cannot answer that question, you have not yet established the patient's baseline.

Why Baseline Prevents Hindsight Bias

One of the greatest dangers in healthcare litigation is evaluating past decisions using information that only became available later.

Baseline Profiling helps prevent that mistake. It reminds us to place ourselves back where the clinicians stood.

- What did they know about this patient?

- What risks already existed?
- How did this patient usually present?
- What did "normal" look like for this individual?

Those questions create fairness. Not only for the clinician. For the patient. For the attorney. And ultimately for the court. Clinical Intelligence therefore uses baseline not to excuse decisions or criticize decisions.

It uses baseline to understand decisions. Only after they have been understood can they be evaluated. A diagnosis describes a condition. A baseline describes a person.

Patients are far more than the diagnoses listed in their medical record. The same disease may produce very different levels of independence, resilience, physiological reserve, and vulnerability in different individuals. Clinical Intelligence therefore reconstructs the patient's baseline before interpreting the significance of any later event.

Understanding the diagnosis without understanding the person is only half the investigation.

Attorneys who distinguish diagnosis from baseline evaluate clinical decisions more accurately, recognize the true significance of deterioration, avoid hindsight bias, and develop stronger opinions regarding causation, prognosis, and damages.

Medicine records diseases. Clinical Intelligence reconstructs people.

Baseline Is the Lens Through Which Every Clinical Decision Must Be Viewed

One of the most important principles in Clinical Intelligence is that a patient's baseline does not simply introduce the investigation.

It remains with you throughout the investigation.

Once you understand who the patient was before the clinical story began to change, you should never put that understanding aside.

Instead, every subsequent question should be viewed through that baseline. When you review imaging... Ask whether the findings represent a change from the patient's normal condition. When you reconstruct the timeline...

Ask when the patient's baseline first began to shift. When you evaluate the standard of care... Ask how the patient's baseline should reasonably have influenced the clinician's decisions. When you analyze causation...

Ask whether the identified departures changed the patient's expected clinical course from that baseline.

When you evaluate damages...

Ask how the patient's life differed after the event compared with the life they were living before it.

The baseline has become more than the beginning of the investigation. It has become the reference point for the entire investigation.

That is why Baseline Profiling occupies such an important place within the Lexcura Clinical Intelligence Model™.

Without it, every later opinion lacks context. With it, every later opinion has meaning.

The Patient's Baseline Should Follow You Through Every Chapter

As you continue reading this book, you will notice that we repeatedly return to the patient's baseline.

That repetition is deliberate. Experienced clinicians do exactly the same thing.

When a patient's condition changes, they compare it with the patient's previous condition.

When new symptoms appear, they ask whether those symptoms are new or longstanding.

When treatment is considered, they ask what the patient was capable of before becoming ill.

Clinical Intelligence adopts exactly the same discipline. The patient's baseline should remain beside the attorney throughout the investigation. Not as background information.

As the constant point of comparison against which every later observation is interpreted.

This is one of the reasons Clinical Intelligence feels different from traditional medical record review.

Traditional review often progresses through the records chronologically.

Clinical Intelligence continually returns to the patient's baseline because that baseline explains the significance of everything that follows.

Case example: The CT Scan That Meant Two Different Things

A sixty-nine-year-old man presents with sudden confusion and weakness.

A CT scan demonstrates chronic small vessel ischemic changes together with a new area of low attenuation within the left parietal lobe.

An attorney unfamiliar with the patient's history might reasonably conclude that the scan simply demonstrates significant cerebrovascular disease.

Baseline Profiling asks another question.

What did this imaging represent for this patient before today?

Review of earlier records demonstrates that the chronic changes had been present for years without measurable neurological impairment.

The patient had remained independent, continued driving, and managed his own business. The chronic findings were part of the patient's baseline. The new parietal lesion was not. Suddenly, the imaging becomes much more meaningful.

Not because the scan changed.

Because the attorney now understands which findings belong to the patient's past and which belong to the event being investigated.

Baseline transformed anatomy into understanding. That distinction influences every later opinion regarding deterioration, causation, prognosis, and damages. Whenever you identify an abnormal finding, ask yourself:

"Is this part of the patient's baseline...or evidence that the patient's clinical story has changed?"

That single question prevents one of the most common errors in healthcare litigation.

Confusing pre-existing disease with new injury.

Why Baseline Protects the Investigation

One of the greatest strengths of Baseline Profiling is that it protects the attorney from reaching conclusions too quickly.

Without a baseline, normal age-related change may appear pathological. Chronic disease may be mistaken for new injury. Long-standing functional limitation may be interpreted as recent disability. Conversely, genuine deterioration may be dismissed because chronic disease already existed.

Clinical Intelligence avoids both errors.

It asks attorneys to establish what belonged to the patient's life before the event and what truly changed afterwards.

Only then can the significance of the evidence be understood.

That is why Baseline Profiling is far more than a description of the patient's past.

It is the foundation upon which meaningful comparison becomes possible. Every clinical finding acquires meaning only when compared with the patient's baseline.

Clinical findings do not exist in isolation. Their significance depends upon what was normal for the individual patient before the clinical story began to change. Baseline Profiling provides the essential reference point that allows attorneys to distinguish pre-existing conditions from new injury, expected progression from unexpected deterioration, and chronic abnormalities from acute events.

Attorneys who consistently compare every important finding against the patient's baseline develop stronger theories of liability, more accurate causation analyses, better expert instructions, and more persuasive explanations of damages because every conclusion is anchored to the patient's actual clinical reality.

A clinical finding has no meaning until you know what came before it.

Baseline Is the Beginning of Fairness

One of the responsibilities of every healthcare attorney is to evaluate the evidence fairly.

That responsibility extends beyond advocating for a client. It begins with understanding the patient accurately. Clinical Intelligence recognizes that fairness is impossible without context. Imagine meeting someone halfway through a conversation.

You hear one sentence. You form an opinion. Later, you discover you missed everything that came before it. Suddenly, the meaning of that sentence changes completely. Healthcare litigation is no different.

The alleged negligence is often only one chapter in a much longer clinical story.

Without understanding what came before it, attorneys risk drawing conclusions that are incomplete-not because the evidence is weak, but because the context is missing.

Baseline Profiling provides that context.

It reminds us that every patient arrives with a history, a level of health, a degree of physiological reserve, and a life that existed long before the event being investigated.

That understanding creates fairness. Fairness for the patient. Fairness for the clinicians. Fairness for the attorney. And ultimately, fairness for the court. Clinical Intelligence is built upon that principle. The objective is not simply to identify what happened.

The objective is to understand why it happened to this patient, at this point in their life, under these particular circumstances.

Only then can responsibility be evaluated honestly.

Case example: The Same Fall, Two Different Lives

Two patients fall while admitted to hospital. Both sustain fractured hips. On paper, the injuries are identical. The legal question appears identical. Clinical Intelligence begins somewhere else.

The first patient is seventy-two years old, walks three miles each morning, volunteers at a local school, and lives independently with no assistance.

The second patient is ninety-three years old, has advanced Parkinson's disease, requires assistance with every activity of daily living, has experienced multiple falls during the previous year, and resides in a skilled nursing facility.

The fracture is the same. The patient's baseline is not. That difference does not determine liability. It does determine how the investigation should proceed.

- How foreseeable was the fall?
- How vulnerable was the patient?
- What preventative measures were appropriate?
- What recovery could reasonably have been expected?
- How did the injury alter the patient's future?

None of those questions can be answered by looking at the fracture alone.

They require an understanding of the person who sustained it. That is why Baseline Profiling is not simply descriptive. It is analytical.

It changes the investigation before the investigation even reaches the standard of care.

As you establish the patient's baseline, ask yourself one question that should remain with you throughout the entire investigation.

"Am I evaluating this event...or am I evaluating this event as it happened to this particular patient?"

Those are not the same investigation. Clinical Intelligence requires the second approach.

Baseline Creates Perspective

One of the greatest values of Baseline Profiling is that it prevents attorneys from viewing every healthcare event through a single lens.

Medicine is individualized. Clinical decisions are individualized. Outcomes are individualized. Therefore, investigations must also be individualized. A patient's baseline provides that perspective. It reminds us that medicine is never practiced in the abstract.

Every decision is made for one patient, at one moment, under one unique set of circumstances.

Clinical Intelligence asks attorneys to evaluate those circumstances before evaluating the decision itself.

That sequence is deliberate. It is also fair. Fair investigations begin by understanding the patient before judging the decision.

Clinical decisions cannot be evaluated in isolation from the patient for whom they were made. Baseline Profiling provides the context necessary to understand why clinicians made particular decisions, what risks already existed, what options were available, and how the patient's individual characteristics influenced the course of care.

Clinical Intelligence therefore begins with understanding before judgment.

Attorneys who establish the patient's baseline before evaluating the care develop more balanced investigations, reduce hindsight bias, ask more precise expert questions, and build litigation strategies that are grounded in the realities of the patient's circumstances rather than assumptions about them.

Context does not excuse a decision. It explains the decision before it is judged.

The Baseline Gives Meaning to Every Piece of Evidence

As the investigation progresses, the attorney will encounter thousands of individual pieces of evidence.

A laboratory value. A CT scan. An MRI. An ECG. A nursing observation. A physician assessment. An operative report. A pathology result. Each one appears to answer an important question.

Standing alone, however, none of them explains the patient's clinical story.

Every piece of evidence acquires significance only when it is interpreted within the context of the patient's baseline.

An oxygen saturation of ninety-two percent may be entirely acceptable for one patient and a medical emergency for another.

A serum creatinine of 2.0 mg/dL may represent acute kidney injury in a previously healthy individual or normal baseline function in a patient with advanced chronic kidney disease.

A CT scan demonstrating cerebral atrophy may be expected in an elderly patient with longstanding dementia but entirely unexpected in a healthy fifty-year-old.

The evidence itself has not changed. Its meaning changes because the patient changes. Clinical Intelligence therefore teaches attorneys never to evaluate evidence in isolation. Always ask... "What does this finding mean for this patient?"

That single question transforms information into understanding.

Why Objective Evidence Must Always Be Interpreted

Attorneys often think of imaging and laboratory studies as objective evidence. In one sense, they are. The scan exists. The laboratory value exists. The image exists. But objective evidence is not the same as objective understanding.

A CT scan may accurately demonstrate an abnormality. The important question is not simply what the scan shows. The important question is:

What does that abnormality represent in the context of this patient's baseline?

- Was it new?

- Was it chronic?
- Was it progressing?
- Was it incidental?
- Was it expected?
- Did it explain the patient's deterioration?
- Or did it identify something entirely different?

Those are Clinical Intelligence questions. The scan supplies the anatomy. Baseline supplies the context. Together they begin reconstructing the patient's clinical story.

That is why Imaging Analysis naturally follows Baseline Profiling within the Lexcura Clinical Intelligence Model™.

The investigation has earned the right to ask not merely what the image demonstrates, but what that image actually means.

Case example: The MRI That Changed Nothing-and Everything

A sixty-seven-year-old woman presented with sudden dizziness, unsteady gait, and intermittent blurred vision.

An MRI of the brain demonstrated multiple chronic white matter changes together with a small acute cerebellar infarction.

The attorney's first reaction was understandable. The acute stroke appeared to explain the patient's symptoms. Baseline Profiling encouraged the investigation to continue.

Review of earlier neurological records demonstrated that the chronic white matter disease had been present for several years without measurable functional limitation.

The patient's balance had remained normal. She continued working full-time. She exercised regularly. She had never required walking aids. The MRI itself had not changed. The patient's baseline had changed the attorney's understanding of the MRI.

The chronic findings were background. The acute infarction represented the meaningful change. That distinction influenced every later stage of the investigation. The timeline. The neurological assessment. The standard of care.

The causation analysis.

Everything became clearer because the imaging was interpreted within the context of the patient rather than in isolation.

Whenever you review objective evidence, ask yourself:

"Does this image explain the patient's clinical story-or is it simply describing anatomy?"

Clinical Intelligence requires both. Anatomy tells you what exists. The patient's baseline tells you why it matters.

Why Chapter 3 Naturally Leads to Imaging Analysis

By now, you understand who the patient was before the clinical story began to change.

You understand why that baseline becomes the reference point for every later opinion.

You understand that objective evidence has little meaning until it is interpreted within that context.

The investigation has therefore reached another decision point. Not because we have finished learning about the patient. Because we have earned the right to ask a new question. The medical record has described the patient.

The baseline has explained the patient.

Now we must determine what the objective anatomical evidence reveals about the patient's condition.

That question introduces the next stage of the Clinical Intelligence investigation. Objective evidence is only objective. It is not self-explanatory.

Imaging studies, laboratory results, pathology findings, and other objective evidence are among the most persuasive forms of clinical evidence available in healthcare litigation. Yet even the most objective findings require interpretation. Their significance depends upon the patient's baseline, the clinical context, the timing of the event, and their relationship to every other piece of evidence.

Clinical Intelligence therefore teaches attorneys that objective evidence should never be viewed in isolation. It must always be interpreted within the patient's clinical story.

Attorneys who understand how baseline gives meaning to objective evidence ask better questions of radiologists, pathologists, and clinical experts, distinguish chronic findings from acute pathology more accurately, and develop investigations that are substantially more resistant to challenge.

An image shows what is present. Clinical Intelligence explains why it matters.

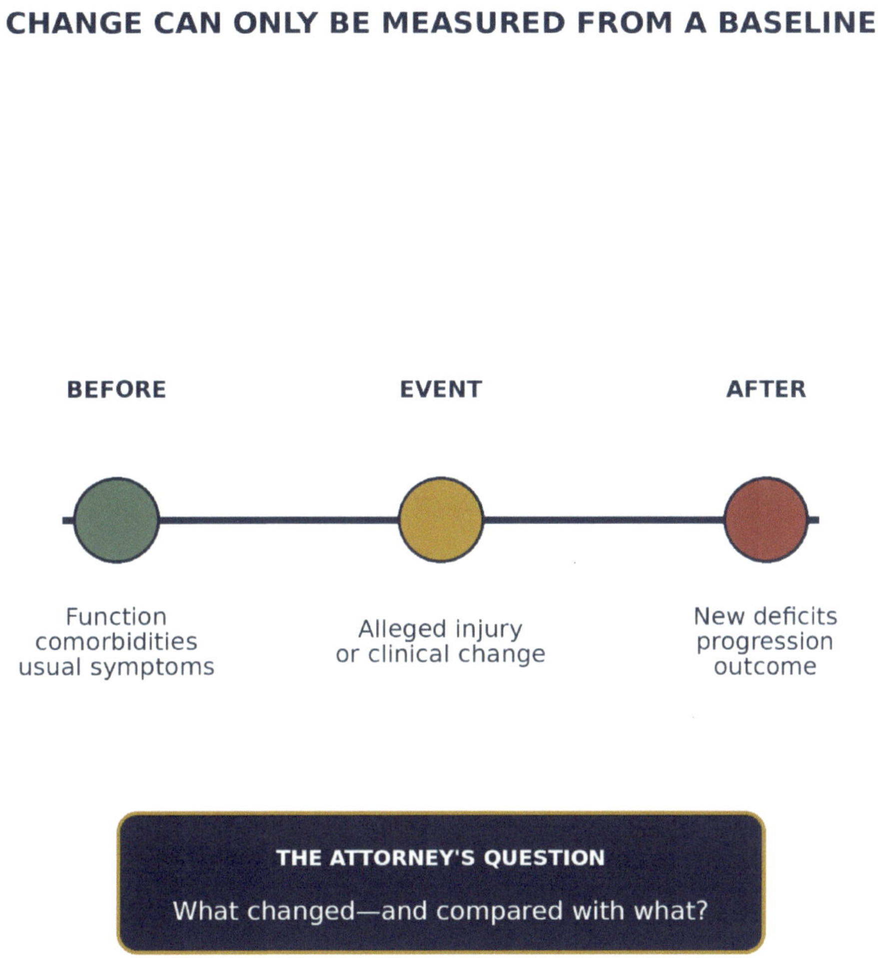

Figure 5 Baseline Profiling gives the attorney a defensible point from which to measure change, injury, function, and damages.

CHAPTER 8

Imaging Analysis

By the time I had become comfortable reconstructing a patient's baseline, I had already learned that the written record could never be treated as the whole story. The documentation provided essential evidence, but it was created by different people, at different times, for different purposes, and always through the perspective of the person making the entry. That did not make it unreliable. It simply meant that every note reflected one part of the patient's journey rather than the journey in its entirety. The more cases I reviewed, the more I found myself looking for another source of evidence that might help me determine whether the clinical story emerging from the documentation was supported by what was actually happening inside the patient's body.

At first, I do not think I saw imaging as a separate part of the investigation. Like most clinicians, I viewed diagnostic studies as another source of information within the medical record. I read the radiology report, considered the findings, and placed them alongside the laboratory results and clinical notes. That was an entirely reasonable way to work, and in many cases it provided everything I needed. Over time, however, I began to realize that imaging often carried a significance that was different from the rest of the documentation. It was not simply another description of the patient. It was often the closest thing available to an objective record of what the patient's body was revealing at a particular moment in time.

That distinction stayed with me because so much of healthcare litigation depends upon interpretation. A nurse describes what they observed. A physician explains what they believed was happening. A family member remembers how the patient appeared. An expert later reviews the same evidence and offers another interpretation. Each perspective may be honest and clinically valuable, but each is still shaped by knowledge, experience, and the circumstances in which the observation was made. Imaging does not remove interpretation, because every study still has to be read and understood, but it introduces something different into the investigation. It provides a physiological reference point against which the developing clinical narrative can be tested.

I remember reviewing cases where the documentation and the imaging aligned almost perfectly. The patient's symptoms, examination findings, progression, and diagnostic studies all appeared to be telling the same story. In those cases, the imaging strengthened the confidence I could place in the clinical narrative because the objective findings supported what clinicians had been observing and responding to. I also reviewed cases where the imaging seemed to challenge the story contained within the written record. A patient described as stable had objective evidence of significant disease. A condition documented as acute appeared, on closer review, to have been developing for much longer. A study reported as showing no important change became far more significant when compared with earlier imaging that had not initially been obtained.

Those cases made me stop and think because I had previously treated imaging as confirmation of a diagnosis rather than as a witness to the patient's progression. Once I began to see it differently, I could no longer read a radiology report simply to identify the final finding. I wanted to understand where that study sat within the patient's journey, what had prompted it, what the body was showing at that moment, and whether the finding supported or challenged everything else I thought I understood.

That change in thinking was gradual. There was no single case where Imaging Intelligence suddenly appeared as a fully formed discipline. It emerged because the same questions kept returning. Did the image support the documented clinical impression? Was the abnormality new, longstanding, or evolving? What had been visible on earlier studies? Had the patient's symptoms begun before the objective finding was recognized? Did the study reveal a level of disease that should have influenced urgency, treatment, or escalation? Were later interpretations being applied retrospectively to images that had been less clear at the time?

The more I asked those questions, the more I understood that imaging could not be separated from baseline, chronology, or clinical decision-making. A study captures the body at one point in time, but it does not explain the entire journey that led there. A CT scan may show a stroke, but it does not automatically establish when the vascular event began, when the symptoms first became clinically meaningful, or whether treatment opportunity still existed earlier. An X-ray may show a fracture, but it does not by itself establish how the injury occurred or whether the appearance reflects an acute event, an older injury, or underlying disease. An MRI may reveal significant spinal pathology, but the significance of that pathology depends upon the patient's symptoms, function, baseline, progression, and the decisions made before and after the study.

That was when I began to appreciate that imaging was not simply about what could be seen. It was about what the findings meant in relation to the patient.

There is a natural tendency to view diagnostic imaging as especially authoritative because it appears objective. I understand that. Images are physical records of anatomy, structure, function, blood flow, tissue change, or electrical activity. They often feel more concrete than a narrative note because they are not dependent upon someone remembering what happened or describing what they observed in words. Yet I learned not to confuse objectivity with certainty. An image may be objective, but its significance still has to be interpreted. Findings may be subtle, nonspecific, chronic, incidental, evolving, or dependent upon the quality and timing of the study. Two experts may review the same image and disagree, not because one is necessarily careless, but because medicine does not always offer the level of certainty litigation would prefer.

That realization made me more cautious rather than less confident. It reminded me that the purpose of Imaging Intelligence was never to elevate imaging above all other evidence. It was to understand what imaging could reliably contribute and what it could not. A scan does not replace the patient's symptoms. It does not replace clinical examination. It does not replace laboratory findings, chronology, or professional judgment. It becomes most valuable when it is placed alongside those sources and considered as part of one continuous clinical story.

I began to notice how often imaging was discussed as though it marked the beginning of the disease process. The abnormality appeared on the study, so the investigation naturally focused on that moment. The more cases I reviewed, however, the more often I found that the image represented the point at which the disease became visible rather than the point at which it began. The patient's body had frequently been changing before the study was performed, sometimes gradually and sometimes rapidly. Symptoms, vital signs, laboratory values, pain, function, or neurological findings may already have been signaling that something was wrong. The image did not create the condition. It revealed a condition that had already been developing.

That distinction became particularly important in delayed diagnosis and failure-to-recognize cases. If the investigation concentrates only on the moment imaging confirmed the diagnosis, it may miss the earlier period during which the patient's physiology was already changing. At the same time, it would be equally unfair to assume that because imaging later showed significant disease, the diagnosis should have been obvious much earlier. The central question was not whether the image eventually confirmed the condition. It was whether the information available before the study reasonably supported a different level of concern, investigation, or response.

I remember reviewing a postoperative case where the patient developed increasing abdominal pain, tachycardia, reduced urine output, and a gradual decline in blood pressure. Each finding had been documented, but the significance of the pattern was not fully appreciated until a CT scan demonstrated intra-abdominal bleeding. The scan became central to the case because it confirmed the diagnosis, yet the more important question was not what the CT showed. The more important question was what the patient's body had been showing before the CT was ordered.

The imaging made the earlier observations more meaningful, but I had to be careful not to use the later diagnosis to make every earlier sign appear obvious. Pain after surgery is common. Mild tachycardia may have several explanations. Blood pressure can fluctuate. Reduced urine output may occur for reasons unrelated to bleeding. None of those findings established the diagnosis on its own. What mattered was how they accumulated, whether the pattern became increasingly difficult to explain, and when the possibility of significant bleeding should reasonably have entered the clinical decision-making.

That case taught me that imaging often looks backward as well as forward. It tells us what was present when the study was performed, but it may also help us understand the significance of findings that appeared earlier. The discipline lies in using that information carefully. The later image can help explain the journey, but it should not be allowed to rewrite the uncertainty that genuinely existed before the diagnosis became clear.

I found the same issue in stroke cases. A patient may present with weakness, speech difficulty, dizziness, confusion, or other neurological symptoms, and the initial CT may show no acute hemorrhage or no obvious infarction. Later imaging may demonstrate an evolving ischemic stroke. Once the outcome is known, it becomes tempting to read the first presentation as though the diagnosis should have been immediately apparent. In some cases, the pattern was indeed sufficiently concerning to require urgent neurological evaluation and additional imaging. In others, the early findings remained nonspecific, fluctuating, or difficult to distinguish from competing explanations.

Imaging Intelligence did not allow me to decide that earlier treatment would have changed the outcome simply because later imaging showed extensive injury. It required me to ask more disciplined questions. What did the initial study exclude? What did it fail to exclude? What symptoms were present? When did the neurological pattern become clearer? What additional imaging was available? When did the tissue injury become established? What treatment opportunities remained at each stage? The image mattered enormously, but only when it was interpreted within the patient's baseline, clinical presentation, and timeline.

That was one of the reasons I eventually stopped thinking of imaging as a separate document category. It was part of a relationship between what clinicians observed and what the body revealed. Sometimes those two sources were strongly aligned. The documentation described progressive neurological deterioration, and the imaging demonstrated evolving infarction consistent with that progression. The clinical narrative became more coherent because each part supported the other.

In other cases, the documentation and imaging appeared to be saying different things. A patient was described as improving, yet the imaging showed progressive pathology. A scan was reported as stable, but comparison with earlier studies revealed a meaningful change. A severe abnormality was documented, yet the patient's function and symptoms appeared inconsistent with the significance later attributed to the finding. Those discrepancies did not automatically prove that the documentation was wrong or that the imaging had been misinterpreted. They told me that I had not yet fully understood the relationship between the sources.

That relationship became increasingly important because healthcare litigation often depends upon whether different forms of evidence support one another. When the documentation, examination findings, laboratory values, imaging, and patient progression all point in the same direction, confidence in the clinical understanding naturally increases. When they do not, the disagreement deserves careful investigation. The purpose is not to choose one source and dismiss the others. It is to understand why the evidence appears to diverge and whether the divergence reflects timing, interpretation, incomplete information, chronic disease, or a genuine failure to recognize what was happening.

I learned to pay close attention to comparison studies because they often provided the context that a single image could not. A radiology report may describe a finding as chronic, unchanged, or newly developed, but the reliability of that conclusion depends upon what previous studies were available. Earlier imaging can reveal whether a lesion was longstanding, whether disease had progressed, whether a postoperative complication was new, or whether the current finding reflected a known condition rather than the event under investigation. In some cases, the most important study was not the one performed during the disputed admission. It was the one completed months or years earlier.

That brought me back to Record Integrity. If prior imaging existed but had not been obtained, the interpretation of the current study might remain incomplete. A radiologist may have referred to previous films that were not included in the litigation file. A specialist may have compared findings with a study performed at another institution. A patient may have undergone outpatient imaging that changed the understanding of what was new and what was pre-existing. The investigation could not rely only on the studies that happened to be included with the hospital record. It had to determine what imaging existed across the patient's broader healthcare journey.

The actual images also became important in some cases, rather than relying entirely on written reports. I want to be clear that I have never believed attorneys or non-radiologist clinicians should attempt to replace qualified imaging specialists. Formal interpretation belongs with appropriately trained experts. At the same time, I learned that the report does not always answer every litigation question. The radiologist may accurately describe the findings without addressing whether they were subtle, obvious, evolving, or clinically concordant with the patient's presentation. A specialist review of the original study can sometimes clarify whether the image supports the interpretation given at the time or whether reasonable disagreement existed.

That distinction mattered because hindsight can influence imaging review just as it influences every other part of the case. Once the final diagnosis is known, subtle findings may appear more obvious than they did prospectively. An expert may identify an abnormality retrospectively that was genuinely difficult to appreciate on the original study. That does not necessarily mean the earlier interpretation fell below the standard of care. The investigation must consider image quality, clinical information available to the radiologist, the subtlety of the finding, the limits of the modality, and what a reasonably competent specialist would have been expected to recognize at that time.

Conversely, there are cases where the abnormality was sufficiently apparent that the failure to identify or communicate it becomes difficult to defend. The discipline lies in distinguishing between those situations rather than assuming that every missed finding represents negligence or that every interpretation is protected by uncertainty. Imaging Intelligence provides the clinical context needed to frame the right questions for the appropriate expert, but it does not replace that expert's formal opinion.

The timing of imaging also became central to my investigations. I found that there were often several relevant times rather than one. The time the study was ordered, the time it was performed, the time it was interpreted, the time the report became available, the time a critical result was communicated, and the time someone acted upon it could all be different. In routine cases, those differences may have little significance. In time-sensitive deterioration, stroke, bleeding, pulmonary embolism, spinal compression, or other acute conditions, they may become central to understanding whether meaningful opportunity remained.

A report timestamp alone rarely answered the full question. The study may have been read preliminarily before the final report was entered. A physician may have viewed the images directly. A radiologist may have communicated urgent findings by telephone. An electronic alert may have been generated but not acknowledged. A result may have been available without being connected to the patient's changing clinical condition. Each part of that sequence had to be reconstructed before I could understand whether the imaging contributed to timely care or whether the communication pathway failed somewhere along the way.

This was another area where imaging and regulatory analysis eventually connected. A delayed response to a critical study may reflect an individual failure, but it may also reveal weaknesses in communication systems, after-hours coverage, escalation procedures, electronic alerts, or responsibility for follow-up. The image may identify the pathology, while the broader investigation explains why the finding did or did not lead to an appropriate response.

I also began to appreciate that imaging can carry very different weight depending upon the clinical question. In some cases, it provides direct evidence of injury or disease. In others, it excludes an important possibility. A normal study may be just as significant as an abnormal one, but only if the limitations of the modality are understood. A normal CT does not exclude every early ischemic stroke. A normal X-ray does not rule out every fracture. A negative ultrasound may have limitations depending upon timing, technique, and the condition being investigated. Imaging Intelligence requires an understanding not only of what a study shows, but of what it is capable of showing.

That became particularly important when later opinions relied too heavily on negative findings. There were cases where a normal or nondiagnostic early study was treated as proof that no significant disease existed at the time. The more appropriate conclusion was often that the disease had not yet become visible on that modality, that the study had limitations, or that further investigation was required if the clinical concern remained high. The image had to be interpreted within the strength of the clinical suspicion rather than allowed to end the investigation automatically.

The opposite problem also occurred. An abnormal finding could be treated as though it explained every symptom and every later outcome, even when the relationship remained uncertain. Incidental abnormalities are common, particularly in older patients and those with complex medical histories. Degenerative changes, chronic vascular disease, old infarcts, benign lesions, and longstanding structural abnormalities may appear significant on imaging without being responsible for the event under investigation. Baseline and comparison studies become essential in distinguishing pre-existing findings from new injury and clinically relevant pathology from incidental disease.

I remember reviewing a spinal injury case where extensive degenerative changes were described on MRI. The report sounded severe, and it would have been easy to assume that the abnormalities explained the patient's neurological complaints. When the imaging was considered alongside the baseline, chronology, and specialist assessments, however, the picture became less straightforward. Some findings were longstanding. The timing of symptom progression did not align neatly with the theory being proposed. The imaging was important, but it did not support the level of causal certainty initially attributed to it.

In another case, relatively subtle imaging became highly significant because it aligned closely with a new and progressive clinical deficit. The images were not dramatic, but they were new, they corresponded anatomically with the patient's symptoms, and they appeared within the correct timeframe. The importance of the finding came not from its visual severity alone, but from its relationship with the patient's baseline and progression.

These cases reminded me that imaging severity and clinical significance are not always the same. A dramatic image may represent chronic disease with limited relevance to the allegation. A subtle change may become central when it corresponds with new symptoms and a clear deterioration from baseline. The investigation has to understand that relationship before the image can be given its proper weight.

I also became more cautious about the language used in reports. Terms such as possible, suspicious for, cannot exclude, consistent with, likely, stable, and unchanged each carry different levels of certainty. They are not interchangeable, and they should not be converted into stronger or weaker conclusions simply because the litigation prefers a definitive answer. A radiologist's language often reflects the genuine uncertainty of the study, and that uncertainty should be preserved unless additional evidence supports a more confident interpretation.

At the same time, I learned not to treat cautious language as though it made the finding unimportant. A report stating that a condition cannot be excluded may be clinically significant when the patient's symptoms and progression strongly support the concern. The wording has to be interpreted alongside the rest of the evidence. Imaging Intelligence is not an exercise in extracting phrases from reports. It is an exercise in understanding what the study contributed to the clinical decision-making at that moment.

Pathology eventually became part of this same way of thinking. Although pathology is not traditionally grouped with radiology, it also provides objective evidence of disease. Tissue findings can confirm diagnosis, characterize malignancy, demonstrate chronicity, or clarify mechanisms of injury. As with imaging, pathology does not interpret itself. The findings have to be connected to the patient's presentation, treatment, and progression. A pathological diagnosis may explain what disease was present without establishing when it became clinically detectable or whether earlier intervention would have altered the outcome.

The same principle applied to ECGs, echocardiograms, angiography, ultrasound, fetal monitoring tracings, and other objective physiological studies. Each captured a different aspect of the patient's condition. An ECG could demonstrate ischemic change or arrhythmia. An echocardiogram could reveal function, structure, and hemodynamic effects. Fetal monitoring could provide a continuous record of physiological response over time. These studies were not simply attachments to the medical record. They were forms of objective evidence that could confirm, refine, or challenge the clinical narrative.

I gradually realized that the common feature was not the type of image or study. It was the question I was asking. What did the patient's body objectively reveal, and how did that evidence relate to what clinicians observed, documented, and did?

That question eventually became the foundation of what I now describe as Imaging Analysis.

Imaging Analysis is the disciplined interpretation and integration of diagnostic imaging and other objective physiological evidence within the context of the patient's baseline, clinical presentation, progression, and the decisions made throughout the healthcare journey. Its purpose is not to replace specialist interpretation or to treat images as more important than the rest of the record. Its purpose is to determine whether the objective evidence supports the clinical story, challenges it, or reveals a part of the patient's progression that has not yet been fully understood.

The definition became important to me because I wanted to separate Imaging Intelligence from simple image review. A radiologist interprets the study. A cardiologist may interpret an ECG or echocardiogram. A pathologist examines tissue. Those specialties remain essential. Imaging Intelligence asks what those findings mean when integrated into the entire case. It considers when the evidence was obtained, what was visible, what was communicated, how it related to baseline, and whether it should have influenced recognition, treatment, escalation, or causation.

That integration is what makes the discipline useful to attorneys. The attorney does not need to become a radiologist, but they do need to understand why the imaging matters. They need to know whether the image supports the theory of the case, whether comparison studies are missing, whether specialist review is necessary, whether timing affected treatment opportunity, and whether the objective findings align with the opinions being offered. Without that understanding, imaging can appear persuasive while remaining disconnected from the actual legal and clinical questions.

I have seen expert opinions that relied heavily on imaging without adequately addressing baseline or chronology. I have also seen opinions that discussed the clinical course in detail while giving little attention to objective studies that contradicted the narrative. Both approaches left the analysis incomplete. Imaging Intelligence requires the image and the patient's journey to be understood together because neither can be interpreted responsibly without the other.

This became particularly clear in cases where one side focused on the dramatic final image while the other emphasized the uncertainty present earlier. Both positions might contain truth. The final study may show severe disease, while the earlier signs remained nonspecific. The role of Clinical Intelligence is not to choose whichever version is more persuasive. It is to reconstruct how the patient moved from uncertainty to objective confirmation and identify when the evidence reasonably required a different response.

That is why Imaging Intelligence and Timeline Reconstruction eventually became so closely connected in my thinking. Imaging provides objective points within the journey, while the timeline explains what happened between them. A series of studies can demonstrate progression, stability, or response to treatment. The timing of each study can reveal whether deterioration was recognized promptly or whether important opportunities were lost. At the same time, the timeline prevents the image from being interpreted in isolation by showing what the patient was experiencing before and after it was obtained.

I remember reviewing a case involving a patient with respiratory deterioration where serial chest imaging had been performed over several days. Each report was read as a separate study, and no single one appeared dramatic enough to explain the eventual decline. When the studies were reviewed together and placed alongside oxygen requirements, respiratory rate, laboratory findings, and nursing observations, the progression became much clearer. The patient's condition had not changed suddenly. The objective evidence showed a gradual worsening that had been visible across several sources long before the final crisis.

That case reinforced something I had begun to understand in many other investigations. Objective evidence is often most meaningful when viewed as a pattern rather than as an isolated finding. One image may raise a question. Several images may show a trajectory. One ECG may be nonspecific. Serial changes may reveal evolving ischemia. One laboratory result may be mild. A trend may demonstrate deterioration. The body often communicates through progression, and Imaging Intelligence has to preserve that progression rather than reducing it to the final abnormal study.

At the same time, I learned that progression on imaging does not automatically establish preventability. The question still remained whether the disease was recognizable, what intervention was available, and whether earlier action probably would have changed the outcome. Imaging may define the pathology and help establish timing, but it does not answer causation by itself. It becomes one part of the larger reasoning process that eventually leads to that conclusion.

The more I worked with objective evidence, the more I became aware of how easily it could create false confidence. Images feel definitive because they can be displayed, measured, and shown to a jury. They carry visual power that written documentation often lacks. That power makes disciplined interpretation even more important. A compelling image may still be clinically ambiguous. A severe abnormality may be unrelated to the alleged breach. A subtle finding may be more significant than it appears. The image must earn its place within the case just as every other piece of evidence must.

I came to believe that one of the most useful questions an attorney can ask is not simply, "What does the imaging show?" but, "What does this imaging prove, and what does it not prove?" That question creates space for both confidence and restraint. It allows the study to contribute fully without being asked to carry more weight than the evidence can sustain.

In some cases, the imaging establishes that an injury occurred. In others, it helps define when it occurred or how it progressed. It may identify alternative explanations, demonstrate pre-existing disease, or reveal that the proposed mechanism is physiologically unlikely. It may support the standard-of-care analysis by showing what information was available to clinicians, or it may become central to causation by demonstrating whether meaningful tissue remained salvageable. The contribution varies from case to case, which is why the image has to be understood within the exact question the litigation is asking.

I also found that imaging could protect against unfair conclusions in both directions. It could prevent a provider from being blamed for an outcome that objective evidence showed was already largely established before the alleged delay. It could also demonstrate that disease was visible and progressive despite documentation suggesting the patient remained stable. The image did not belong to the plaintiff or the defense. It belonged to the patient's clinical story.

That is how I eventually came to view all objective physiological evidence. It was not there to strengthen one side. It was there to test the story.

The discipline required me to remain open to whichever direction the evidence led. There were cases where imaging strengthened concerns about delayed recognition or inappropriate response. There were others where it challenged a theory that initially appeared compelling. Occasionally it revealed that the case was more uncertain than either side had acknowledged. I learned not to see that uncertainty as a failure. It was often the most honest conclusion available.

By the time Imaging Intelligence had become a formal part of the Lexcura Clinical Intelligence Model™, I no longer thought of it as a specialist subsection of the review. It had become another way of asking whether the case I believed I understood was supported by the patient's body. Baseline had shown me who the patient was before everything changed. Imaging now allowed me to examine what the body was revealing as the journey unfolded.

Once that evidence had been identified and placed into context, another question naturally followed. An image captured a moment, but a healthcare case was never only a moment. I still needed to understand how the patient had moved from one clinical state to another, when isolated findings had become a recognizable pattern, and where meaningful opportunity to intervene had appeared or disappeared.

The objective evidence had shown me what was present. Now I needed to understand how the patient had reached that point.

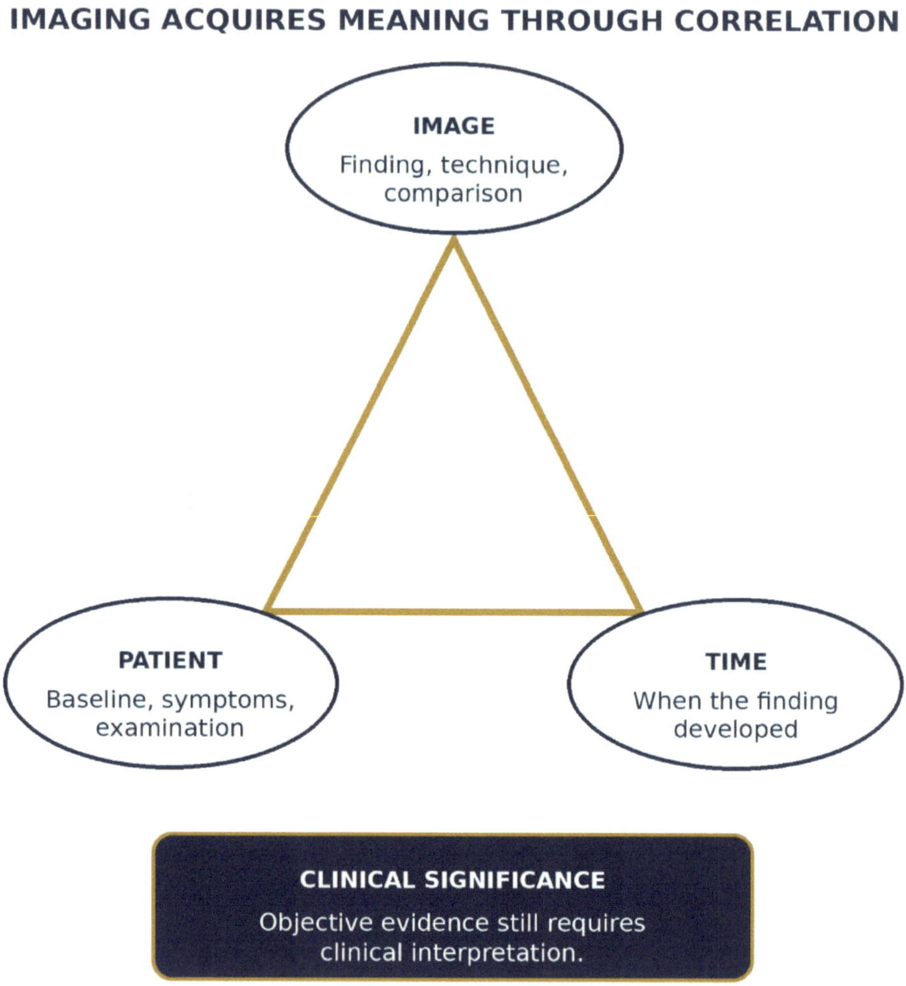

Figure 6 Imaging findings become useful only when they are correlated with the patient, the clinical examination, comparison studies, and time.

CHAPTER 9

Timeline Reconstruction

When I first began reviewing healthcare litigation, I do not think I appreciated how much of my attention was being drawn toward the major events in the case. I would naturally focus on the operation, the deterioration, the cardiac arrest, the stroke, or whatever event had eventually brought the patient into litigation. It seemed like the obvious place to begin because those were the moments everyone was talking about. They were the events that appeared to explain why the patient had suffered harm, so I assumed that was where I needed to concentrate my attention.

Looking back now, I think I was missing one of the most important parts of the patient's story. It was not because I was failing to read the records carefully. I was reading every page, comparing the documentation, and trying to make sense of each decision as it appeared. The difficulty was that I was following the record in the same way it had been written, one entry at a time, without fully appreciating that the patient's condition was not unfolding in neat sections simply because the documentation was organized that way.

The documentation moved from one note to the next. The patient did not. The patient was living continuously while the record captured only selected moments along that journey. Once I began thinking about that difference, I found myself becoming much more interested in the spaces between the entries because those were often the places where the patient's condition had begun changing before anyone had recognized the significance of what was happening.

A nurse might document that the patient appeared comfortable at eight o'clock in the morning, followed by another entry several hours later describing increasing pain, a rising heart rate, or a change in mental status. The record showed me what had been observed at those two points in time, but it could not tell me exactly when the patient's condition began to change or how quickly that change had developed. It could not tell me whether there had been subtle signs in between that nobody considered significant enough to document, or whether the deterioration had occurred more suddenly than the chart appeared to suggest.

I found myself thinking more and more about those spaces because patients do not deteriorate every three hours simply because observations are recorded every three hours. Their physiology changes continuously. The documentation gives us only occasional windows through which we can observe that progression. Once I understood that, I stopped seeing the medical record as a complete timeline of the patient's journey and began seeing it as a series of glimpses that had to be brought together carefully before the progression could be understood.

That change in thinking affected the way I approached every case that followed. Instead of asking only what had been documented, I began asking what was likely happening to the patient while nobody happened to be documenting anything at all. I was not trying to speculate or fill gaps with assumptions. I was trying to understand whether the available observations formed a pattern that continued across the spaces in the record, even when that pattern had not yet been recognized at the time.

The more I did this, the more I realized that a chronology and a reconstructed timeline were not the same thing. A chronology could tell me that the patient's temperature rose at one time, the heart rate increased later, the blood pressure fell several hours after that, and treatment eventually began. Those facts were useful, but they did not automatically explain when the patient's condition became clinically concerning or when a different response should reasonably have been considered. The chronology placed events in order. It did not always explain their meaning.

That distinction became especially clear in cases where no single finding appeared dramatic. A slightly elevated heart rate could be explained by pain, anxiety, fever, dehydration, medication, or any number of other possibilities. A mild reduction in blood pressure might not appear alarming in isolation. A patient who seemed more tired or less communicative might simply be recovering from surgery. Each finding could be explained, and sometimes those explanations were entirely reasonable at the time.

What changed the investigation was not necessarily the presence of one abnormal observation. It was the way those observations began to relate to one another. A rising heart rate became more significant when it continued despite pain control. Reduced urine output became more concerning when it appeared alongside falling blood pressure.

Confusion took on a different meaning when accompanied by fever, increasing respiratory effort, or worsening laboratory values. The patient's story gradually shifted as each new piece of information changed the meaning of the information that had come before it.

I think that was one of the most important lessons Timeline Reconstruction eventually taught me. Clinical significance rarely sits inside one isolated fact. It develops through relationships. The more accurately those relationships are reconstructed, the more clearly the patient's progression begins to emerge.

I remember reviewing a postoperative case involving an older patient who later returned to surgery with significant internal bleeding. The allegation centered on a delay in recognition, and everyone involved seemed to have a different view of when the deterioration should have become apparent. The family believed the patient had looked unwell for hours. The nursing documentation described pain, nausea, and increasing restlessness, but none of those findings was particularly unusual after major surgery. The physician notes referred to expected postoperative symptoms, and the early laboratory changes were not dramatic enough to establish the diagnosis.

When I first read the records, I understood why the disagreement existed. If the individual entries were read separately, each one could support a relatively reassuring interpretation. The patient had pain, but pain was expected. The heart rate had risen, but not to a level that immediately demanded one explanation. The blood pressure had fallen from the patient's earlier readings, but it remained within a range that did not necessarily indicate shock. The hemoglobin had decreased, although not enough at that stage to confirm significant bleeding.

The more I reconstructed the sequence, however, the more difficult it became to view those findings as unrelated. The heart rate had not simply risen once. It had continued to rise. The blood pressure remained technically acceptable, but it was steadily moving away from the patient's own baseline. Urine output had declined. Pain became more persistent despite treatment. The patient appeared pale and increasingly unsettled. No single finding established the diagnosis, but the pattern was beginning to tell a story that routine postoperative recovery no longer fully explained.

That case stayed with me because it showed how easily a patient's deterioration can remain hidden when the record is read by discipline or by event rather than as one continuous clinical journey. Nursing documented the symptoms. Laboratory testing showed the changing blood values. The medical team considered several explanations. Imaging eventually confirmed the bleeding. Each part of the record contained something important, but the significance only became clear when those pieces were placed alongside one another and viewed over time.

The question was no longer whether the patient had been obviously unstable at the beginning. They had not been. The more difficult question was when the accumulating information had reached a point where continued observation was no longer enough and the possibility of bleeding should reasonably have changed the clinical response.

That was a much fairer question than asking why the diagnosis had not been made at the first abnormal observation. It recognized the uncertainty that genuinely existed earlier while still examining whether that uncertainty had been allowed to continue for too long. I came to believe that this was one of the most important safeguards within Timeline Reconstruction because it prevented hindsight from making the earliest sign appear more obvious than it had been, while also preventing a developing pattern from being dismissed simply because no single finding was diagnostic.

I found the same issue repeatedly in sepsis cases. A fever, mild tachycardia, reduced appetite, or increasing fatigue may not appear particularly concerning on its own, especially in patients with several competing explanations for those findings. The significance changes when the pattern continues, new abnormalities appear, and the patient begins moving away from their baseline. The point of concern is not always the first abnormal value. It is often the point at which the abnormalities begin forming a pattern that should reasonably change clinical thinking.

That point can be difficult to identify retrospectively because the later outcome makes the earlier signs feel more connected than they may have appeared at the time. Once we know the patient developed septic shock, every temperature, heart rate, and laboratory result seems to be part of an obvious progression. The clinicians caring for the patient did not have that certainty. They were dealing with possibilities, some more likely than others, and often with incomplete information.

The challenge for the investigator is to understand both perspectives at the same time. We have to reconstruct the full progression with the benefit of everything that eventually became known, but we also have to return to each decision point and ask what the information reasonably meant at that moment. I found that this required a conscious effort because hindsight is difficult to remove once the ending is known. It does not disappear simply because we remind ourselves to be objective.

Over time, I developed the habit of stopping at each important point in the timeline and temporarily setting aside everything that happened afterward. I would ask myself what the clinician knew at that time, what they did not know, what possibilities remained open, and whether the available information reasonably required a different response. I wanted to understand not whether the correct diagnosis was obvious in retrospect, but whether the patient's condition had become sufficiently concerning that the next step should have changed.

That distinction became central to my understanding of clinical decision-making. Medicine does not always move directly from symptom to diagnosis. More often, it moves from uncertainty to increasing concern, then toward investigation, treatment, and, eventually, confirmation. Timeline Reconstruction allowed me to examine whether that movement occurred at a reasonable pace in relation to the patient's progression.

I also learned that a medical record may contain several different times for the same event, and those differences can become important. There is the time the patient experienced the change, the time someone observed it, the time it was documented, the time it was communicated, and the time action was taken. Those moments may be close together, but they may also be separated by minutes or hours. In time-sensitive cases, the difference can influence the entire analysis.

A laboratory result may be collected at one time, processed later, posted electronically, acknowledged by a clinician, and acted upon after another delay. An imaging study may be ordered, performed, interpreted preliminarily, finalized, communicated, and then translated into treatment. A nurse may assess the patient at one time but enter the note later in the shift. A physician note may describe an earlier examination while carrying the timestamp of the final entry. If those distinctions are ignored, the reconstructed sequence may appear more precise than the evidence allows or may attribute delays to the wrong part of the process.

I became particularly cautious about relying on documentation time as though it always represented clinical time. Sometimes it did. Other times, the note reflected an event that had occurred earlier. Medication administration records, orders, laboratory collection times, imaging metadata, telephone records, and electronic audit trails often helped clarify the true sequence. The purpose was not to create an artificial level of precision. It was to establish the most reliable progression the evidence could honestly support and to identify where uncertainty remained.

That uncertainty mattered because timelines can easily become more authoritative than the evidence behind them. Once events are placed into a clean table with precise times, the sequence begins to look certain even when the source records were not. I learned to resist that. If the evidence supported only an approximate time, I wanted the timeline to preserve that limitation. If two records conflicted, the conflict needed to remain visible until it could be resolved. A timeline should clarify the evidence, not make it appear more complete than it is.

I think this was another place where Record Integrity continued influencing the investigation. Timeline Reconstruction depends upon reliable source material, but it also helps test the integrity of that material. When the sequence is assembled carefully, gaps and contradictions often become visible in ways they were not when the records were read separately. A medication appears to have been administered before the order was entered. A physician note describes an assessment that does not align with the nursing observations. A critical result appears in the chart without any clear response. A transfer occurs without documentation explaining why it became necessary.

Those inconsistencies do not automatically establish wrongdoing. They may reflect delayed entry, different documentation practices, or missing records. What they do establish is that the story has not yet been fully understood. Timeline Reconstruction gives those questions a place to become visible.

The more cases I reviewed, the more I also came to understand that time carries different meaning in different clinical situations. A delay of thirty minutes may be inconsequential in one case and devastating in another. Several hours may be clinically acceptable when a condition is stable and uncertainty remains reasonable, while a much shorter delay may be significant when the patient is actively deteriorating and effective treatment is time-dependent.

That is why I stopped thinking of delay simply as elapsed time. The number of minutes or hours mattered, but only in relation to what was happening physiologically during that period. I wanted to know whether the patient remained stable, whether the disease process was progressing, what treatment options remained available, and whether the opportunity to alter the outcome was narrowing while the patient waited.

This gradually led me to think about what I now describe as the intervention window. I did not begin with that term, and I certainly did not think of it as a formal concept in the early years. I simply noticed that there were periods in some cases when a different response still had a realistic chance of changing what followed, and other periods when the same response would probably have made little difference because the injury or disease process had already progressed too far.

The intervention window is not always easy to identify. It may begin before the diagnosis is confirmed, at the point where the pattern becomes sufficiently concerning that investigation or escalation is required. It may remain open for hours, or it may narrow rapidly. It may affect survival, functional recovery, the severity of injury, or the duration of treatment rather than determining whether harm occurs at all.

That understanding became particularly important because healthcare litigation often treats causation as an all-or-nothing question. Either earlier intervention would have prevented the outcome or it would not. The clinical reality is often more nuanced. Earlier treatment may not have prevented every consequence, but it may have reduced the severity of injury, preserved more function, shortened hospitalization, or increased the probability of survival. Timeline Reconstruction helps identify which possibilities remained available at each stage rather than assuming that one moment determined everything.

I remember a stroke case where the disagreement centered on when the patient's symptoms had become sufficiently clear to require urgent neurological evaluation. The early presentation was uncertain. The patient had intermittent weakness, mild speech changes, and periods where the symptoms appeared to improve. The initial imaging did not show hemorrhage or a clearly established infarction. Later, the patient deteriorated significantly, and further imaging confirmed a large ischemic stroke.

Once the final diagnosis was known, it was tempting to treat the early symptoms as an obvious stroke presentation. The more carefully I reconstructed the sequence, however, the more I understood why the initial uncertainty existed. Some findings were subtle. Others fluctuated. Competing explanations had been considered. The early study had not provided a definitive answer.

That did not end the investigation. It changed the question. Instead of asking why the stroke had not been diagnosed immediately, I began asking when the neurological pattern had become sufficiently consistent and concerning that the remaining uncertainty should no longer have delayed escalation or additional imaging.

That point did not necessarily correspond with the first symptom or the final deterioration. It sat somewhere between them, and identifying it required a careful understanding of what had changed, what was knowable, and what treatment opportunity remained. The timeline did not create certainty where none existed. It showed when the balance of concern should reasonably have shifted.

I found that this was often where timeline analysis became most valuable to attorneys. The legal theory may identify a broad delay, but the reconstructed clinical timeline helps define the actual decision points. It shows when concern first arose, when additional information became available, when communication occurred, when action was taken, and what remained possible during the intervals in between.

Without that level of detail, an allegation of delay can remain too general to withstand scrutiny. Saying that treatment should have begun earlier is not enough. Earlier than what? Based on which findings? What response was reasonably required? What would that response probably have changed? Timeline Reconstruction helps move the analysis from broad criticism to specific, clinically grounded questions.

The same was true in cases where the timeline ultimately weakened the allegation. There were matters where care appeared delayed when viewed only from the time of admission to the time of treatment. Once the sequence was reconstructed, it became clear that much of that interval involved reasonable investigation, genuine diagnostic uncertainty, or a patient whose condition remained stable. The meaningful period of delay was far shorter than originally suggested, and in some cases it occurred after the opportunity to alter the outcome had already narrowed considerably.

Those conclusions were not always comfortable, especially when the outcome was tragic, but I came to believe that the purpose of Timeline Reconstruction was not to strengthen a case. It was to clarify it. Sometimes clarity supports the allegation. Sometimes it challenges it. Often it reveals a more complicated truth that neither side had fully appreciated at the beginning.

I also began to see how easily the patient's story could disappear inside an overly detailed chronology. Earlier in my career, I believed that the best chronology was the one that contained the most information. I worried that leaving out a medication, laboratory value, or brief assessment might mean overlooking something important. That concern made me extremely thorough, but it also taught me that more detail does not always produce more understanding.

A chronology can become so crowded that the patient's progression is almost impossible to see. Every event may be technically relevant, yet the critical pattern becomes buried beneath information that does not change the analysis. I eventually learned to distinguish between preserving detail and presenting meaning. The complete record still had to be available and reviewable, but the reconstructed timeline needed to make the patient's changing condition visible.

That required judgment. I wanted to know which events altered the clinical picture, which decisions affected the next stage of care, which findings demonstrated progression, and which gaps required explanation. The timeline had to remain faithful to the evidence without becoming a transcript of the entire medical record.

I think that was when Timeline Reconstruction became much more than an organizational tool for me. It became a way of thinking about progression. It asked me to understand how one clinical state became another, how recognition developed, how decisions were made, and how opportunity changed as time passed.

Over the years, I also came to appreciate the importance of communication within the timeline. A clinician may recognize deterioration, but the recognition only influences care if it is communicated effectively and reaches someone capable of responding. The time a concern was documented was not necessarily the time it was reported. The time it was reported was not necessarily the time it was understood. The time it was understood was not necessarily the time action occurred.

Those distinctions became especially important in cases involving nursing escalation, critical laboratory results, radiology findings, transfers, and consultation requests. The records might show that communication occurred, but the content, urgency, and response were sometimes unclear. A note stating that the physician was informed does not necessarily tell us what information was conveyed or how the concern was framed. A message may have been sent without confirmation that it was received. An abnormal result may have been visible electronically without anyone connecting it to the patient's deterioration.

The timeline allowed those communication pathways to be reconstructed alongside the physiological progression. I wanted to understand not only when the patient changed, but when that change became known to the people responsible for acting upon it. That relationship often explained why a delay occurred and whether the failure was primarily one of recognition, communication, response, or system capacity.

This eventually connected Timeline Reconstruction with the later Regulatory and Compliance Overlay. A delay that initially appeared to be the responsibility of one individual might reflect an escalation pathway that had failed across several levels. A nurse may have recognized deterioration and contacted the covering physician, but the physician was responsible for several units. A critical imaging result may have been communicated, but the system did not ensure acknowledgment or follow-up. The timeline identified when each part occurred. The regulatory analysis later helped explain why the sequence unfolded as it did.

I learned not to separate those issues too early because the timeline often revealed the difference between an individual decision and a broader system failure. It showed who was present, what they knew, what responsibilities existed, and what barriers influenced the response. Without that sequence, it was easy to assign responsibility based on the person who happened to document the final event rather than understanding the chain that preceded it.

There were also cases where the timeline revealed that several separate opportunities had existed rather than one prolonged delay. The patient may have shown an early sign that justified reassessment, a later pattern that required escalation, and a final deterioration that demanded emergency intervention. Each decision point had to be evaluated independently because the information and available options were different at each stage.

That became important when expert opinions focused only on one moment. One expert might identify the first abnormal sign and treat it as the beginning of the breach. Another might concentrate on the point where the diagnosis became obvious. The reconstructed timeline helped determine whether those were truly the same issue or whether the case contained several distinct questions about recognition, investigation, treatment, and causation.

I came to believe that a strong timeline does not force the case into one continuous theory. It allows the stages of the patient's journey to remain visible. There may have been reasonable care early in the admission, a missed opportunity later, and appropriate emergency treatment after the patient became unstable. Recognizing those distinctions creates a more accurate analysis than describing the entire admission as either negligent or appropriate.

The same principle applied when several providers were involved. Each clinician entered the patient's journey at a different point and had access to different information. A consultant may have evaluated the patient before a significant change. A covering physician may have been called after several hours of deterioration. A nurse beginning a new shift may have inherited a patient whose earlier pattern was not fully communicated. The timeline helped establish what each person could reasonably know and whether they had enough information to understand the significance of what they were seeing.

That perspective protected the analysis from becoming unfairly collective. It was easy to say that "the healthcare team" should have recognized deterioration, but the team was made up of individuals who encountered the patient at different moments. Responsibility had to be tied to the information available to each person and the duties they carried at that stage of the journey.

At the same time, the timeline could reveal when the organization itself possessed knowledge that no single clinician appeared to hold. Information may have been scattered across nursing observations, laboratory systems, imaging reports, and specialist notes. The patient's deterioration was visible within the record as a whole, but no one had brought the pieces together in real time. That raised a different question about whether the system supported integration, escalation, and continuity effectively.

I think this was one of the reasons Timeline Reconstruction became so central to Clinical Intelligence. It did not simply tell me when events occurred. It showed how information moved through the healthcare system and whether that movement kept pace with the patient's changing condition.

Looking back now, I can see that the discipline emerged because I was never satisfied with knowing that something happened before or after something else. I wanted to understand why the sequence mattered. I wanted to know when a finding changed the clinical picture, when uncertainty became concern, when concern required action, and whether action occurred while meaningful opportunity still existed.

That is the understanding I eventually came to describe as Timeline Reconstruction.

Timeline Reconstruction is the disciplined reconstruction of the patient's evolving clinical journey so that progression, recognition, communication, response, and opportunity can be understood within the information available at each moment in time. It is not simply a record of events. It is an attempt to understand how the patient moved from one clinical state to another and how the decisions made along the way influenced that movement.

The definition became important because it separated Timeline Reconstruction from the chronologies I had relied upon earlier in my career. A chronology could be accurate and still fail to reveal the patient's progression. Timeline Reconstruction required me to understand not only the sequence, but the clinical meaning of that sequence.

It also reminded me that time should never be examined independently of physiology. An hour is not inherently significant. Its meaning depends upon what was happening to the patient during that hour. If the patient remained stable and the diagnostic process was reasonable, the interval may carry little concern. If the patient was progressively deteriorating and effective treatment was time-sensitive, the same interval may become central to the case.

This is where baseline and imaging continued shaping the analysis. Baseline told me where the patient began. Imaging and other objective evidence provided points of confirmation within the journey. The timeline connected those points and showed how the patient's condition changed between them. Each discipline remained distinct, but none operated alone.

The more completely those relationships were reconstructed, the more clearly the next question began to emerge. Once I understood what happened, when it happened, what information was available, and how the patient's condition was progressing, I could finally begin evaluating whether the clinical response remained reasonable at each decision point.

I had spent years learning not to ask that question too early. A decision cannot be judged fairly until the patient, the evidence, and the sequence are understood. By this stage of the investigation, those foundations were finally in place.

Now I could begin asking what should reasonably have happened next.

Figure 7 Event time, observation time, documentation time, and action time must be separated before delay can be evaluated fairly.

CHAPTER 10

Standard of Care Review

By the time I reached this point in an investigation, I had usually spent a considerable amount of time understanding the patient before I allowed myself to think seriously about whether the care had been reasonable. That was very different from the way I approached cases in the beginning because, like most people entering healthcare litigation, I was naturally drawn toward the question everyone wanted answered. Had someone made a mistake? It seemed like the most direct place to begin, especially when the allegation already identified the decision, delay, or omission that had brought the case into litigation.

The longer I worked in this field, however, the more uncomfortable I became with asking that question too early. I had seen too many cases change once the records were completed, the patient's baseline was properly understood, the objective findings were placed into context, and the timeline was reconstructed carefully enough to show what had actually been known at each stage. A decision that initially appeared difficult to defend sometimes became far more understandable once the uncertainty surrounding it was restored. In other cases, a decision that seemed routine in the documentation became much more concerning once the patient's progression and the information available at the time were brought together.

That taught me not to begin by deciding whether the care had been right or wrong. I needed to understand the decision before I could judge it.

I think this is one of the most difficult disciplines in healthcare litigation because the final outcome is always present in our minds. By the time the records arrive, we know what happened. We know the diagnosis that was eventually made, the injury that followed, the operation that became necessary, or the outcome the patient did not survive. That knowledge quietly changes the way earlier decisions appear. A symptom that seemed vague at the time may look obvious in retrospect. A laboratory result that carried several possible explanations may seem to point in only one direction once the diagnosis is known. A delay may appear indefensible because we can now see exactly what was developing while the clinicians were still trying to understand it.

I found that I had to work deliberately against that influence. It was not enough to remind myself that hindsight existed. I had to return to the decision point and rebuild the circumstances surrounding it as faithfully as the evidence allowed. What did the clinician know at that moment? What had not yet been discovered? What possibilities were reasonably being considered? What risks were present? What options were available? What would another reasonably competent professional have been expected to recognize and do under the same circumstances?

Those questions became far more useful to me than asking whether I personally would have made the same decision.

That distinction took time to appreciate because clinical experience naturally shapes judgment. When we have spent many years in healthcare, we develop habits, preferences, and ways of responding that feel right to us. We know what we would have done, which questions we would have asked, and what findings would have concerned us. Experience is invaluable, but I learned that personal preference and professional obligation are not the same thing. Two experienced clinicians may choose different but equally reasonable approaches. The fact that I would have ordered another test, escalated sooner, or selected a different treatment did not automatically mean the care provided fell outside the range of reasonable practice.

I became much more cautious about confusing a different decision with a negligent one.

That caution did not make me less willing to identify poor care. In many ways, it made the strongest conclusions clearer because I was no longer criticizing every decision that differed from my own. I was trying to determine whether the response remained within the range of choices that a reasonably competent professional could defend based on the information available at the time. When the evidence showed that several reasonable options existed, I wanted the analysis to preserve that reality. When the evidence showed that the patient's condition had progressed to a point where no reasonable pathway supported continued delay or inaction, I wanted that conclusion to be equally clear.

I think this is where Standard of Care Review began to take shape in my thinking. It was not simply about comparing the care with a guideline, policy, or textbook expectation. It was about understanding what reasonable professional practice required at a specific moment in this particular patient's journey.

The phrase standard of care is used so often in healthcare litigation that it can begin to sound more precise than it really is. When I first became involved in this work, I assumed there would usually be one clear standard against which the care could be measured. Sometimes there was. A medication had been administered despite a documented allergy. A critical result had not been communicated. A patient had not received a required assessment. In those cases, the expectation could be relatively straightforward.

Many cases were not like that.

Medicine often involves judgment under uncertainty. Symptoms may be nonspecific. Several diagnoses may remain possible. Treatments may carry competing risks. A patient's comorbidities may make the usual approach less appropriate. Resources may be limited. The most reasonable response may depend upon information that changes over time. In those circumstances, the standard of care cannot be reduced to whether one specific action occurred. It has to be understood through the quality of the reasoning, the recognition of risk, the timeliness of reassessment, and the appropriateness of the response as the clinical picture evolved.

The more I reviewed cases, the more I realized that the standard of care often becomes visible through a series of responsibilities rather than one isolated rule. A clinician may not be expected to make the final diagnosis immediately, but they may be expected to recognize that the patient requires further investigation. A nurse may not determine the medical cause of deterioration, but they may be responsible for reassessment, documentation, communication, and escalation. A physician may reasonably begin with conservative management, but that approach may become unreasonable if the patient fails to improve or new warning signs appear. The obligation changes as the evidence changes.

That became one of the reasons Timeline Reconstruction was so important before Standard of Care Review. I could not judge a decision fairly without knowing where it sat within the patient's progression. A response that was reasonable at one point may no longer have been reasonable several hours later. A decision to observe may have been appropriate while the symptoms remained nonspecific, but the same decision may become difficult to defend once the pattern of deterioration becomes clearer. The standard does not remain frozen while the patient changes.

I remember reviewing a case involving a patient who developed worsening respiratory distress after surgery. The early symptoms were mild and could reasonably have been attributed to postoperative pain, sedation, or shallow breathing. Oxygen was provided, the patient was encouraged to mobilize, and the condition was monitored. At that stage, I could understand why the team did not immediately pursue an aggressive investigation.

The problem emerged later.

The respiratory rate continued to rise, oxygen requirements increased, and the patient became less responsive. Laboratory findings changed, and nursing documentation showed that concern had been communicated more than once. The early decision to observe had been reasonable. The later decision to continue the same approach without reassessment was much harder to understand.

That case reinforced something I had gradually come to believe. Standard of care is not always about whether the first decision was correct. It is often about whether the clinical response changed when the patient's condition changed.

The more carefully I looked at those cases, the more interested I became in decision points. Broad conclusions such as "the patient was not monitored appropriately" or "escalation was delayed" may be directionally correct, but they are not enough. I wanted to know when monitoring should have intensified, what information made escalation necessary, who carried the responsibility at that moment, and what options remained available. Without that level of detail, the standard-of-care opinion could become little more than criticism after the fact.

A strong opinion needed to show how the obligation arose from the evidence.

This became particularly important when several clinicians were involved. Healthcare litigation often speaks about the care team as though everyone shared the same information and responsibility at all times. In reality, each professional enters the patient's journey at a different point and carries a different role. The bedside nurse may be responsible for recognizing change and reporting it. The covering physician may be responsible for assessing the significance of that report and deciding whether further investigation or treatment is required. A specialist may become responsible only after consultation. An organization may hold responsibility for staffing, supervision, communication systems, and access to resources.

I learned not to ask simply whether the standard of care had been met. I wanted to know whose standard was in question, what that professional's role required, and whether the evidence showed that the obligation was fulfilled.

That distinction often changed the direction of the case. I reviewed matters where the allegation initially focused almost entirely on nursing because the nurse had documented the patient's deterioration. The deeper investigation showed that the nurse had recognized the change, contacted the physician, and followed the instructions given. The more important questions involved the medical response, the quality of the communication, and the system supporting escalation. In other cases, the physician had been contacted but had not received an accurate picture of the patient's condition because key information had not been communicated clearly. Responsibility could not be understood by looking at the final note alone.

Those cases taught me that Standard of Care Review has to follow the flow of responsibility through the timeline. It is not enough to identify the person closest to the adverse event. The investigation has to understand who knew what, who was expected to act, what action was reasonable, and whether the responsibility shifted as the patient's condition evolved.

I also became much more careful about the role of policies, protocols, and guidelines. Early in my work, I sometimes treated them as relatively direct evidence of the standard of care. If a policy required one action and the record showed that action had not occurred, the conclusion appeared straightforward. Over time, I realized the relationship was more complicated.

Policies matter because they reflect organizational expectations and may help define the processes intended to protect patients. Guidelines matter because they describe evidence-based approaches and professional consensus. Protocols can be especially important in time-sensitive situations where a standardized response is designed to reduce variation and delay. None of those materials should be ignored.

At the same time, I learned that a policy is not automatically the legal or professional standard of care. An organization may adopt a policy that exceeds ordinary practice. A guideline may allow clinical discretion. A protocol may not fit every patient. A deviation may be justified by circumstances that were not anticipated when the document was written. Conversely, strict compliance with a policy does not necessarily mean the care was reasonable if the patient's condition required a different or more urgent response.

The written rule was part of the investigation, but it was never the entire answer.

This became especially clear in cases where the policy existed but could not be followed effectively in practice. A facility might require escalation after certain physiological thresholds were met, yet staffing shortages, unavailable physicians, or weak communication systems made timely escalation difficult. The individual clinician's responsibility still required examination, but so did the environment in which that responsibility had to be carried out. That broader question would eventually become central to the Regulatory and Compliance Overlay, but it often first became visible during Standard of Care Review.

The same was true of clinical guidelines. I found them helpful when they clarified what signs should prompt investigation, what treatment windows existed, or what level of monitoring was generally expected. The danger came when a guideline was treated as though it could make the decision for us. Guidelines are designed to support judgment, not replace it. They describe what is generally appropriate, while the standard of care still requires the clinician to consider the particular patient, the competing risks, and the information available at the time.

That individual context mattered especially in patients with complex baselines. A standard treatment may carry greater risk in someone with severe renal impairment, bleeding risk, frailty, or another condition that changes the balance of benefit and harm. A decision that appears conservative may have been reasonable because the alternative carried substantial danger. The investigation had to understand not only what action was possible, but why one option was selected over another.

I came to appreciate that the reasoning behind a decision can be just as important as the decision itself. A clinician may choose not to perform a procedure, start a medication, or pursue aggressive treatment for reasons that are clinically sound. If those reasons are documented clearly and align with the patient's condition, the decision may be entirely defensible. When the reasoning is absent, inconsistent, or unsupported by the evidence, the same decision becomes more difficult to evaluate.

Documentation does not create reasonableness, and lack of documentation does not automatically prove that reasonable care did not occur. Yet documentation often becomes the only evidence available years later to explain what was considered and why. I learned not to equate poor documentation with poor care automatically, but I also understood that undocumented reasoning leaves the investigation with uncertainty that might otherwise have been avoided.

This was another place where intellectual restraint became important. It is tempting to fill in missing reasoning with what a competent clinician might have considered, especially when the decision appears reasonable. It is equally tempting to assume that no reasoning occurred because none was documented. Neither approach is safe. The analysis should distinguish between what the record establishes, what can reasonably be inferred, and what remains unknown.

I found that attorneys often appreciated this distinction because it helped them understand the difference between a clinical concern and a supportable legal theory. A troubling record may raise serious questions without yet establishing a breach. An apparent departure may require expert interpretation before its significance can be determined. A policy violation may be important but still need to be connected to the patient's care. The purpose of the Clinical Intelligence review is not to replace qualified expert opinion. It is to identify the decisions, evidence, and questions that require expert analysis and to ensure that the expert is being asked to evaluate the case from a complete clinical foundation.

This became one of the areas where I saw the quality of expert referrals vary considerably. A broad question such as "Was the standard of care breached?" places an enormous burden on the expert to reconstruct the entire case before reaching the opinion. A more disciplined referral identifies the patient's baseline, the key decision points, the information available at each stage, the response that occurred, and the specific professional obligation requiring evaluation.

The expert remains responsible for the formal opinion, but the quality of the opinion often depends upon the quality of the question.

I think this is one of the reasons Standard of Care Review became so important within the Lexcura Clinical Intelligence Model™. It was not intended to produce a final legal conclusion. It was intended to make the clinical obligations visible enough that the attorney and the appropriate expert could examine them precisely.

Over time, I also became more aware of the difference between an error and negligence. Healthcare professionals make errors because they are human, and healthcare systems are complex. A medication may be given late. A note may be incomplete. A diagnosis may initially be missed despite reasonable assessment. A clinician may choose one acceptable approach where another professional would have chosen differently. Those events may deserve review, improvement, or criticism, but they are not all equivalent.

I learned to separate the imperfect from the unreasonable.

That distinction mattered because a review that criticizes every deviation can become less credible rather than more persuasive. If every documentation gap, delayed entry, or alternative decision is described as a breach, the genuinely significant failures may become buried in unnecessary criticism. I wanted the analysis to focus on the departures that were clinically meaningful, tied to a clear obligation, and connected to a point where a different response remained available.

The stronger the case, the less exaggeration it needed.

I remember reviewing a medication case where the wrong dose had been administered. At first glance, the error appeared obvious, and there was no real disagreement that the medication process had failed. The more difficult question was whether the error had caused the patient's later deterioration. The patient had several serious underlying conditions, was already unstable, and experienced complications that had multiple possible explanations.

Standard of Care Review identified the medication error clearly. It did not allow me to assume causation simply because the error existed. That distinction was essential because breach and outcome impact belong to different stages of the analysis. The failure may be undeniable while the causal significance remains uncertain.

The reverse can also occur. A patient may suffer a severe and clearly related injury even though the care remained within reasonable standards. Complications happen. Treatments fail. Diseases progress despite timely recognition and appropriate intervention. A devastating outcome does not prove negligence any more than an obvious error proves causation.

I think that was one of the most important balances I learned to maintain. Standard of Care Review defines what the professional should reasonably have done. It does not decide what the outcome would have been if they had done it.

That question belongs later.

Before reaching it, I needed to understand whether the alleged departure occurred while meaningful opportunity remained. Timeline Reconstruction had already begun identifying the intervention window, but Standard of Care Review helped determine whether there was an obligation to act within that window. The two disciplines were closely connected. Time showed when action could matter. Standard of care showed when action was reasonably required.

I reviewed a case involving a patient with progressive neurological symptoms after spinal surgery. The early symptoms were subtle and could be explained by postoperative pain, medication effects, or temporary weakness. The initial response involved observation and reassessment, which appeared reasonable. Over several hours, however, the weakness progressed, sensation changed, and bladder function became impaired. The evidence gradually moved from ordinary postoperative uncertainty toward a pattern requiring urgent specialist evaluation and imaging.

The standard-of-care question was not whether the diagnosis should have been made at the first complaint. It was when the progression became sufficiently concerning that continued observation was no longer reasonable. That decision point mattered because urgent decompression may have remained capable of preserving neurological function for a limited period. The standard and the intervention window came together around the same moment.

That case reinforced why I had learned not to begin with the outcome. If I had started with the permanent injury and worked backward, every earlier complaint might have appeared diagnostic. If I had focused only on the uncertainty of the early symptoms, I might have overlooked when the pattern became unmistakably concerning. The fair analysis sat between those extremes.

I came to believe that fairness in Standard of Care Review requires us to recognize uncertainty without allowing uncertainty to become an excuse for inaction. Medicine does not require immediate certainty before clinicians respond to risk. There are times when the diagnosis remains unclear, but the patient's condition is concerning enough to justify further investigation, closer monitoring, consultation, or escalation. The standard may require action because of the risk, even before the final diagnosis is known.

That became particularly important in deterioration cases. The question was often not whether the clinician should have known exactly what was wrong. It was whether they should have recognized that the patient was no longer following the expected course and required a different level of attention.

The distinction is subtle but important. Clinical care is not only diagnosis. It is also recognition of change, management of uncertainty, and protection against foreseeable harm while the diagnosis is being established.

I found that nurses often understood this instinctively because bedside care depends heavily on recognizing when the patient no longer looks or behaves as expected. A nurse may not be able to identify the precise disease process, but they may recognize that the patient is deteriorating. The standard may then require reassessment, communication, and escalation. The physician's responsibility begins with understanding the significance of that information and determining the appropriate response.

When those responsibilities connect well, the healthcare system can respond before the patient becomes critically unstable. When they do not, the investigation may reveal a chain of failures rather than one isolated mistake.

This is where Standard of Care Review began leading naturally toward the broader system analysis. A clinician may recognize deterioration but be unable to obtain timely review. A physician may be covering too many patients. A policy may require escalation, but the practical pathway may be unclear. Equipment, imaging, specialist support, or transfer capacity may be unavailable. The individual decision still matters, but it exists within an environment that can either support or undermine safe care.

I had not fully appreciated that in the early years because I tended to evaluate the clinician closest to the event. The more cases I reviewed, the more I realized that responsibility often extends outward. The question is not only whether one person acted reasonably. It is whether the system made reasonable care possible.

That broader question did not remove individual accountability. It made the analysis more complete.

I also became increasingly interested in what was foreseeable at the time. Foreseeability in healthcare is rarely about predicting the exact outcome. It is about recognizing risks that a reasonably competent professional should consider. A patient with escalating respiratory distress may be at risk of failure even if the precise cause remains uncertain. A patient with new neurological deficits may be at risk of permanent injury even before imaging confirms the diagnosis. A patient receiving a high-risk medication may require monitoring because known complications are possible.

The standard of care often emerges from the relationship between foreseeable risk and reasonable response. The greater the risk and the more serious the potential consequence, the more important it may become to investigate, monitor, or escalate even when uncertainty remains. At the same time, the response should remain proportionate. Not every possibility requires the most aggressive intervention.

That balance is one of the reasons clinical judgment is so difficult to evaluate retrospectively. The clinician has to act without overreacting to every minor abnormality and without overlooking the pattern that signals real danger. Standard of Care Review has to respect that difficulty while still identifying when the balance was no longer reasonable.

I think this is where experience helped me most, but it also required the greatest humility. The more clinical patterns I had seen, the easier it became to recognize what might be developing. That did not mean the treating clinician had the same perspective at the same moment. They may have encountered only one part of the sequence, worked within another specialty, or lacked information that later became available. My role was not to ask what the most experienced reviewer could see retrospectively. It was to ask what a reasonably competent professional in that role should have recognized prospectively.

That question became the center of the discipline.

Looking back now, I think Standard of Care Review evolved because I needed a way to examine professional obligation without allowing hindsight, personal preference, or the severity of the outcome to determine the answer. I wanted to understand what reasonable care required in the circumstances that genuinely existed, not in the cleaner and more certain version of the case created after the outcome was known.

That understanding eventually became the definition I continue to use.

Standard of Care Review is the disciplined evaluation of whether the recognition, decisions, communication, monitoring, treatment, and escalation provided at each meaningful point in the patient's journey remained within the range of reasonable professional practice based on the information and circumstances available at that time.

The definition mattered because it placed the standard inside the patient's timeline rather than outside it. It recognized that obligation can change as information develops, that different professionals carry different responsibilities, and that the reasonableness of care depends upon context rather than outcome alone.

It also reminded me that the standard of care is not a promise of the best possible result. It is a professional obligation to provide care that remains reasonable under the circumstances. Healthcare cannot guarantee recovery. It can only be expected to recognize risk, respond appropriately, and make defensible decisions based on the evidence available at the time.

The more carefully I applied that discipline, the more balanced my reviews became. I could identify genuine departures without turning every imperfection into negligence. I could recognize reasonable uncertainty without allowing it to justify prolonged inaction. I could understand the clinician's perspective while still asking whether the patient received the response their condition required.

That balance became especially important when I explained the case to attorneys. They did not need another opinion that simply stated whether the standard had been met. They needed to understand the reasoning. They needed to know which decisions mattered, when the obligation changed, what evidence supported the conclusion, and where the opinion remained vulnerable to challenge.

A strong Standard of Care Review should make that reasoning visible.

It should show why a response was reasonable or unreasonable. It should distinguish the strongest concerns from the weaker ones. It should identify where qualified expert opinion is required and frame the questions with enough precision that the expert can address the real clinical issue rather than reconstructing the entire case from the beginning.

I came to see this as another form of litigation risk management. Cases are often weakened not because the care was defensible, but because the theory of breach was too broad, too early, or disconnected from the patient's actual progression. A disciplined review helps the attorney focus on the decisions the evidence can support and avoid building the case around criticisms that may not survive deeper scrutiny.

The same discipline helps defense counsel identify where the care is strongest and where genuine exposure exists. A case does not become more defensible because every action is justified. It becomes more defensible when the reasonable decisions are separated from the ones that require explanation. Clarity strengthens both sides because it replaces general accusation and general denial with specific clinical understanding.

By the time I had completed Standard of Care Review, I usually understood which professional responsibilities had existed and whether the care had departed from them. Yet another question remained, and experience had taught me not to move beyond it too quickly.

A clinical decision never occurs in a vacuum.

Even the most competent professional works within a system that influences staffing, communication, supervision, resources, policies, technology, and access to care. I had spent years looking at individual decisions before I began appreciating how often the environment shaped what became possible.

Once I saw that, I could no longer judge the clinician without also asking what was happening around them.

CHAPTER 11

Regulatory & Compliance Overlay

Once I began looking beyond the individual clinician, I started to notice how often the conditions surrounding the care had already influenced what happened before anyone reached the decision that later became the focus of the case. At first, I do not think I appreciated how much those conditions mattered because my attention was naturally drawn toward the people who were directly involved with the patient. The nurse documented the deterioration. The physician made the treatment decision. The pharmacist verified the medication. The therapist assessed the function. Those were the people whose actions appeared most visible in the record, so they became the people I examined most closely.

The longer I worked in healthcare litigation, however, the more often I found myself asking why competent professionals had failed to respond in the way I would normally have expected. Sometimes the explanation was straightforward. A warning sign had been overlooked, a decision had been delayed, or a clinician had failed to recognize the significance of the information available at the time. In other cases, the explanation was much harder to isolate because the care appeared to have been shaped by circumstances that extended far beyond one person's judgment.

A nurse may have recognized that a patient was deteriorating but been responsible for too many patients to provide the reassessment the situation required. A physician may have been contacted but covering several units at the same time. An imaging study may have been ordered appropriately but delayed because the service was unavailable overnight. A critical laboratory result may have entered the electronic record without reaching the clinician who needed to act upon it. A policy may have required escalation, yet the actual escalation pathway may have been unclear, understaffed, or routinely ignored because it did not work in practice.

Those cases made me stop and think because they did not fit neatly into the way I had previously approached standard of care. I could identify the professional obligation, and I could see that the patient had not received the response their condition required, but I was not always convinced that the failure could be understood by examining one person alone. Something else was happening around the clinicians, and I began to realize that if I ignored that environment, I might reach a conclusion that was technically defensible but clinically incomplete.

Healthcare is delivered by individuals, but it is organized by systems. That became increasingly difficult for me to overlook because almost every action taken at the bedside depends upon something beyond the person providing the care. Staffing determines how much time is available. Communication systems determine whether information reaches the right person. Policies influence how risk is managed. Technology controls how findings are displayed, transmitted, and acknowledged. Training determines whether staff recognize what they are seeing. Leadership decisions influence resources, supervision, and the culture in which clinicians work.

None of those factors automatically excuses poor care, but neither can they be separated from it.

I remember reviewing a case involving an older patient who developed sepsis during a hospital admission. The early concern centered on the bedside nurse because the patient's physiological observations had been changing throughout the afternoon, yet escalation did not occur until the deterioration had become much more obvious. The nursing notes documented increasing concern, and the electronic observation system had generated alerts. On the surface, the case appeared to involve a failure to respond to the patient's worsening condition.

The more I reconstructed the environment, however, the more complicated the picture became. The nurse was caring for an unusually heavy assignment. The charge nurse was also carrying patients. Several other patients on the unit required urgent attention, and the physician covering the ward was responsible for multiple clinical areas. The early warning system generated alerts, but the process for ensuring that those alerts resulted in timely medical review depended heavily on staff already working beyond reasonable capacity.

None of that changed the fact that the patient required a more timely response. It did change the question I was asking. I was no longer looking only at whether the nurse had escalated appropriately. I was trying to understand why a system that had recognized deterioration through its own monitoring process had still failed to respond effectively.

That distinction became central to the investigation because it revealed something I had previously underestimated. Healthcare systems can possess information without converting that information into action. An alert can be generated. A result can be posted. A note can be entered. A concern can be documented. Yet unless the system ensures that someone receives, understands, and responds to that information, the existence of the data does not necessarily protect the patient.

I began to think much more carefully about the difference between a policy and a functioning process. A hospital may have an excellent escalation policy. It may specify when vital signs should trigger review, who should be contacted, and how quickly the patient should be reassessed. On paper, the process appears safe. The more important question is whether staff can actually follow it under ordinary working conditions. If the policy depends upon resources that are rarely available, responsibilities that are poorly defined, or communication pathways that routinely fail, the existence of the document may create the appearance of safety without ensuring that safety exists in practice.

That was difficult to appreciate at first because policies carry a certain authority. When they are well written, they make organizational expectations appear clear. The longer I reviewed cases, the more I learned that the written policy is only one part of the story. I wanted to know whether staff had been trained, whether the process was monitored, whether compliance was realistic, and whether previous problems had already shown that the system was not working as intended.

I found myself becoming interested in documents that I had not always requested earlier in my career. Staffing rosters, assignment sheets, training records, competency assessments, audit data, quality reviews, incident reports, meeting minutes, and escalation logs began to matter because they helped explain the environment in which the care occurred. These records did not replace the clinical record. They added another layer of understanding that the clinical documentation alone could not provide.

A nursing note may show that the patient was not reassessed promptly. The staffing record may show that the nurse was responsible for an unsafe number of patients. A policy may require hourly monitoring, while the assignment structure made that expectation unrealistic across the unit. An electronic audit trail may show that an alert was generated and acknowledged, but no one was assigned clear responsibility for ensuring that action followed. Each source answered a different part of the question, and only when they were brought together did the system begin to become visible.

I think this was one of the moments where my understanding of healthcare litigation expanded beyond the patient's immediate care. I had spent years reconstructing clinical journeys, and I was now beginning to reconstruct the organizational journey that surrounded them. I wanted to understand how staffing decisions were made, how communication was supposed to occur, how risk was monitored, and whether the system had already been given opportunities to recognize the problem before the event under investigation.

That last question became increasingly important because serious healthcare failures are not always unexpected from the organization's perspective. A similar incident may have occurred before. Staff may have raised concerns. Audit findings may have shown repeated noncompliance. Quality reviews may have identified a weakness that had not been corrected. The event involving the patient may appear isolated within the medical record while representing a pattern within the broader organization.

I learned not to assume that such a pattern existed, but I also learned not to assume that it did not. The investigation had to determine whether the event reflected a one-time failure, a breakdown in an otherwise functioning system, or a recurring risk that the organization had already recognized. Those distinctions could change the entire understanding of responsibility.

I remember a case involving delayed communication of an abnormal imaging result. The radiologist had identified a finding requiring urgent follow-up and documented that the result had been communicated. The treating team maintained that the significance had not been understood, while the family believed the result had simply been ignored. At first, the disagreement appeared to center on individual recollection and documentation.

The electronic data revealed a more complicated sequence. The result had entered the system, an automated notification had been sent, and a message had been acknowledged. What remained unclear was who had assumed responsibility for ensuring that the patient received the necessary follow-up. The referring clinician believed the specialist would manage it. The specialist believed the primary team retained responsibility. The electronic system documented communication, but the organizational process had not established ownership.

That case taught me that information can be transmitted successfully while responsibility remains lost.

The failure was not necessarily that nobody saw the result. The failure was that the system allowed several people to believe someone else would act. Once I understood that, the event no longer looked like a simple communication error. It reflected a weakness in the way the organization assigned and tracked responsibility.

This was where regulatory and compliance analysis began to feel less like a review of rules and more like an examination of how the healthcare organization functioned. Regulations, accreditation requirements, policies, and professional standards all mattered, but their value came from the responsibilities they created and the safety processes they were intended to support. I wanted to know whether those expectations had been translated into practice and whether the organization had reasonable systems for making compliance possible.

I became especially cautious about treating compliance as evidence that care was safe. An organization may meet a staffing ratio while still assigning patients in a way that creates unreasonable clinical demands. Required training may have been completed online without demonstrating practical competence. A policy may have been reviewed annually without anyone examining whether it worked. Audit results may show high compliance while excluding the shifts, units, or circumstances where risk is greatest.

Compliance can be important, but it does not always equal effectiveness.

The reverse is also true. A technical deviation from a policy does not automatically establish that the system failed or that the patient was harmed. Staff may depart from a process for clinically sound reasons, or the policy may not fit the circumstances. The question remained whether the organization had created and maintained a reasonable environment for safe care and whether the identified system factor contributed meaningfully to what happened.

The more I worked through these issues, the more I realized that organizational responsibility often exists at several levels. The frontline clinician has responsibilities. The immediate supervisor has responsibilities. Department leadership, quality teams, administrators, and governing bodies may each carry obligations related to staffing, policy, training, oversight, and resource allocation. A failure visible at the bedside may have developed through decisions made far away from the patient and long before the event occurred.

That did not mean every adverse event should be attributed to senior leadership or treated as evidence of corporate negligence. It meant the investigation should follow responsibility as far as the evidence reasonably led. If the bedside failure resulted from an individual lapse within a functioning system, the analysis should say so. If the evidence showed that the individual was working within conditions that repeatedly undermined safe care, the analysis should not stop at the bedside simply because that was where the harm became visible.

I found this especially important in long-term care, home health, behavioral health, and other settings where staffing, supervision, documentation, and continuity can influence care over long periods. A pressure injury may be documented as a wound-care issue, but the deeper investigation may involve staffing, repositioning schedules, nutrition, equipment availability, care-plan implementation, and oversight. A fall may appear to involve one missed precaution while reflecting a broader failure to update risk assessments, communicate changes, or provide adequate supervision. A medication event may involve one administration error but also reveal weaknesses in ordering, pharmacy verification, storage, handoff, and monitoring.

The patient experiences the combined effect of the system, even when the record divides responsibility across multiple departments.

I think this is one of the reasons healthcare litigation sometimes becomes overly focused on the final person in the chain. That person is visible. Their name appears in the record. Their action or omission sits closest to the outcome. It is much more difficult to trace how earlier organizational choices shaped the circumstances in which that final decision occurred.

The visible failure is not always the originating failure.

I learned to ask what had to go wrong before the event became possible. Was the clinician appropriately trained? Was supervision available? Were policies clear? Were staffing levels adequate for the acuity of the patients? Did technology support the workflow or create additional risk? Were earlier warnings recognized? Had the organization already identified the problem? Were corrective actions implemented and sustained?

Those questions often led the investigation into areas that had not been part of the original allegation. Sometimes they revealed meaningful organizational exposure. Other times they showed that the system had functioned reasonably and that the failure remained primarily individual. The value was not in broadening the case automatically. The value was in understanding responsibility accurately.

I also came to appreciate how organizational culture influences whether staff speak up, escalate concern, and report problems. Culture is difficult to evaluate because it rarely appears directly in the medical record. It becomes visible through patterns. Staff may repeatedly document concern without challenging ineffective responses. Incident reports may be discouraged or treated as blame rather than learning. Nurses may hesitate to activate escalation pathways because previous attempts were dismissed. New employees may learn quickly that policies exist on paper but are not followed in practice.

I did not want to make assumptions about culture based on one event, but I learned to recognize when the evidence justified deeper inquiry. Repeated similar incidents, staff turnover, unresolved complaints, poor audit results, and inconsistencies between policy and actual practice could all suggest that the environment deserved closer examination.

This was particularly important in cases where the formal hierarchy made escalation difficult. A nurse may have been expected to contact a physician, but what happened if the physician did not respond? Was there a clear next step? Could the nurse contact another clinician without fear of criticism? Was rapid response available? Did the organization support staff who escalated concerns, or did the culture quietly encourage them to wait?

A policy may state that anyone can activate a rapid response team, yet staff behavior may reveal that the process is rarely used until the patient is already critically unstable. The difference between what the organization says and what people actually do can become one of the most important findings in the case.

I remember reviewing a matter where nursing documentation showed repeated concern about a patient's neurological status. The physician had been contacted several times, but no urgent assessment occurred until the patient became profoundly unresponsive. The escalation policy appeared comprehensive. It allowed nursing staff to seek a higher level of review if the initial response was inadequate.

The deeper investigation showed that staff were reluctant to use that pathway because previous escalations had led to conflict and criticism. The policy existed, but the culture surrounding it made the protection less effective than it appeared. That did not remove the responsibility of the individual nurse to escalate, but it changed my understanding of why the delay occurred and where corrective responsibility belonged.

I came to believe that a safe system must do more than permit appropriate action. It must make appropriate action reasonably possible.

That principle influenced the way I looked at staffing. Staffing discussions often become reduced to numbers, yet numbers alone rarely tell the whole story. The ratio may appear acceptable while patient acuity, admissions, discharges, supervision needs, and staff experience create demands far beyond what the ratio suggests. A unit staffed primarily with inexperienced clinicians may require more support than the numbers show. A nurse assigned fewer patients may still face an unsafe workload if several require complex monitoring, frequent interventions, or behavioral management.

I wanted to understand not only how many staff were present, but whether the staffing model matched the needs of the patients at that time.

This required looking at the assignment rather than only the schedule. Which patients were allocated to each clinician? What was their acuity? Were breaks covered? Was the charge nurse carrying a full assignment? Were agency or temporary staff familiar with the unit? Were vacancies filled? Was overtime excessive? Did the staffing pattern change after the event, suggesting that the organization recognized a weakness?

These questions could not always be answered, but when the records were available, they provided important context. A missed reassessment means something different when the clinician was caring for a manageable assignment than when they were responsible for several unstable patients with limited support. The standard of care remains, but the system analysis helps explain whether the organization had created conditions in which meeting that standard was realistic.

I became equally interested in competency and training because a completed orientation does not necessarily establish that a clinician was prepared for the responsibilities assigned. Healthcare organizations often rely on documentation showing that education was provided, but the more meaningful question is whether the individual demonstrated the knowledge and skills required in practice. Was competency assessed? Were weaknesses identified? Was supervision appropriate? Was the employee assigned responsibilities beyond their experience?

I reviewed a case where a newly hired nurse failed to recognize a significant deterioration in a high-risk patient. The organization produced training records showing that the nurse had completed mandatory modules. The deeper review revealed that orientation had been shortened because of staffing pressures, preceptors changed repeatedly, and the nurse had expressed concern about readiness for independent practice. The failure could not be understood fully by pointing only to the completed training checklist.

That case reminded me that systems sometimes document completion more effectively than capability.

The difference matters because regulatory compliance may require education, but patient safety depends upon competence. A signature, test score, or online module can provide evidence of exposure to information. It does not always establish that the person can apply that information under pressure in a complex clinical environment.

Technology introduced another set of questions. Electronic health records, monitoring systems, medication scanners, alerts, and decision-support tools are designed to improve safety, and many do. At the same time, they can introduce new risks when the workflow is poorly designed, alerts are excessive, information is fragmented, or staff become dependent on systems that do not display the complete clinical picture.

I began to see cases where important information existed electronically but was difficult to locate. Alerts became so frequent that staff stopped distinguishing the meaningful ones from the routine ones. A medication warning was overridden because it appeared repeatedly for clinically insignificant reasons. A patient's deterioration was documented across several screens without any one view showing the complete pattern. Technology had not failed in the traditional sense. It had functioned exactly as designed, but the design did not support clinical understanding as well as everyone assumed.

That was a difficult issue because technology carries an appearance of precision. Timestamps, alerts, and audit trails make the process look highly controlled. The investigation still had to ask whether the system provided usable information to the people delivering care and whether the workflow supported timely action.

I learned to distinguish between data availability and information usability. A result may be available somewhere in the record, but that does not mean it is displayed in a way that makes its significance clear. A trend may exist across multiple values, but clinicians may see only one result at a time. An alert may trigger, but the recipient may have no direct responsibility for the patient. The system can capture everything while helping no one understand what matters most.

This connected back to Clinical Intelligence in a way I had not initially expected. The same problem that appears in litigation can also exist during patient care. There is no shortage of information. The difficulty lies in bringing the information together into meaningful understanding. A well-designed healthcare system should help clinicians do that in real time. When it does not, the organization may contribute to the same fragmentation that later makes the case so difficult to reconstruct.

I also became more attentive to transitions of care because they create predictable points of vulnerability. Admissions, transfers, handoffs, shift changes, and discharges all require information to move from one person or setting to another. The patient continues through one clinical journey, while responsibility changes hands. Each transition creates an opportunity for important information to be lost, delayed, misunderstood, or assumed.

A patient may leave the emergency department with one working diagnosis and arrive on the ward with another. A transfer summary may omit the concern that prompted escalation. A night nurse may inherit a patient whose gradual deterioration was recognized by the day team but not communicated clearly. A discharge may occur before pending results are assigned to someone for follow-up. None of these failures is unusual enough to surprise experienced healthcare professionals, which is precisely why systems should be designed to prevent them.

I reviewed a case involving a patient transferred from a community hospital to a tertiary center. The receiving team focused on the condition present at arrival, while the referring hospital records later showed that deterioration had begun much earlier. Important information had been discussed verbally but not included clearly in the transfer documentation. The receiving clinicians did not fully understand the progression, and the referring clinicians assumed the urgency had been communicated.

The failure did not belong neatly to one person. It sat inside the transition.

That case taught me to examine handoffs as clinical events in their own right. What information was transferred? What was omitted? Who was responsible for follow-up? Did the receiving team understand the concern? Was there confirmation rather than assumption? A handoff is not merely administrative. It can determine whether the next clinician begins with an accurate understanding of the patient or spends valuable time reconstructing what should already be known.

I became increasingly aware that regulatory and compliance requirements often exist because the risks are already well understood. Medication reconciliation, critical-result reporting, fall-risk assessment, infection prevention, restraint monitoring, informed consent, emergency preparedness, and many other requirements were developed in response to recurring patient-safety problems. When compliance fails, the significance lies not only in the broken rule, but in the known risk the rule was intended to control.

That perspective helped me avoid treating regulation as a separate legal layer placed on top of clinical care. The best regulatory standards are closely connected to patient safety. They exist because experience has shown what can happen when systems are left to informal practice alone.

At the same time, I learned to remain careful about regulatory interpretation. Requirements vary by setting, jurisdiction, payer, accreditation status, and the period in which the care occurred. A standard may have changed. A recommendation may not be mandatory. A federal condition of participation may apply differently from a state licensing rule or an accreditation expectation. Formal legal interpretation belongs with counsel and appropriately qualified experts.

My role was to identify the relevant organizational responsibilities and determine how they related to the patient's care. I wanted the attorney to understand which regulations, policies, or compliance issues deserved further legal analysis rather than presenting every deviation as a definitive legal violation.

This distinction became important because regulatory findings can be persuasive and easily overstated. A policy failure may strengthen the understanding of how the event occurred, but it does not automatically establish causation. A staffing concern may explain delayed response without proving that a different staffing model would have changed the outcome. A compliance issue may reveal organizational weakness while remaining peripheral to the patient's injury.

The analysis had to remain connected to the patient.

I often returned to the same question: how did this organizational condition influence the care that this patient actually received? If the connection could not be demonstrated, the issue might still matter for quality improvement or regulatory review, but it should not be given more weight in the litigation than the evidence supported.

That discipline protected the analysis from becoming a catalogue of every policy or regulatory concern in the organization. The purpose was not to prove that the facility was imperfect. Every healthcare organization is imperfect. The purpose was to identify the system conditions that materially shaped recognition, communication, treatment, escalation, or outcome in the case under review.

I think this is where the phrase overlay became meaningful to me. The regulatory and compliance analysis does not replace the clinical investigation. It sits across it, helping explain the environment in which each decision occurred. The patient's baseline, imaging, timeline, and standard-of-care findings remain central. The overlay adds context that may clarify why care succeeded, why it failed, or why an apparently simple event was actually the result of several interacting weaknesses.

Over time, I came to define the discipline more precisely.

Regulatory & Compliance Overlay is the structured evaluation of the organizational, regulatory, policy, staffing, communication, technology, training, supervision, and governance conditions that influenced how care was delivered throughout the patient's clinical journey.

That definition mattered because it kept the focus on influence rather than mere existence. Every organization has policies, technology, staffing structures, and governance processes. The relevant question is how those systems affected the care in this case.

I found that attorneys often understood the importance of this analysis once they saw how it changed the narrative. A case initially framed as one nurse failing to monitor a patient may become a broader examination of staffing, assignment practices, escalation pathways, and supervision. A delayed diagnosis may reveal gaps in test-result follow-up across departments. A medication event may expose weaknesses in reconciliation, order entry, pharmacy review, and bedside administration. The event remains clinical, but the explanation becomes organizational.

For plaintiff counsel, the overlay may reveal additional sources of responsibility and evidence required in discovery. For defense counsel, it may distinguish a system that functioned reasonably from one isolated lapse or identify where exposure genuinely exists. For both, it creates a more accurate understanding of how the event became possible.

I also found that organizational analysis could protect individual clinicians from being made solely responsible for conditions beyond their control. Healthcare professionals are expected to exercise reasonable judgment, but they do not control every staffing decision, every technology design, or every resource limitation. When the system materially contributes to the failure, fairness requires that responsibility be examined at the appropriate level.

That does not mean individual clinicians are absolved whenever the environment is difficult. Professionals still have obligations to recognize risk, communicate concern, escalate appropriately, and refuse assignments or seek support when necessary. The existence of a system problem does not erase professional responsibility. It helps define the circumstances in which that responsibility had to be exercised.

I came to see individual and organizational responsibility as interacting rather than competing. A clinician may make an unreasonable decision within a poor system. A competent clinician may be placed in conditions that make safe performance increasingly difficult. An organization may have reasonable systems that an individual fails to follow. The investigation has to identify which combination the evidence supports.

That was much more useful than choosing between blaming the person and blaming the system.

I think one of the most persistent weaknesses in healthcare investigations is the tendency to simplify responsibility. Simplicity is appealing because it produces a clear narrative. One person failed. One policy was broken. One delay caused the outcome. The reality is often far more complicated. Several small weaknesses may align in a way that allows harm to occur, while any one of them alone might not have produced the same result.

The Regulatory and Compliance Overlay helped me understand those interactions. A nurse's delayed reassessment may combine with inadequate staffing, unclear escalation, and poor medical coverage. A missed test result may involve the person who received it, the electronic system, the assignment of responsibility, and the absence of follow-up auditing. A fall may involve patient risk, environmental design, staffing, communication, and failure to update the care plan after earlier changes.

The system does not experience these factors separately, and neither does the patient.

I remember reviewing a long-term care case involving repeated falls. The final fall resulted in a serious fracture and became the focus of the litigation. The early review concentrated on whether staff had followed the fall-prevention plan on that day. The deeper investigation showed that the patient's mobility and cognition had been changing over several weeks, yet the risk assessment and care plan had not been updated meaningfully. Staffing patterns limited supervision during the period when most falls occurred. Equipment recommendations were delayed, and family concerns had been documented without clear action.

The final event appeared sudden. The system failure was gradual.

That case stayed with me because it showed how a serious injury can emerge from a sequence of ordinary omissions. No single decision looked catastrophic. The harm became possible because the organization failed to respond as the patient's needs changed. The clinical timeline demonstrated the progression, while the regulatory overlay showed that the care system had not adapted alongside it.

I found similar patterns in home health cases. The patient may receive visits from several professionals, each documenting their own assessment, while no one integrates the changes into a complete understanding of deterioration. Orders may remain unsigned. Communication with the physician may be delayed. Visit frequency may not increase despite worsening risk. The agency may comply with the scheduled plan of care while failing to recognize that the plan no longer matches the patient's condition.

This reminded me that compliance with a plan does not guarantee that the plan remains appropriate.

Healthcare systems need mechanisms for recognizing when the patient has changed enough that the existing approach must change as well. A process can be followed perfectly and still produce poor care if the process is no longer responsive to the clinical reality.

That principle applied in almost every setting. A postoperative pathway may be appropriate for routine recovery but inadequate for a patient who begins deteriorating. A behavioral health observation plan may meet the original risk level but become unsafe after new suicidal behavior. A staffing model may work under average demand but fail during a surge in acuity. The system has to be capable of adapting rather than merely repeating.

I think this is where governance becomes relevant. Governance is sometimes treated as a distant administrative concept, yet it determines how organizations recognize risk, respond to patterns, and hold themselves accountable. Boards, executives, quality leaders, and clinical managers may not provide direct care, but their decisions influence whether safety concerns are identified and corrected.

I became interested in whether the organization had mechanisms for learning. Were incidents investigated thoroughly? Were corrective actions specific and measurable? Did the organization examine whether changes were sustained? Were similar events recurring despite previous reviews? A system that documents an incident without changing the conditions that produced it has completed paperwork, not learning.

This mattered because litigation often occurs years after the event, when organizations can produce policies, training records, and corrective plans that create an appearance of careful oversight. I wanted to understand what existed at the time of the patient's care and whether the safety processes were functioning then. Later improvements may be important, but they do not establish that the earlier system was adequate.

I also learned to be cautious about hindsight in organizational analysis. After a serious event, almost any process can be improved. The question was not whether the organization could have designed a perfect system. The question was whether the systems in place were reasonable in light of known risks, applicable requirements, prior experience, and the resources available at the time.

That standard of reasonableness was similar to the one applied to individual clinicians. Organizations cannot eliminate every possibility of error. They can be expected to identify foreseeable risks, create workable safeguards, monitor performance, and respond when evidence shows that those safeguards are failing.

This approach helped me avoid judging the organization simply because harm occurred. A robust system can still experience an isolated failure. At the same time, the absence of prior harm does not prove that a weak system was reasonable. The investigation had to examine design, implementation, monitoring, and response rather than relying on outcome alone.

The more I worked through these cases, the more I realized that the organizational environment often influenced causation indirectly. A staffing shortage may not cause the underlying disease, but it may delay recognition. A communication failure may not create the abnormal imaging finding, but it may delay treatment. Inadequate training may not cause the patient's vulnerability, but it may prevent the warning signs from being understood. The system factor becomes causally meaningful through its effect on the clinical response.

That connection had to be mapped carefully. It was not enough to identify an unsafe condition and assume it caused the outcome. I wanted to understand the pathway. What did the system weakness change? Did it affect monitoring, recognition, communication, access to treatment, or the timing of escalation? Did that effect occur while meaningful intervention opportunity remained? If the system had functioned reasonably, what would probably have happened differently?

Those questions prepared the investigation for Causation Mapping. By the end of the Regulatory and Compliance Overlay, I usually understood not only where the clinical response had failed, but why it had failed and which individual or organizational responsibilities had contributed. The remaining question was whether those failures had actually changed the patient's outcome.

I learned not to assume that they had.

A system may be poorly designed, a policy may have been breached, and staffing may have been inadequate, yet the patient's injury may already have become unavoidable. Conversely, a seemingly minor organizational delay may become highly significant if it occurred during a narrow intervention window. The seriousness of the system problem and the seriousness of its causal effect are not always the same.

That distinction was essential because healthcare litigation can become overwhelmed by evidence of poor process. A troubling organizational record may create a powerful impression, but causation still has to be established through the patient's physiology and timeline. The regulatory overlay explains the conditions. It does not replace the final analysis of outcome impact.

Looking back now, I think this discipline changed the way I understood accountability. I had once viewed accountability primarily through the actions of individuals. Over time, I came to see that true accountability requires us to understand both the person and the environment. It is unfair to place the entire burden on a clinician when the system repeatedly undermined safe care. It is equally unfair to blame the system so broadly that individual judgment and responsibility disappear.

Clinical Intelligence required both to remain visible.

That balance became one of the reasons I valued the overlay so highly. It allowed me to examine system influence without losing the patient, the clinician, or the specific decision at the center of the case. The analysis remained grounded in what actually happened rather than drifting into a general criticism of the organization.

I also began to recognize that the same organizational factor could have different significance for different patients. A delayed laboratory result may have little impact in a stable patient and profound consequences in someone actively deteriorating. Limited overnight imaging access may be reasonable in one setting but dangerous if the facility accepts patients requiring immediate advanced diagnostics without a reliable transfer process. Staffing that is adequate for routine care may become unsafe when several high-acuity patients are admitted simultaneously.

The system has to be evaluated in relation to the clinical demands placed upon it.

That is why I never believed the Regulatory and Compliance Overlay could be completed by comparing the organization with a list of requirements. The requirements matter, but the patient's journey determines which ones become clinically meaningful. A regulation becomes relevant because it was intended to control a risk present in the case. A staffing issue matters because it influenced care. A policy failure matters because it affected recognition, communication, or treatment. The overlay remains connected to the patient from beginning to end.

There were cases where the organizational analysis revealed no meaningful contribution. The systems were reasonable, staffing was appropriate, communication pathways functioned, and the adverse event resulted primarily from the disease process or an individual judgment that fell outside expected practice. That conclusion was just as important as identifying systemic failure because it prevented responsibility from being broadened without evidence.

There were other cases where the overlay changed the case entirely. What appeared to be a single missed assessment became evidence of chronic understaffing and inadequate supervision. What appeared to be a delayed consultation revealed a service model that routinely left one clinician responsible for an unreasonable volume of patients. What appeared to be a failure to follow policy showed that the policy had never been operationalized in a workable way.

In those cases, the patient had been failed long before the final event became visible.

The failure began when the organization accepted a known risk without creating an effective response, when warnings were identified but not corrected, or when the system depended upon individuals compensating for structural weaknesses until someone eventually could not.

I found those cases particularly difficult because the harm often felt preventable at several levels. A different individual decision might have changed the outcome, but so might better staffing, clearer communication, stronger supervision, or a more reliable escalation process. Responsibility could not be reduced to one moment because the conditions had developed over time.

That was when I understood why the overlay had to come before causation. I needed to know not only what happened clinically, but how the healthcare system shaped the path that led there. Only then could I determine which failures were causally meaningful and which were concerning but ultimately unrelated to the outcome.

By this stage of the investigation, the patient's journey had become much clearer. I understood who they had been before the event, what their body revealed, how the condition progressed, what reasonable care required, and how the organization influenced the response. The case no longer appeared as a collection of separate records or isolated decisions. It had become one connected clinical and operational story.

That story still did not answer the final question.

A departure from reasonable care may exist. A system failure may be clear. The patient may have experienced a devastating outcome. None of those findings, on its own, establishes that the identified failures changed what happened.

I had learned not to move directly from criticism to causation, no matter how compelling the criticism appeared. The patient's physiology still had to support the conclusion. The timeline still had to show meaningful opportunity. Alternative explanations still had to be considered. The outcome had to be compared with what was realistically possible for this particular patient.

Everything we had reconstructed so far had been preparing the investigation for that moment.

Now I could finally ask whether the failures we had identified probably altered the patient's clinical course.

CHAPTER 12

Causation Mapping

By the time I reached causation, I usually understood the case far more completely than I had when it first arrived. I knew whether the evidence was reliable enough to support meaningful analysis, I understood who the patient had been before the event, I had examined the objective physiological findings, reconstructed the progression, identified the professional obligations, and considered the system in which the care had been delivered. Even then, I had learned not to assume that the final question would be easy.

It rarely was.

One of the first things healthcare litigation taught me was that poor care and preventable harm are not the same thing. A clinician may make an unreasonable decision without changing the outcome. A system may fail without causing the injury alleged. A patient may experience a devastating result despite timely recognition and appropriate treatment. Those distinctions can be difficult to accept, particularly when the record contains obvious failures, but causation cannot be inferred simply because the care deserves criticism.

Earlier in my career, I think I sometimes moved too quickly from identifying a departure to assuming that the departure explained what followed. The sequence appeared logical. Something should have happened and did not. The patient later deteriorated. It was easy to connect the two. The more cases I reviewed, however, the more I realized that the connection had to be demonstrated through the patient's physiology, timeline, baseline, and realistic treatment opportunity. Without that work, the conclusion remained possible, but possibility was not enough.

That distinction became one of the most important in my thinking. Healthcare litigation often begins with possibility because possibility is what prompts the investigation. Could earlier treatment have changed the outcome? Could a delay have worsened the injury? Could another response have preserved function or life? Those are entirely appropriate questions. Causation begins later, when the evidence is examined closely enough to determine whether the proposed relationship is not merely conceivable, but clinically supportable.

I found myself returning again and again to the same question: if the identified failure had not occurred, what would probably have happened differently for this patient? The answer could not be separated from who the patient was, how advanced the disease process had become, what intervention remained available, and how likely that intervention was to change the course. In some cases, the answer was relatively clear. In others, the evidence supported only a narrower conclusion than the allegation originally suggested.

I remember reviewing a sepsis case where the delay in recognition was difficult to defend. The patient's observations had been worsening, the laboratory findings were becoming more concerning, and escalation occurred only after significant deterioration. At first, it appeared reasonable to conclude that earlier treatment would have prevented the death. The deeper analysis, however, revealed that the patient had advanced disease, limited reserve, and evidence of organ dysfunction before the most significant delay occurred. Earlier treatment may have improved the chance of survival, but the evidence did not allow me to say with confidence that survival was probable.

That case stayed with me because it forced me to separate several questions that I might once have treated as one. Did the delay matter? Yes. Did it reduce the patient's opportunity? Probably. Did it worsen the clinical course? The evidence supported that possibility strongly. Did it probably cause the death? That conclusion was much harder to sustain.

The care could still be criticized. The patient may still have lost a meaningful opportunity. The delay may still have increased suffering, accelerated deterioration, or reduced the possibility of recovery. None of those findings required me to overstate what the evidence could prove.

I came to believe that honest causation analysis often depends upon recognizing the difference between preventing an outcome and changing its severity. Earlier treatment may not have prevented every consequence, but it may have reduced the extent of injury. A stroke may still have occurred, but the neurological loss may have been less severe. An infection may still have required hospitalization, but progression to shock may have been avoided. A postoperative complication may still have required intervention, but organ damage, prolonged ventilation, or permanent disability may have been reduced.

That is why causation is not always a single yes-or-no question. The outcome has several dimensions. Survival, function, severity, duration, pain, treatment burden, and quality of life may each be affected differently. The analysis has to identify which part of the outcome the evidence supports rather than forcing every case into the question of whether the entire event would have been avoided.

Baseline became essential here because causation requires a comparison between the actual clinical course and the course that was realistically available to that patient. The comparison is not made with a perfectly healthy person or an idealized recovery. It is made with the patient who actually existed before the event, carrying all of their strengths, vulnerabilities, chronic disease, and prior trajectory.

I reviewed a case involving an older adult who suffered a serious neurological injury after delayed treatment. Before the event, the patient lived independently, managed personal affairs, drove, and remained actively involved with family despite several chronic conditions. The defense emphasized age and medical complexity, while the plaintiff emphasized independence and loss. Both descriptions were true.

The causation analysis had to hold those truths together. The patient's chronic disease may have influenced recovery and life expectancy, but it did not erase the functional life that had existed. Earlier treatment may not have guaranteed a complete return to baseline, yet the evidence supported a meaningful probability of preserving greater function. The honest conclusion sat between total recovery and inevitable decline.

That middle ground is often where the strongest causation opinion exists, although it may be less dramatic than the position either side initially prefers. I learned not to treat nuance as weakness. A conclusion that accurately defines the extent of probable impact is more defensible than one that claims certainty beyond the evidence.

Imaging also became central to causation because it could help establish how far the disease or injury had progressed and whether tissue, function, or organ capacity remained salvageable. In stroke cases, the timing and extent of infarction could influence whether treatment opportunity remained. In spinal compression, imaging could help identify progression and the likely effect of delayed decompression. In bleeding, serial studies and physiological changes could clarify when the patient moved from compensation toward irreversible shock.

Even then, the image could not answer the entire question. It had to be interpreted through the timeline. A severe final image did not establish what was present several hours earlier. A subtle early study did not prove that intervention would have been ineffective. The analysis required an understanding of progression between the objective points.

I became especially cautious about retrospective certainty in causation opinions. Once the final outcome is known, it is easy to construct a clean explanation that moves directly from failure to injury. Real physiology is rarely that simple. Several causes may be operating simultaneously. Chronic disease may interact with acute injury. Treatment may help one problem while creating another risk. The patient may deteriorate despite appropriate intervention because the disease process is unusually aggressive or advanced.

The purpose of Causation Mapping was not to identify one explanation and eliminate every other possibility. It was to examine the competing factors, determine how they interacted, and assess which ones probably influenced the outcome in a clinically meaningful way.

I found the term mapping helpful because causation rarely followed one straight line. There might be an underlying disease process, a delayed recognition, an organizational barrier, a treatment response, a complication, and a later failure to rescue. Each contributed at a different stage. Some factors created vulnerability. Others narrowed opportunity. Others directly worsened injury.

The map allowed those contributions to remain visible without pretending they were equal.

I remember a postoperative case where the patient developed respiratory failure. The allegation focused on delayed escalation, but the patient also had severe chronic lung disease, obesity, sleep apnea, and a history of difficult recovery after anesthesia. Those conditions increased vulnerability, yet they did not fully explain why the patient progressed without timely reassessment. The delayed response did not create every risk, but it likely reduced the opportunity to intervene before respiratory failure became severe.

The causation map therefore included the patient's pre-existing vulnerability, the effect of sedation and surgery, the evolving respiratory changes, the delay in recognition, and the later emergency response. The final outcome could not be attributed honestly to one cause alone. The meaningful question was how each factor contributed and whether the identified departure materially changed the course.

This way of thinking protected the analysis from two common extremes. One extreme treats pre-existing disease as though it caused everything and the healthcare event changed nothing. The other treats the alleged failure as though it created the entire outcome in a patient who had no prior vulnerability. Both can be misleading. The patient entered the event with one physiological reality, and the care then influenced what happened within that reality.

Causation Mapping had to preserve both.

I also learned to distinguish between a condition that made harm possible and an event that made harm more likely. A patient's chronic disease may create susceptibility. A delay may allow the disease process to advance. A system failure may prevent timely treatment. The final injury may emerge from the interaction of all three. Saying that the patient was already vulnerable does not answer whether the care materially worsened the outcome.

The same was true in medication cases. A patient may be at increased risk because of age, kidney function, other medications, or underlying disease. The medication error may then trigger bleeding, sedation, arrhythmia, or another complication. The baseline explains vulnerability. The error explains exposure. The timeline and objective evidence help determine whether the exposure probably produced the injury.

I came to believe that a reliable causation opinion should make each step visible. What was the patient's condition before the event? What physiological process was already present? What departure occurred? How did that departure affect recognition, treatment, or progression? What injury followed? Could the same outcome reasonably have occurred without the departure? What alternative explanations remain?

If the reasoning cannot be traced, the conclusion may sound persuasive without being clinically secure.

That mattered particularly when experts used language such as "more likely than not," "substantial factor," or "proximate cause." Those terms carry legal significance, and the applicable standard belongs with counsel and the retained expert. My responsibility was to make sure the clinical reasoning underneath the language was sound. The phrase cannot repair a weak physiological connection.

I saw opinions where the final conclusion was expressed with great certainty while the steps connecting breach to outcome remained largely assumed. The report might state that earlier treatment would have prevented the injury without explaining what treatment would have been provided, how quickly it would have acted, what condition the patient was in at that time, or what evidence showed that the outcome remained reversible.

Those missing steps became the focus of my review. Earlier intervention is not a treatment. It is a time.

The analysis still has to identify what would have occurred during that time and why it probably would have mattered.

In a delayed diagnosis case, earlier recognition may have led to additional testing, specialist consultation, surgery, medication, monitoring, or transfer. Each step has its own timing and probability. The patient may not have received definitive treatment immediately after recognition. Resources, consent, stability, and clinical judgment still influence what would likely have happened.

Causation Mapping therefore had to reconstruct the probable alternative pathway rather than assuming that recognition automatically produced the best possible treatment outcome.

I found this especially important in cancer cases. An earlier diagnosis may appear likely to improve prognosis, but the analysis depends on tumor type, stage, biology, available treatment, and the length of the delay. Some cancers progress rapidly. Others remain relatively indolent. A delay may change staging or treatment options, while in another case the disease may already have been advanced when detection first became reasonably possible.

The existence of a delay does not establish that the prognosis changed.

At the same time, uncertainty in cancer progression does not mean the delay had no significance. Earlier diagnosis may have preserved less invasive treatment, reduced disease burden, or improved the probability of survival. The conclusion has to reflect the evidence available for that disease and that patient.

I learned not to search for absolute certainty where medicine could provide only probability. Causation in healthcare is often based on the weight of evidence rather than direct proof. The patient cannot live the alternative course so that the outcomes can be compared. We reconstruct what probably would have occurred using clinical science, timing, response patterns, and the patient's individual circumstances.

That reconstruction requires restraint because the alternative path can easily become idealized. It is tempting to assume that every correct decision would have occurred immediately, every treatment would have worked as intended, and no complication would have followed. Real care does not operate that way. The alternative course should be clinically reasonable, not perfect.

I often asked myself what would probably have happened in ordinary practice if the departure had been avoided. Would the clinician have ordered the study? How quickly would it have been performed? Would the result have led to treatment? Was the treatment available? How likely was the patient to respond? What risks would the intervention have carried? These questions made the alternative pathway more realistic and the eventual conclusion more defensible.

There were cases where the alternative pathway remained too uncertain to support a strong causation opinion. The breach may have created concern, but several additional events would have needed to occur before the outcome could have changed. Each added another layer of uncertainty. In those situations, the analysis needed to acknowledge the limits rather than compressing a chain of possibilities into one confident conclusion.

I did not see that as abandoning the patient or weakening the case. It was the same intellectual honesty that had guided Record Integrity from the beginning. The patient deserved an accurate explanation, not the strongest explanation available.

There were also cases where the causal pathway became remarkably clear. The patient showed a recognizable deterioration, effective treatment remained available, the response was delayed without reasonable explanation, and the injury progressed during that interval. The baseline supported meaningful recovery potential, and the objective evidence aligned with the timeline. In those cases, each part of the Model strengthened the same conclusion.

The opinion became strong because the reasoning was connected, not because the language was forceful.

I think that is one of the most important contributions of the seven disciplines working together. Causation did not have to be constructed from the final outcome backward. It emerged from the evidence forward. Record Integrity established the foundation. Baseline defined the patient's starting point. Imaging showed the objective pathology. Timeline identified progression and opportunity. Standard of Care Review defined obligation. The Regulatory and Compliance Overlay explained how the response was shaped. Causation brought those findings together and asked what they meant for the outcome.

By the time I reached that stage, I was not looking for a new theory. I was testing whether the theory that had emerged could survive every part of the patient's story.

That testing included evidence that challenged the conclusion. If the opinion was that earlier treatment would have changed the outcome, I wanted to understand the strongest reason it might not have. Was the disease already advanced? Was the treatment benefit uncertain? Did the patient have limited reserve? Was another cause equally plausible? Had appropriate treatment already failed?

I found that an opinion becomes more credible when it addresses those questions directly. Ignoring competing explanations does not make them disappear. It simply leaves the report vulnerable to the first person who raises them.

I sometimes approached causation as though I were reviewing the case for the opposite side. If I believed the care had probably changed the outcome, what evidence would I use to challenge that conclusion? If I believed the outcome was largely unavoidable, what evidence might show that meaningful opportunity remained? That exercise forced me to examine whether I had treated supportive and contradictory evidence with the same discipline.

The strongest conclusions usually survived. The weaker ones became narrower or changed. Both outcomes improved the analysis.

I think attorneys sometimes worry that too much internal challenge will weaken the theory of the case. My experience has been the opposite. A theory that cannot survive disciplined internal challenge is unlikely to survive expert review, deposition, or trial. It is far better to identify the weakness while the case can still be evaluated honestly than after everyone has become committed to a position.

Causation Mapping also influenced case valuation because the significance of harm depends upon what probably changed. A breach that caused death carries a different exposure from one that prolonged hospitalization without altering the final outcome. A delay that produced permanent neurological loss differs from one that temporarily worsened symptoms. The clinical map helps the attorney understand the nature and extent of the probable impact before damages are assessed.

It can also reveal that the case contains several causal layers. One failure may have caused the original injury, while another increased its severity. A delayed diagnosis may allow disease progression, and a later failure to rescue may further worsen the outcome. The patient's final condition may therefore reflect more than one period of preventable harm.

I reviewed a case where an early delay reduced the patient's chance of avoiding surgery, while a later postoperative failure contributed to permanent disability. Treating the matter as one continuous causal event obscured the different responsibilities and outcomes. Mapping the stages allowed each contribution to be examined separately.

This became particularly important in multi-provider cases because different clinicians or organizations may influence different parts of the outcome. One provider may be responsible for delayed recognition, another for delayed transfer, and another for inadequate postoperative monitoring. The causation analysis has to determine which stage each failure affected and whether the contributions overlap.

The existence of several contributors does not mean every participant caused the entire outcome. Responsibility should remain connected to the effect the evidence supports.

I also became careful about language such as loss of chance or lost opportunity because the legal treatment varies and belongs with counsel. Clinically, however, the concept remained important. There are cases where the evidence cannot establish that a better outcome was probable, but it can show that the patient lost a meaningful opportunity for improvement, survival, or reduced injury.

That clinical finding may or may not satisfy the applicable legal standard. My responsibility was to describe the opportunity accurately, including how substantial it appeared, when it existed, and how the identified failure affected it.

The intervention window became central here. A patient may have several hours during which treatment remains likely to help, followed by a period where benefit becomes less certain, and finally a point where irreversible injury is largely established. The alleged delay may cross more than one of those stages. Causation Mapping should reflect how the probability of benefit changed over time rather than treating the entire interval as equal.

I found that visualizing the window often clarified the analysis. It showed when recognition was reasonably required, when treatment could have occurred, and when the opportunity narrowed or closed. Even without a formal diagram, thinking in that way prevented me from assuming that every minute carried the same clinical significance.

I remember a spinal compression case where the patient's neurological deficits progressed gradually. Early symptoms justified reassessment, later findings required urgent imaging, and the final deficits indicated severe injury. The causal question was not simply whether surgery occurred late. It was whether decompression during the earlier stage probably would have preserved more neurological function.

The literature provided general information about timing, but the patient's own progression remained essential. Baseline function, severity of compression, duration of deficits, and the response after surgery all contributed to the analysis. The evidence supported a probable reduction in function from the delay, but not the certainty of complete recovery.

That conclusion was less absolute than one side wanted, but it was clinically sustainable.

I came to value that phrase: clinically sustainable. An opinion should remain stable when it is examined through physiology, timing, competing explanations, and the limits of medical knowledge. It should not depend upon one favorable sentence in the record or one expert assumption. The reasoning should continue holding together even when challenged from another direction.

That became the standard I applied to causation.

- Could the conclusion survive the patient's baseline?
- Could it survive the imaging?
- Could it survive the timeline?
- Could it survive the strongest alternative explanation?
- Could it survive the uncertainty that genuinely existed?

If it could, I felt far more confident presenting it to the attorney.

If it could not, the conclusion needed more work.

I also learned that causation opinions should explain the degree of confidence honestly. Some relationships are strongly supported. Others remain probable but uncertain. Some are merely possible. The language should reflect the evidence rather than presenting every conclusion with the same level of certainty.

This was not an invitation to become vague. It was an invitation to become precise.

Saying that an event "may have contributed" is not enough unless the report explains how and why. Saying that an outcome was "more likely than not" is not enough unless the physiological pathway supports it. Precision comes from explaining the mechanism, timing, and probable effect.

I found that mechanism often became the bridge between breach and injury. How did the delay produce harm? Did untreated infection progress to shock? Did continued compression produce neurological damage? Did hypoxia lead to brain injury? Did unrecognized bleeding cause prolonged hypotension and organ failure? The mechanism had to be coherent and consistent with the objective evidence.

When the proposed mechanism conflicted with the imaging, pathology, laboratory trends, or clinical progression, the theory required reconsideration. A causal story cannot be sustained simply because the sequence appears plausible. The body must support it.

This is where Clinical Concordance began to emerge in my thinking, although I did not use that name at first. I wanted to know whether the different forms of evidence were telling the same story. Did baseline, symptoms, imaging, laboratory findings, timeline, and outcome align with the proposed mechanism? When they did, confidence increased. When they did not, the discordance had to be explained.

Sometimes the explanation was straightforward. Chronic disease altered one finding. Treatment changed the later course. Documentation was incomplete. In other cases, the disagreement exposed a weakness in the theory itself.

I learned not to fear that moment. A theory should change when the evidence requires it.

That may be one of the hardest lessons in litigation because cases develop momentum. Attorneys invest time and resources. Experts form opinions. Families develop expectations. Organizations adopt defensive positions. Changing the theory can feel like failure.

From a Clinical Intelligence perspective, refusing to change a theory after the evidence changes is the greater failure.

The patient's story does not owe consistency to the position we preferred at intake.

I think this is where causation became the strongest test of intellectual honesty within the Model. Every earlier discipline required me to remain open, but causation was where the pressure to reach a desired conclusion became greatest. The outcome might be tragic. The breach might be obvious. The client might need clarity. Even then, the physiological connection had to be earned.

Looking back now, I believe Causation Mapping is the disciplined integration of the patient's baseline, objective evidence, clinical progression, professional departures, system influences, and alternative explanations to determine whether, how, and to what extent the identified failures probably changed the patient's outcome.

That definition developed slowly because I wanted it to preserve the complexity I had encountered in real cases. Causation was not one final box to complete after the rest of the review. It was the point where every earlier finding was tested against the outcome.

The phrase "to what extent" mattered just as much as whether. It allowed the analysis to recognize partial contribution, increased severity, lost function, prolonged suffering, and reduced opportunity without overstating that the entire outcome had been caused by one failure.

I think attorneys find this particularly useful because it translates clinical complexity into a more realistic understanding of litigation strength. A case may contain a strong breach but limited causal impact. Another may involve a subtle departure with profound consequences because it occurred during a narrow treatment window. The seriousness of the error and the seriousness of the outcome do not automatically tell us the strength of the connection between them.

Causation Mapping makes that connection visible.

For plaintiff counsel, it helps determine whether the case theory can be supported before substantial resources are committed. For defense counsel, it identifies where breach may exist but causation remains vulnerable, or where the objective evidence makes denial of outcome impact difficult to sustain. For both, it improves expert selection and referral because the relevant causal questions are defined clearly.

I also found that it improves communication with families and clients. Healthcare outcomes can be emotionally overwhelming, and people understandably want a clear explanation. Sometimes the evidence provides one. Sometimes it provides a more complicated answer. Explaining that poor care occurred but probably did not determine the final outcome can be difficult. So can explaining that chronic illness contributed but did not make the harm inevitable.

A disciplined analysis allows those conversations to be honest without becoming dismissive.

I never believed that acknowledging a patient's vulnerability diminished the significance of avoidable harm. Nor did identifying a breach require me to attribute every consequence to it. The patient deserved an explanation that respected both their prior condition and what the care changed.

That balance remained at the center of my work.

By the time Causation Mapping was complete, the investigation had traveled a long way from the original allegation. The records had become evidence, the evidence had reconstructed the patient, the objective findings had revealed the body, the timeline had shown progression, the standard had defined obligation, and the regulatory overlay had explained the environment. Causation determined what those findings meant for the outcome.

No one discipline could have answered that question alone.

A strong timeline without baseline could overstate reversibility. A clear breach without imaging could misunderstand the pathology. A system failure without an intervention window could appear causally significant when the outcome was already established. Each part of the Model corrected and strengthened the others.

That was when I finally understood why the questions had organized themselves in this order. They were not seven separate areas of review. They were one investigation moving toward a conclusion.

I had begun years earlier by trying to understand medical records.

What emerged was a way of understanding the patient's entire clinical journey before deciding what that journey meant.

Once all seven disciplines were brought together, another change occurred. The case stopped feeling fragmented. The records, opinions, imaging, decisions, and organizational factors no longer competed for attention as separate issues. They formed one connected explanation.

That explanation was what I had been searching for from the beginning. It was Clinical Intelligence.

We have completed the seven disciplines in Part II through Causation Mapping. The next chapter should bring them together and show why they operate as one continuous investigation rather than seven separate reviews.

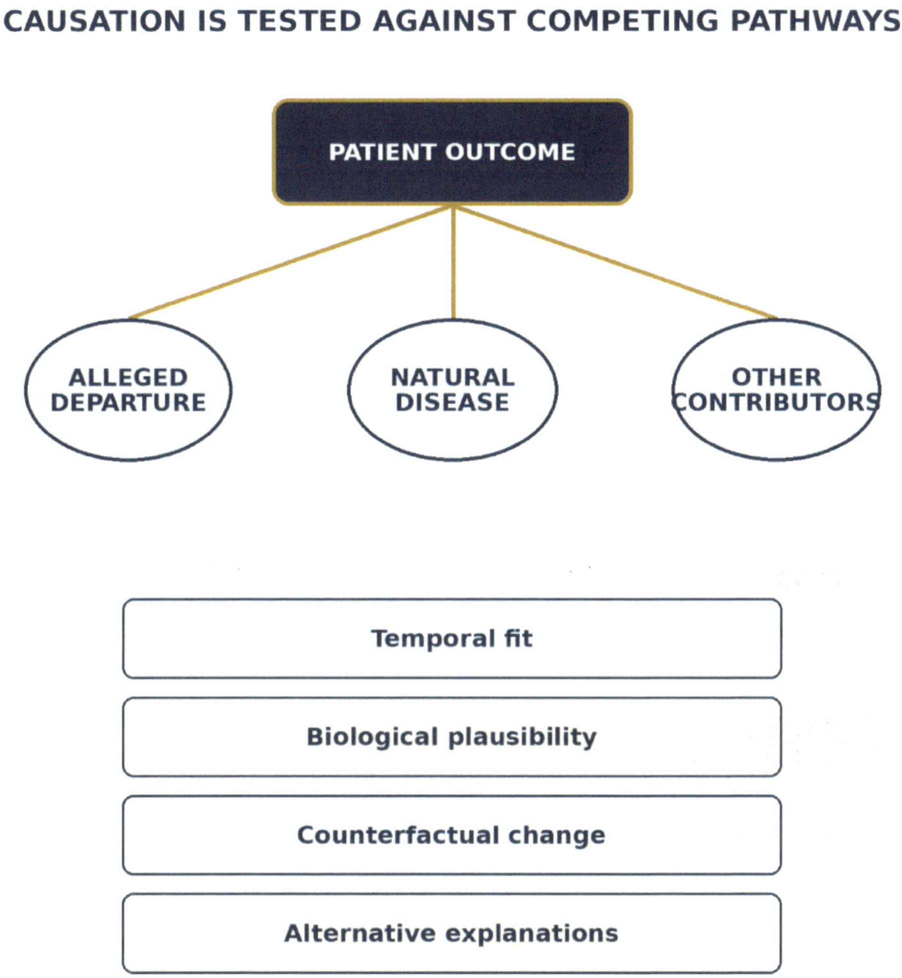

Figure 8 Causation Mapping tests the alleged pathway against natural disease, patient vulnerability, and other contributors.

CHAPTER 13

From Seven Pillars to Litigation-Ready Output

When I finally reached the point where all seven disciplines were operating together, I realized I was no longer reviewing healthcare cases in the way I had when I first entered this field. The change had occurred gradually, and for many years I probably would not have been able to explain it clearly. I knew that my reviews had become more structured and that I was asking more disciplined questions, but I still thought of those questions as separate parts of the work. I checked the evidence, understood the patient's baseline, examined the imaging, reconstructed the timeline, reviewed the standard of care, considered the system, and then addressed causation. It seemed logical to describe them as individual stages because each one had a distinct purpose.

The more I looked back over the cases, however, the more I realized that none of those disciplines had ever truly operated alone. Record Integrity influenced how confidently I could reconstruct the baseline. The baseline changed the meaning of the later findings. Imaging helped clarify progression, but only when it was placed inside the timeline. The timeline identified the decision points that Standard of Care Review needed to examine. The regulatory overlay explained the environment in which those decisions occurred. Causation depended upon all of them because it could not determine what had changed without first understanding the evidence, the patient, the pathology, the opportunity, the obligation, and the system.

What I had been treating as separate questions were actually parts of one continuous investigation. Each answer changed the question that followed, and each later discipline tested the conclusions reached earlier. A baseline that initially appeared clear might need to be reconsidered after imaging revealed longstanding disease. A timeline theory might change when audit data clarified when information became available. A standard-of-care concern might become less significant if causation showed that meaningful opportunity had already passed. Nothing remained untouched by everything else.

That was probably when I first understood what Clinical Intelligence had become.

It was not the addition of seven reports or seven opinions. It was the integration of seven different ways of understanding the same patient until the case could be seen as one connected clinical journey. The disciplines gave the investigation structure, but the value came from the way they interacted. No single finding was allowed to carry more meaning than the rest of the evidence could support, and no conclusion was considered complete until it had survived examination through the entire Model.

Looking back now, I think this is where Clinical Intelligence differs most significantly from a traditional record review. A record review may be accurate, thorough, and clinically informed while still concentrating primarily on what the documents contain. Clinical Intelligence uses those documents to reconstruct relationships. It asks how the patient's prior condition influenced later vulnerability, how objective findings aligned with the documented progression, how time changed the available options, how professional obligations developed, how the system shaped the response, and whether those combined factors probably altered the outcome.

The difference is not simply that more information is considered. The difference is that the information is brought together before its legal significance is decided.

I had seen how easily a case could become fragmented when each issue was examined independently. One expert focused on the imaging. Another concentrated on the standard of care. The attorney built the chronology. A regulatory consultant reviewed the policies. Each person might complete excellent work, yet the conclusions could remain disconnected because no one had been responsible for reconstructing how all of those findings related to the patient's complete journey.

That fragmentation often explained why intelligent professionals reached very different opinions after reviewing the same case. They were not necessarily disagreeing about the facts. They were giving different weight to different parts of the story. One saw the severe final image. Another saw the compromised baseline. One emphasized the obvious breach. Another concentrated on the limited intervention window. Each perspective contained truth, but none necessarily explained the whole case.

Clinical Intelligence required those truths to remain in the same room.

I found that once the seven disciplines were integrated, disagreements became easier to understand. The question was no longer simply which expert was right. I could identify which part of the patient's journey each expert was emphasizing, what evidence supported that emphasis, and what other findings had not been fully incorporated into the opinion. Sometimes one view became clearly stronger. Sometimes the case remained genuinely uncertain. In either situation, the attorney had a much better understanding of why the disagreement existed and where further expert analysis was needed.

This was particularly valuable in cases that initially appeared simple. A delayed diagnosis might look like one event, but the integrated review could reveal incomplete records, a declining baseline, ambiguous early imaging, several reasonable periods of uncertainty, one later missed decision point, and a narrow causal effect. The case did not disappear, but it became more precise. The strongest issue could be separated from the parts that would not survive challenge.

The same integration could strengthen a case that initially appeared weak. A seemingly routine postoperative decline might become more concerning when the patient's strong baseline, progressive objective changes, delayed escalation, inadequate staffing, and preserved intervention window all supported the same explanation. No single fact transformed the case. The alignment between them did.

Over time, I came to think of that alignment as clinical concordance. I wanted to know whether the different forms of evidence were supporting the same clinical understanding. Did the patient's baseline make the proposed recovery realistic? Did the imaging correspond with the symptoms and timeline? Did the alleged breach occur before irreversible injury? Did the system failure explain the delayed response? Did the final outcome fit the proposed mechanism?

When the disciplines aligned, the conclusion became much more stable because it did not depend upon one favorable interpretation. When they did not align, the disagreement required explanation before the opinion could be trusted. Sometimes the discordance reflected missing evidence or a misunderstanding that could be corrected. At other times, it revealed that the theory itself was not clinically sustainable.

I learned to value discordance because it often prevented me from becoming too confident in a case that looked persuasive on the surface. A severe outcome might not fit the alleged mechanism. The imaging might show chronic rather than acute disease. The baseline might demonstrate that recovery potential was more limited than expected. The timeline might place the departure after the intervention window had largely closed. Those findings did not make the investigation fail. They made it honest.

Clinical Intelligence was never intended to prove the allegation. It was intended to test whether the allegation could survive the patient's complete clinical story.

That principle mattered regardless of which side the attorney represented. Plaintiff counsel needed to know whether the case could support the investment, expert work, and emotional burden that would follow. Defense counsel needed to know whether a denial remained realistic or whether the evidence showed meaningful exposure. Both needed more than a list of strengths and weaknesses. They needed to understand how those strengths and weaknesses interacted.

I found that the integrated analysis also changed the questions asked of experts. Instead of sending thousands of pages with a broad request to determine whether malpractice occurred, the attorney could identify the exact decision points, the competing physiological explanations, the unresolved imaging issue, the regulatory condition, or the causal question requiring formal opinion. The expert's time could be directed toward the issues that genuinely required specialty judgment rather than spent reconstructing a case that should already have been organized.

That did not diminish the expert's role. It made the role more effective.

The same was true in depositions. Once the patient's journey had been reconstructed, questions could follow the clinical reasoning rather than the order of the chart. A clinician could be asked what information was available, how it influenced the differential diagnosis, what change would have required escalation, and whether the system supported the expected response. The deposition became an examination of reasoning rather than a search for isolated admissions.

In mediation, the integrated Model helped explain why the case was strong, weak, or mixed without reducing the discussion to competing conclusions. The attorney could show how the evidence moved from baseline through progression to outcome and identify exactly where the parties disagreed. A case grounded in connected clinical reasoning was often easier to evaluate because the uncertainty was visible rather than hidden behind absolute positions.

I also began to understand that the integration protected the patient's story from being owned by either side. Plaintiff and defense theories naturally organize the facts toward different legal objectives. Clinical Intelligence does not pretend those objectives do not exist, but it reconstructs the patient independently before determining which parts of either theory the evidence supports.

That independence became essential to the credibility of the work. I did not want the Model to become a more sophisticated way of defending a predetermined position. The same discipline had to be applied regardless of who retained the reviewer, and the findings had to be allowed to lead wherever the evidence supported. A model that produces only favorable answers for the person paying for it is not Clinical Intelligence. It is advocacy disguised as analysis.

The attorney remains the advocate. The clinical investigation has a different responsibility.

I think this is why the sequence of the Model matters so much. It deliberately delays the legal conclusion until the patient has been understood from every necessary direction. The evidence is tested before the allegation is evaluated. The patient is reconstructed before the loss is measured. The progression is understood before the decision is judged. The obligation is defined before causation is assumed.

Each discipline slows the investigation just enough to prevent the next conclusion from arriving before it has been earned.

That does not mean the process is inefficient. In many cases, it saves time because weak theories are identified earlier, missing evidence becomes visible before expert retention, and the issues requiring deeper review are narrowed. The discipline may appear slower at the beginning, but it prevents the far greater waste that occurs when months of litigation are built on an incomplete understanding of the case.

I had seen that happen too often. An attorney retained several experts before obtaining prior imaging. A causation theory developed before the baseline was reconstructed. Depositions were taken before the communication pathway was understood. The case became more expensive and more difficult because the investigation had moved forward without a stable clinical foundation.

Clinical Intelligence brought the order back.

The more I used the Model, the more I also understood that integration does not mean every case requires the same depth of review. Some matters can be screened relatively quickly because the key facts align and the clinical questions are limited. Others require extensive specialty review, regulatory analysis, or multiple causal pathways. The Model provides the same disciplined sequence, while the complexity of the patient and the case determines how deeply each discipline must be explored.

That flexibility matters because a framework should support judgment rather than replace it. The purpose is not to produce unnecessary analysis. It is to ensure that no essential question is overlooked simply because the case appears familiar or the allegation seems obvious.

I often returned to the concern I had felt years earlier when a case looked complete but still did not make sense. Clinical Intelligence gave that discomfort somewhere to go. If the story remained unclear, I could ask which discipline had not been resolved. Was the evidence incomplete? Was the baseline poorly understood? Did the imaging conflict with the documentation? Was the timeline missing a decision point? Had the system influence been overlooked? Did the causation theory require more than the physiology could support?

The Model did not guarantee that every question would be answered. Some cases remain uncertain because medicine is uncertain and evidence has limits. What it did provide was confidence that the uncertainty had been reached through disciplined investigation rather than through fragmentation or omission.

That distinction became increasingly important to me. There is a difference between not knowing because the case has not been investigated adequately and not knowing because the available evidence cannot support a more definite conclusion. The first demands more work. The second may be the most honest answer.

Clinical Intelligence helped me recognize which one I was facing.

By the time the seven disciplines had been integrated, I could usually explain the case in a way that was both more complete and more concise. That may sound contradictory after such an extensive investigation, but depth often creates clarity. Once I understood the relationships, I no longer needed to describe every event with equal weight. I could identify the evidence that shaped the patient's journey, the decisions that mattered, the system conditions that influenced them, and the causal effect the evidence supported.

The final explanation became simpler because the thinking behind it had been thorough.

That was the purpose of the Clinical Intelligence Report™. It was not intended to reproduce the entire investigation or overwhelm the attorney with every piece of information reviewed. It was intended to present the integrated understanding that emerged from the Model in a form that could guide litigation decisions.

The report begins with the evidence because every conclusion depends upon it. It explains the patient's baseline because outcome has no meaning without a starting point. It identifies the objective findings and clinical progression because the body and the timeline show how the case unfolded. It defines the professional and system responsibilities because accountability requires context. It maps causation because breach alone cannot explain outcome.

Most importantly, it shows how those findings relate.

I never wanted the report to read as though seven separate specialists had contributed seven unrelated sections. The reader should feel that one investigation has moved continuously from the first record to the final conclusion. The language, reasoning, and evidence should remain connected enough that the attorney can follow exactly how each opinion developed.

That transparency became important because a strong conclusion should not depend upon authority alone. The attorney should not have to accept an opinion because the reviewer is experienced or highly qualified. They should be able to see why the conclusion makes sense. They should understand which facts support it, what uncertainty remains, and what additional expert opinion is required.

I think that is one of the central responsibilities of Clinical Intelligence. It translates complex healthcare evidence without simplifying it beyond truth. It gives the attorney access to the reasoning rather than only the answer.

The distinction matters because attorneys cannot make sound strategic decisions from conclusions they do not understand. They may rely on experts appropriately, but they still need to know how the medicine shapes intake, discovery, valuation, settlement, deposition, and trial. Clinical Intelligence gives them a structured clinical understanding from which legal judgment can operate.

It also gives clinicians a clearer view of how their decisions enter litigation. The Model does not treat them as characters in a legal story. It reconstructs the information, uncertainty, pressure, and system conditions surrounding their actions. That does not excuse unreasonable care. It ensures the care is judged in the reality in which it occurred.

I have always believed that attorneys and clinicians need one another in this work. Attorneys understand legal standards, evidentiary rules, strategy, and the burdens the case must satisfy. Clinicians understand physiology, progression, treatment, risk, and the realities of care. Clinical Intelligence does not ask either profession to surrender its role. It creates a way for those roles to work from the same patient story.

When that happens, the quality of the litigation improves. Experts receive better questions. Attorneys understand weaknesses earlier. Clinicians are evaluated more fairly. Families receive clearer explanations. Cases with genuine merit become stronger because the reasoning can withstand challenge, while cases built on assumption are identified before they consume years of effort.

The Model is not neutral because it avoids conclusions. It is neutral because it earns them.

That understanding became central to the doctrine that followed. Once I could see how the seven disciplines worked together, I began asking why the approach felt different from other forms of medical-legal review. The answer was not simply that it was more comprehensive. Comprehensive review can still produce disconnected information. The difference was that Clinical Intelligence created a disciplined relationship between evidence, patient, progression, obligation, system, and outcome.

It was a way of knowing when a conclusion had become reliable enough to influence a legal decision.

I did not appreciate at first that this carried a responsibility beyond case review. If Clinical Intelligence was going to become a professional discipline, it required standards for how the Model was applied, how conclusions were documented, how uncertainty was communicated, and how technology could support the work without replacing judgment. A method this influential could not depend only upon individual intuition.

That realization eventually led to the Doctrine of Clinical Intelligence, the training and licensing system, and the governance structures designed to protect the integrity of the Model. Those developments came later, but their foundation was already present in the integrated investigation. The more powerful the analysis became, the more important it was to ensure that the discipline remained evidence-based, clinically governed, and resistant to misuse.

The Model had emerged from questions. The doctrine emerged from responsibility.

At this stage of the book, however, the most important thing is not the system that later grew around Clinical Intelligence. It is the change that occurs when the attorney begins seeing the healthcare case as one clinical journey rather than a collection of records, experts, and allegations.

Once that change occurs, the case cannot be approached in quite the same way again.

The attorney begins asking whether the evidence is complete before relying on the chronology. They want to know the patient's prior function before discussing damages. They ask what the imaging proves and what it does not. They look for the point where the pattern became clinically meaningful rather than simply identifying the first abnormal result. They distinguish between an error and a causally important departure. They ask whether the system made safe care possible. They test the outcome theory against the patient's physiology rather than the severity of the harm alone.

Those questions become part of the way the case is understood.

That is when Clinical Intelligence stops being a model someone applies and becomes a discipline someone practices.

Looking back now, I think this was the destination I had been moving toward throughout my career without knowing its name. I began by reading records because I wanted to understand what happened. Over time, patients taught me that understanding required more. It required evidence that could be trusted, a patient who could be seen, a body that could be heard, a progression that could be reconstructed, decisions that could be judged fairly, a system that could be examined honestly, and an outcome that could be connected without assumption.

Together, those disciplines produced something no individual review could provide. They produced Clinical Intelligence.

PART III

CLINICAL INTELLIGENCE IN LITIGATION PRACTICE

How disciplined clinical understanding changes legal preparation

CHAPTER 14

Professional Roles and Boundaries

The value of Clinical Intelligence depends on clear professional boundaries. Healthcare litigation brings together people who have different authority, training, and responsibilities. Confusion begins when one participant quietly assumes another participant's role.

The attorney

The attorney controls the legal representation, selects legal theories, determines litigation strategy, evaluates procedural and evidentiary requirements, retains experts, and advises the client. Clinical Intelligence should give counsel a more reliable understanding of the medical evidence. It should never present a clinical reviewer as a substitute for legal judgment.

The treating clinician

The treating clinician made decisions within a real clinical environment. Information arrived over time. Staffing, competing needs, urgency, and the patient's response affected what was possible. Retrospective review must reconstruct that position before evaluating the decision. A later result cannot be treated as though it had been known earlier.

The medical legal analyst

The analyst organizes and tests the evidentiary foundation. The work may include record-integrity review, baseline development, imaging correlation, timeline reconstruction, identification of clinical and system issues, alternative-explanation testing, and preparation of questions for an appropriately qualified expert. The analyst makes reasoning visible and preserves the distinction between what the evidence shows and what requires expert opinion.

A nurse brings clinical knowledge and experience with patient care. A paralegal brings legal-process discipline, document control, issue organization, and an understanding of how evidence is used within litigation. Either background can contribute to medical-legal analysis when the individual is properly educated, works within competence, and uses a governed method. Neither background authorizes the person to act as an attorney, treating clinician, radiologist, toxicologist, life-care planner, or retained expert without the qualifications required for that role.

The independent expert

The expert applies specialized knowledge and reaches an independent opinion. A well-prepared evidence package can reduce time spent locating essential material, but it must not narrow the expert's view to a preferred theory. Contrary evidence, missing records, uncertainty, and competing explanations belong in the material provided for review.

The specialty reviewer

Some questions require focused review before an expert is retained or while a broader analysis is being completed. A specialty reviewer may clarify terminology, identify the significance of an imaging pattern, test whether a proposed physiological pathway is plausible, or explain what additional evidence is needed. The scope must be explicit. A limited consultation should not be represented as a comprehensive expert opinion.

The quality reviewer

Quality review tests whether the work follows the method and whether the report accurately represents the evidence. It checks source traceability, internal consistency, conclusion boundaries, terminology, calculations, chronology, and delivery controls. Quality review is not a search for stronger language. Its purpose is to find unsupported language before the report reaches the decision-maker.

Independence and candor

Clinical Intelligence must remain useful when the findings are unfavorable to the party who requested the work. A weak causal pathway, a well-documented reasonable decision, or a significant pre-existing condition may change the value of a claim. Identifying that early is not a failure of advocacy. It protects counsel from investing in a theory the evidence cannot sustain. The same discipline also identifies strong matters that administrative screening may have underestimated.

Competence and escalation

Competence is specific to the question. A reviewer may be capable of reconstructing a medication timeline but not qualified to interpret a disputed neuroradiology finding. Another may understand intensive-care documentation but need assistance with a product-exposure pathway. The analyst should recognize that boundary before the conclusion is written.

Escalation is not an admission of weakness. It is a control. The file should record the question referred, the information supplied, the professional consulted, and the way the response affected the analysis. When the answer remains outside the analyst's scope, the report should say so plainly and preserve the issue for the appropriately qualified expert.

Communication with counsel

Counsel should know early when the record set is incomplete, the original allegation is inaccurate, or a specialty question is likely to determine the case. Waiting until the final report to disclose a material limitation wastes time and may distort strategy. Interim communication should be concise and decision-focused: what has changed, why it matters, what remains unknown, and what action is recommended.

The analyst should also understand the difference between receiving direction and receiving a desired conclusion. Counsel may define the question, deadline, scope, and legal context. Counsel should not determine what the clinical evidence must show. That separation protects both the analysis and the attorney who must rely on it.

Respect for the patient and the record

Medical records contain intimate information gathered for care, payment, and operations, not for public storytelling. Review should be limited to what the engagement requires, handled through approved systems, and discussed with professional restraint. The patient is not a collection of dramatic facts. The patient is the person whose experience the evidence is being used to reconstruct.

Working Across Professional Boundaries

Shared work becomes reliable when responsibility is explicit. The attorney defines the legal decision, jurisdictional context, privilege strategy, and authorized use. The analyst controls the integrity of the clinical analysis within scope. Specialty reviewers and experts answer questions requiring their qualifications. Quality reviewers test the work without quietly becoming authors of unsupported conclusions.

These roles may overlap in knowledge but not in authority. A nurse analyst may understand why a radiology finding matters clinically without being qualified to interpret the image independently. A paralegal may identify a decisive inconsistency in the record without offering a medical diagnosis. An attorney may recognize the legal importance of an omission without determining the clinical standard. The model allows each professional to contribute fully while preserving the point at which another role is required.

The handoff between analyst and expert

A well-prepared referral identifies the question, relevant period, record universe, important conflicts, and known limitations. It does not tell the expert what answer is needed. The expert should receive material that could weaken as well as support the theory. After the response, the analyst records what changed and whether the broader analysis requires revision.

The handoff between analyst and counsel

Interim communication should occur when a material assumption fails, a deadline is threatened, a specialty need emerges, or missing evidence could change the investment decision. Counsel should not discover those facts for the first time in the final report. The communication should be concise: what was found, why it matters, what remains unknown, and what action is recommended.

Disagreement

Professional disagreement is not automatically a quality failure. The question is whether each view rests on an accurate record and visible reasoning. When two qualified reviewers interpret the same evidence differently, the report should identify the point of divergence. They may differ on the weight of a symptom, the plausibility of a mechanism, or the significance of an interval. Naming that point gives counsel a useful issue. Concealing it creates false certainty.

Protecting independence

The analyst should not adopt counsel's preferred wording when it claims more than the evidence supports. The expert should not be given a curated file that hides contrary evidence. The quality reviewer should not strengthen language merely to make the report appear decisive. Each role protects the others by remaining answerable to the evidence.

CHAPTER 15

Uncertainty and Competing Explanations

Complex healthcare matters rarely arrive with every important fact established. Missing records, inconsistent timestamps, unclear exposure, incomplete imaging, and competing physiological explanations are common. The analyst's task is not to remove that uncertainty through confident wording. The task is to define it accurately enough that counsel can decide what to do next.

Four levels of statement The revised method uses four levels of statement throughout the analysis.

Documented fact identifies what a traceable source directly establishes. The source, date, author, and relevant content should be recoverable.

Supported inference explains a conclusion that reasonably follows from several facts but is not directly stated in one source. The facts and reasoning supporting the inference must be visible.

Competing interpretation identifies another explanation that a qualified professional could reasonably draw from the evidence. The analysis should explain what supports it and what weakens it.

Unresolved question identifies a material issue that cannot responsibly be decided from the current evidence. The report should state what additional evidence or expertise could resolve it, if resolution is possible.

These levels prevent a possibility from becoming a fact simply because it has been repeated. They also prevent excessive caution from obscuring a relationship that the evidence reasonably supports.

Testing the preferred explanation

Every important conclusion should be tested against at least four questions. What evidence supports it? What evidence challenges it? What assumptions does it require? What would have to be true for the main alternative to be correct? The reviewer should then ask whether any missing source is likely to change the analysis. A missing document is material when its contents could alter a decision, not merely because the record set is imperfect.

Stop rules

More evidence is not always better. Repeated requests can consume time and cost without changing the decision. A stop rule weighs the importance of the missing fact, the likelihood that the source exists, the cost and delay required to obtain it, and the effect it would have on the analysis. Counsel makes the litigation decision. Clinical Intelligence supplies the information needed to make that decision honestly.

Language that preserves meaning

Words such as proves, confirms, demonstrates, consistent with, supports, suggests, and cannot exclude are not interchangeable. The strength of the language should match the strength of the evidence. A report should avoid both exaggeration and defensive vagueness. The reader should be able to see why a conclusion was stated at a particular level of confidence.

When evidence conflicts

Conflicting sources should not be resolved by choosing the version that best supports the case. The reviewer examines the purpose of each source, proximity to the event, opportunity to observe, internal consistency, later correction, and relationship to objective evidence. A contemporaneous bedside note may deserve more weight on observed symptoms than a summary written days later. A medication administration entry may be stronger evidence of administration than a narrative note that lists the medication as planned. Neither rule is absolute; the circumstances decide the weight.

The report should preserve a material conflict when it cannot be resolved. It may explain which account appears better supported and why, but should not erase the other account. Counsel and the expert need to know that the conflict exists before it appears in deposition or trial.

Counterfactual discipline

Many causation questions ask what would probably have happened if an action had occurred earlier or differently. The counterfactual cannot be answered by assuming that the alternative action would have worked perfectly. The analysis must consider the patient's baseline, the available intervention, the time required for it to take effect, the biological course already underway, and the range of outcomes that remained possible.

A responsible counterfactual may remain conditional. The evidence may support that earlier intervention would have improved the chance of a better outcome without establishing that it would probably have prevented all injury. The language must reflect that difference and leave the ultimate legal application to counsel and the qualified expert.

Decision impact

Uncertainty should be prioritized by its effect on the decision. A missing note may be frustrating but immaterial. An unverified exposure date may determine whether the biological theory is possible. The report should identify the uncertainty that could change the screening decision, expert need, damages analysis, or settlement posture. That is how uncertainty becomes useful rather than merely descriptive.

Calibrating Confidence

Confidence is not a personality trait and should not be communicated as one. It is a judgment about the relationship between the evidence and the statement being made. The reviewer should be able to explain what supports the level of confidence, what limits it, and what additional evidence could change it.

A documented fact may still require qualification. A note can establish that an author recorded a statement without establishing that the statement was correct. A medication record can establish administration while leaving dose effect or causation unresolved. A report should be precise about what the source proves.

A supported inference is strongest when several independent facts converge and weaker when it depends on one uncertain assumption. The analyst should show the reasoning rather than hide it behind phrases such as "clearly" or "obviously." Those words add emphasis but no evidence.

Competing interpretations should be presented in their strongest responsible form. A weak caricature of the opposing view does not test the preferred explanation. The analyst identifies the evidence each interpretation explains, the assumptions each requires, and the fact most likely to distinguish between them.

An unresolved question should be tied to decision impact. Some uncertainty can be accepted because it would not change screening, expert selection, or causation. Other uncertainty is controlling. An unverified exposure, missing imaging study, absent medication administration record, or unknown event time may prevent a responsible conclusion.

Confidence can change

Early screening may justify a provisional conclusion based on a limited record set. Later discovery may strengthen, narrow, or reverse it. The report should identify its evidentiary date and scope so that a provisional statement is not reused as though it were final after the record changes.

The organization should not treat revision as embarrassment. A conclusion that remains unchanged despite material new evidence may be less credible than one that changes for a documented reason. The duty is to the best supported account, not to consistency for its own sake.

Communicating uncertainty to counsel

Counsel needs more than the statement that "more records are required." The analyst should identify which source is missing, what question it may answer, how likely it is to change the analysis, and whether a decision can reasonably proceed without it. That turns uncertainty into an actionable part of strategy.

The final language should allow a reader to distinguish: established fact, reasonable inference, issue for expert opinion, competing explanation, and unresolved question. When those categories are visible, uncertainty strengthens rather than weakens professional decision-making.

CHAPTER 16

Clinical Intelligence Across the Litigation Lifecycle

From Understanding to Litigation Decisions

Clinical Intelligence should produce the amount of analysis required for the decision at hand. A screening decision does not require the same depth as a causation opinion or deposition strategy. The scope must be defined before the work begins, and the report must state what was reviewed, what was not reviewed, and what decision it is intended to support.

Attorney Case Brief

The Attorney Case Brief supports the first investment decision. It identifies the patient and event, the available records, the strongest clinical issue, material weaknesses, missing evidence, specialty needs, and recommended next step. It is not a compressed expert report. Its value lies in disciplined screening before substantial litigation cost is committed.

Clinical Intelligence Review

The Clinical Intelligence Review is the comprehensive integrated analysis. It brings the seven pillars together and explains the relationships between baseline, objective findings, chronology, professional decisions, organizational factors, alternative explanations, and causation. It should make both supporting and contrary evidence visible.

Medical Chronology and Narrative Summary

A chronology establishes an accurate sequence and provides source traceability. A narrative summary explains the clinical meaning of that sequence. They may be used together, but they are not interchangeable. A chronology without analysis can leave the reader with dates but no understanding. A narrative without traceability can make it difficult to test the account against the record.

Standard of Care Screening Review and Causation Analysis

The Standard of Care Screening Review identifies concerns that may warrant appropriately qualified expert review and frames the questions the expert should address. The Causation Analysis examines whether a supported pathway connects an event or decision with the outcome, while considering baseline risk and alternatives. Neither should be represented as a legal conclusion.

Defense-Oriented Clinical Review

The Defense-Oriented Clinical Review tests the leading theory against contrary evidence, alternative causal pathways, baseline vulnerability, reasonable decision-making, and weaknesses that opposing counsel may expose. It should be performed with the same candor whether the client represents the claimant or the defense. A theory that survives serious challenge is more useful than one protected from it.

Expert and deposition preparation

Expert Witness Preparation organizes the evidence and the questions without directing the opinion. Deposition Preparation tests reasoning, source support, terminology, assumptions, and likely competing interpretations. Both should preserve expert independence and the distinction between preparation and testimony.

Additional applications

Damages and life-care planning support requires reliable injury characterization, functional baseline, prognosis, and traceable assumptions. Rebuttal work requires precise identification of what the opposing opinion assumes, omits, or interprets differently. Mass-tort support requires claimant-specific analysis within a governed portfolio method so that volume does not replace evidence. In every application, the report follows the decision; the decision should never be forced to fit a prefabricated report.

Selecting the right output

The correct output can often be identified by asking what counsel must decide next. If the decision is whether to investigate further, a concise brief may be sufficient. If the decision concerns expert retention, the work should identify the clinical questions, the relevant specialty, and the evidence the expert will need. If the case is approaching deposition, the analysis must test the reasoning and identify the records most likely to be used in questioning. If settlement posture depends on causation, a chronology alone will not answer the question.

This discipline prevents unnecessary work as well as incomplete work. A comprehensive report should not be ordered simply because it is the largest product available. The engagement should be built around the decision, the evidence, and the risk of proceeding without greater clarity.

Writing for the legal reader

The legal reader needs clinical meaning without unsupported simplification. Reports should define unfamiliar terms, explain why a finding matters, and connect the conclusion to the source. Long clinical descriptions should not be included merely to demonstrate effort. Detail belongs in the report when it changes the analysis, supports traceability, or allows another professional to test the reasoning.

The report should also separate the headline finding from the evidentiary explanation. Counsel should be able to identify the principal issue quickly and then follow the reasoning to its source. That structure respects both the demands of legal practice and the complexity of the patient journey.

Clinical Intelligence changes as the matter develops because the decision changes. The method remains stable; the depth, emphasis, and output do not. A useful engagement identifies where the matter stands and what counsel must decide next.

Intake and case selection

At intake, speed and proportionality matter. Counsel needs to know whether the allegation is clinically coherent, whether the supplied records support it, what is missing, whether a viable causal pathway is apparent, and which specialty may be required. The analysis should identify both the strongest issue and the most serious weakness. Its purpose is not to prove the case before investigation. It is to prevent an early administrative decision from being mistaken for a clinical one.

Pre-suit investigation

During pre-suit investigation, the work expands from screening to evidence development. The analyst can identify targeted record requests, reconstruct the baseline, distinguish event time from documentation time, correlate imaging and laboratory trends, and frame questions for potential experts. A well-designed investigation may reveal that the intake theory is inaccurate while identifying a different concern that deserves attention.

Pleadings and early theory development

Clinical Intelligence does not draft legal claims or defenses. It helps counsel ensure that the medical account underlying them is supportable. The work can identify where the proposed theory assumes a fact not established by the record, attributes an outcome to the wrong interval, overlooks baseline vulnerability, or fails to address an obvious competing explanation.

Discovery planning

Once litigation begins, the evidence inventory becomes a discovery map. Missing audit data, outside records, communications, policy versions, staffing information, device logs, pharmacy detail, imaging, and prior treatment can be tied to the questions they may answer. This makes requests more precise and helps counsel distinguish material evidence from volume.

Expert identification and retention

The analysis should identify the specialty question before the expert is selected. A matter may require more than one discipline because the decision, mechanism, and outcome cross professional boundaries. The evidence package should include contrary material and known limitations. The expert must remain free to reach an independent opinion.

Deposition preparation

Deposition preparation tests what a witness knew, when the information became available, what the witness did, and how that account aligns with contemporaneous evidence. The analyst can identify source documents, terminology, unresolved conflicts, and likely alternative interpretations. Preparation should improve precision without scripting testimony or replacing counsel's examination strategy.

Damages and prognosis

Damages analysis begins with a defensible comparison between pre-event and post-event function. The reviewer should distinguish new impairment, aggravation, disease progression, treatment burden, and limitations that predated the event. Prognosis and future care require appropriately qualified opinions; the Clinical Intelligence foundation helps ensure those opinions begin with an accurate baseline and injury description.

Mediation and settlement

At mediation, the value of the work lies in clarity. Counsel should be able to explain the supported clinical pathway, important uncertainties, contrary evidence, expert dependencies, and vulnerabilities likely to affect a fact-finder. A concise decision-oriented analysis is often more useful than reproducing the entire record.

Trial preparation

Trial preparation requires traceability. Material statements should be tied to admissible or potentially admissible sources, and demonstratives should not simplify the evidence beyond what the witnesses can support. The analyst may assist with chronology, exhibit organization, terminology, and consistency checks while leaving legal argument and expert opinion to the professionals responsible for them.

Post-resolution learning

After resolution, the matter can inform the discipline without exposing confidential information. Recurring record gaps, workflow failures, misunderstood terminology, quality issues, and successful controls should be incorporated into education and process improvement. A governed discipline learns from completed work rather than treating every matter as isolated.

Designing Outputs Around Decisions

The final work product should not be selected by habit. Each output answers a different professional need, and each should disclose its scope. A chronology cannot silently become a causation opinion. A screening brief should not imply that a complete expert review has occurred. A comprehensive report should not bury the decision beneath an inventory of facts.

The Attorney Case Brief

The brief supports a defined early decision. It should identify the decision question, record universe, patient baseline, principal issue, strongest supporting evidence, most important contrary evidence, missing material, specialty need, and recommended next action. The brief is concise because the decision is focused, not because uncertainty has been omitted.

The opening finding should be understandable without reading the entire document. Counsel should then be able to follow the finding to the evidence and limitation that shaped it. A useful brief may conclude that further investment is warranted, that a narrower issue should be pursued, that additional records are required before a decision, or that the current theory is not clinically supportable.

The Clinical Intelligence Review

The comprehensive review integrates all seven pillars. It should explain how the record was tested, how baseline was constructed, what objective evidence contributed, how the sequence was rebuilt, which professional decisions require evaluation, how organizational conditions affected the event, and what causal pathways remain supportable.

The report should not read as seven unrelated mini-reports. Relationships must remain visible. A missing record may change the timeline. The corrected timeline may change the standard-of-care question. The changed question may alter the expert specialty required. The expert issue may narrow causation. Integration is the value of the final product.

Chronology and narrative

The chronology should identify clinically material events and maintain source traceability. It should distinguish the types of time when that difference matters. A narrative should explain change, response, turning points, and outcome. The two products may be paired, but the narrative should not repeat every row and the chronology should not conceal interpretation inside neutral-looking entries.

Standard of Care Screening Review

This output identifies decisions that may warrant expert assessment. It should state the conduct at issue, information available at the time, relevant context, evidence supporting and weakening the concern, missing facts, and recommended specialty. It must state that the screening analysis is not a substitute for the independent opinion required in the matter.

Causation Analysis

The causation output should identify the alleged pathway, verified starting facts, baseline susceptibility, temporal relationship, proposed mechanism, objective support, alternatives, counterfactual, and unresolved expert questions. It should make clear whether the evidence supports a pathway, merely permits it, weakens it, or cannot distinguish it from another responsible explanation.

Defense-Oriented Clinical Review

The Defense-Oriented Clinical Review tests the leading allegation against the complete clinical record. It examines inaccurate premises, omitted baseline, reasonable alternative explanations, actions that occurred, system context, causal gaps, and damages attribution. Its purpose is not to manufacture a defense. It is to determine which aspects of the allegation survive disciplined challenge and which do not.

The same candor applies when the review identifies a serious concern. A defense-oriented engagement loses value if unfavorable evidence is minimized. Counsel needs the vulnerability before opposing counsel, an expert, or a witness exposes it.

Expert preparation

An expert package should make the relevant evidence accessible without narrowing the expert's view. It may include the record inventory, issue chronology, imaging list, baseline summary, principal conflicts, questions requiring specialty judgment, and sources that challenge the apparent theory. The analyst should not direct the opinion or remove inconvenient material.

Deposition preparation

Deposition analysis identifies the clinical sequence, decision points, terminology, material records, conflicts, and assumptions likely to be tested. It can show where a witness's later account aligns with or departs from contemporaneous evidence. It should not script testimony. The witness and counsel remain responsible for truthful preparation and legal strategy.

Rebuttal and competing-opinion analysis

Rebuttal work begins by stating the opposing opinion accurately. The analyst identifies the facts and assumptions on which it depends, evidence omitted or weighted differently, terminology that may confuse the issue, and the point at which the reasoning diverges. A strong rebuttal does not attack a conclusion merely because it is unfavorable. It shows why another interpretation is better supported or why the existing opinion exceeds its foundation.

Damages and functional change

The damages foundation compares pre-event and post-event function with attention to disease progression, prior assistance, treatment burden, new impairment, aggravation, and recovery. Future-care or life-care opinions require the appropriate qualifications. Clinical Intelligence helps ensure that those opinions begin with an accurate account of the patient's starting point and the change reasonably attributable to the event.

Making limits visible

Every output should identify the materials reviewed, the relevant period, known omissions, professional scope, and whether specialty review occurred. Conclusions should be labeled in language matching their support. Material contrary evidence belongs in the analysis. The reader should never have to infer whether a statement is documented fact, supported inference, competing interpretation, or unresolved question.

Final delivery control

After substantive approval, a separate delivery check confirms the intended recipient, correct matter, approved final document, version, and secure channel. This control belongs on each core report checklist as the last release step. It is deliberately separate from clinical and quality review because it protects against a different failure. The report may be analytically sound and still be mishandled at delivery.

Applying the Discipline in Different Care Settings

The model remains stable across settings, but the evidence and operational context change. A hospital, long-term-care facility, outpatient office, home-health episode, emergency transport, and product-exposure matter do not preserve the patient's journey in the same way. The analyst must understand the setting before deciding what a complete record should contain or what a missing source may mean.

Emergency and inpatient care

Emergency and hospital matters often contain dense time-sensitive evidence: triage, orders, administration records, monitoring, consultation, imaging, laboratory interfaces, handoffs, and transfers. The analytical risk is fragmentation. Each department may document a coherent part of the event while no source explains the whole course. Parallel timelines and clear turning points are often essential.

High-acuity care also magnifies the difference between information that existed and information that was available to a particular decision-maker. A result may have posted without being communicated. A bedside change may have been observed before it appeared in a physician note. A remote order may reflect a telephone discussion preserved elsewhere. The review must connect the streams without assuming access or knowledge.

Outpatient and ambulatory care

Outpatient matters may involve longer intervals, multiple independent providers, portal messages, telephone encounters, referral systems, prior authorization, and patient follow-through. The question is often not a single bedside response but whether information moved through the system and whether responsibility for follow-up remained clear.

The analyst should distinguish an order from completion, a referral from attendance, and a result from communication. Patient choice, access barriers, insurance requirements, and care received outside the organization may materially affect the sequence. A gap in one chart may be filled by another provider's record rather than indicating no care occurred.

Long term care and residential settings

Long-term-care analysis depends heavily on baseline function, care planning, assistance needs, skin and nutrition records, behavior, family communication, certified nursing assistant documentation, and change-in-condition processes. The resident's course may evolve gradually. A monthly summary can conceal daily decline, while isolated flow-sheet entries may make ordinary variation appear more significant than it was.

The regulatory environment is more prominent, but regulatory language should not replace clinical analysis. The reviewer must connect assessment, plan, implementation, response, and outcome. Staffing information becomes meaningful only when tied to the care the resident required and what actually occurred.

Home health and community care

Home-health records reflect intermittent professional observation within a setting largely managed by the patient, family, and other caregivers. Visit notes may be accurate while leaving long intervals undocumented. Medication reconciliation, access to supplies, caregiver capacity, environmental risk, and communication with ordering professionals may be central.

The analyst should avoid treating the absence of continuous documentation as though the service provided continuous observation. The scope and frequency of authorized visits, goals of care, and responsibilities assigned to each participant must be understood.

Behavioral health and observation

Behavioral-health and observation matters require careful separation of diagnosis, expressed intent, observed behavior, risk assessment, environment, monitoring, communication, and changes in presentation. A risk score is one source, not the patient. The analysis should examine how information was gathered, whether collateral sources were available, what precautions were selected, and what changes required reassessment.

Risk to the patient and risk to others may involve different evidence and controls. Retrospective knowledge of an event should not be projected backward as though the final behavior was certain. The question is what risk was reasonably identifiable and what response was supportable at the time.

Product exposure and mass claims

Exposure matters require claimant-specific verification. Product identification, dose or frequency, duration, timing, indication, competing exposures, baseline risk, latency, diagnosis, and alternative causes must be established for the individual. Portfolio allegations and general literature cannot substitute for proof of the relevant exposure and outcome window.

The same governed fields should be collected across claimants, but uniform process should not force uniform conclusions. Some files will support exposure and timing. Others will contain gaps that plausibility cannot bridge. Clinical Intelligence protects the portfolio from both weak claims advanced by assumption and strong claims missed by administrative screening.

The setting changes the evidence not the standard of honesty

In every setting, the analyst asks the same foundational questions while respecting the evidence the environment actually produces. The discipline does not expect an outpatient chart to resemble an intensive-care flow sheet or a home-health note to provide continuous surveillance. It expects the reviewer to understand what should exist, what does exist, what remains absent, and how those limits affect the decision.

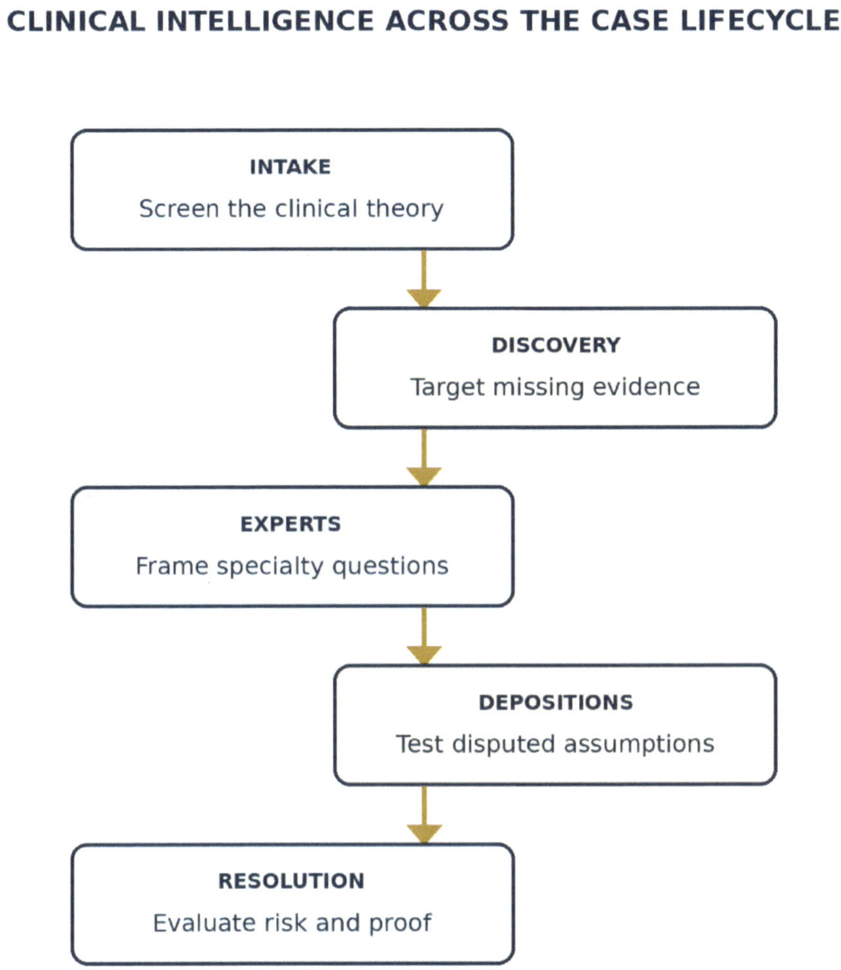

Figure 9 Clinical Intelligence supports different decisions at intake, discovery, expert review, deposition, and resolution.

CHAPTER 17

Quality Assurance Governance and Limits

Quality Assurance and Governance

A named methodology is only credible when its use is governed. Governance protects the client, the patient, the analyst, and the discipline itself. It defines who may perform the work, which review is required, how uncertainty is recorded, and what must occur before a report is released.

Scope control

Every engagement should identify the decision to be supported, the record set, the time period, the requested deliverable, the relevant jurisdiction, known deadlines, and any specialty questions. When the scope changes, the change should be documented. Analysts should not quietly extend a screening review into an expert opinion or treat a partial record set as complete.

Source traceability

Material factual statements should be traceable to a source. Dates should distinguish event time, collection time, result time, entry time, and filing time when the difference matters. Images should be identified by study and date. Calculations, quotations, and policy provisions should be capable of verification.

Analytical controls

The review should confirm that all seven pillars were considered, even when a pillar is not material to the conclusion. Contrary evidence and alternative explanations must be addressed. The report should state unresolved issues and distinguish analyst findings from questions reserved for specialty or expert review.

Clinical and specialty review

Clinical review tests whether the interpretation is medically coherent and whether terminology accurately reflects the evidence. Specialty review is required when a conclusion depends on knowledge outside the analyst's competence. The reason for referral, materials supplied, response received, and effect on the analysis should be documented.

Quality review and release

Quality review confirms scope, source support, internal consistency, terminology, conclusion strength, confidentiality, and formatting. Final release should also confirm the correct matter, recipient, document version, and delivery channel. These controls are operational, but they protect substantive integrity. A sound report sent to the wrong recipient is still a failed report.

Correction and learning

No discipline becomes credible by pretending errors will never occur. Corrections should be documented, communicated, and incorporated into training or process improvement when appropriate. Recurring errors may reveal a weakness in the method, the workflow, or the available education. Governance turns those findings into improvement rather than concealment.

Version control

The working record set should be locked or clearly versioned before substantive review. Additional records must be logged, deduplicated, and connected to the matter. The final report should identify the record universe on which it relied. When new evidence changes a conclusion, the updated report should preserve the relationship to the earlier version so the reader can see what changed and why.

Version control is especially important when several professionals work on the same matter. A reviewer cannot test a conclusion reliably if each participant is using a different chronology, imaging set, or policy version. One governed source of truth reduces avoidable disagreement and prevents stale analysis from reappearing later in the case.

Separation of analytical and delivery controls

Substantive approval and delivery confirmation answer different questions. Substantive review asks whether the report is clinically coherent, traceable, within scope, and appropriately qualified. Delivery confirmation asks whether the approved report is being sent to the correct recipient for the correct matter through the correct secure channel. Both are required. Combining them into one informal final check makes each easier to overlook.

Competency and authorization

Training should teach the method, but completion of training does not eliminate the need for demonstrated competency. Reviewers should be assessed on source handling, clinical reasoning, recognition of limits, written explanation, and application to a complete matter. Authorization to use a proprietary model should also define scope, renewal, quality expectations, and consequences for misrepresentation. These controls protect the meaning of the designation and the professionals who rely on it.

Auditability

An auditable matter allows the organization to reconstruct who received the records, what version was reviewed, what questions were referred, which changes were made, who approved the final report, and how it was delivered. Auditability does not require exposing internal deliberation to every reader. It requires the organization to maintain a defensible record of its own process.

Governing a Discipline in Daily Practice

Governance becomes meaningful when it controls ordinary work. Written standards are not enough if analysts cannot identify which version applies, reviewers do not know what they are approving, or exceptions are resolved informally without a traceable decision.

Authorization and assignment

The organization should define who may perform each level of work and what supervision is required. Assignment should consider the decision question, clinical complexity, record volume, jurisdiction, specialty issues, and deadline. Experience in one setting does not establish competence in every specialty or matter type.

Matter opening

At opening, the organization confirms conflicts, engagement scope, confidentiality controls, authorized recipients, record-transfer method, deadline, and expected output. The initial decision question should be recorded in language specific enough to guide the review. Later scope changes should be documented rather than absorbed silently.

Record control

The record universe should be identifiable at every material stage. New productions are logged and deduplicated. Superseded working sets remain distinguishable. Analyst-created chronologies and summaries should not be mixed with source evidence. When a conclusion is revised after new material arrives, the relationship between versions should be visible.

Analytical supervision

Supervision should test reasoning, not merely appearance. The reviewer asks whether the correct question was answered, all seven pillars were considered, material facts are traceable, alternative explanations were tested, professional boundaries were respected, and the strength of the wording matches the evidence. Review should become more rigorous as the consequence of the decision increases.

Specialty escalation

Referral criteria should be clear enough that analysts do not wait until final drafting to disclose that an essential question exceeds their competence. The referral records the question, information supplied, professional consulted, response, and effect on the work. A limited consultation should not be represented as a comprehensive opinion.

Corrections and adverse quality findings

Errors should be classified by their effect. A typographical correction differs from a source error, reasoning error, confidentiality event, wrong-recipient delivery, or conclusion-changing omission. The response should match the risk and include communication to affected recipients where required. Recurring findings should change education or workflow.

Measures that do not distort judgment

Quality should not be measured by how often the analysis supports the client, how many issues are found, or how long the report becomes. Better measures include source-traceability rate, timely identification of material gaps, appropriate escalation, correction frequency, delivery accuracy, review findings, and whether the work supported the stated decision.

Independence within a client relationship

The analyst serves the engagement by remaining candid. Pressure may be subtle: a request to strengthen a phrase, omit an inconvenient fact, or characterize uncertainty as absence. Governance should give the analyst a clear route to preserve the evidence and escalate concerns. Commercial importance cannot change what the record supports.

Limits Validation and the Duty to Remain Correctable

Clinical Intelligence is designed to improve understanding, not to promise certainty. Its credibility depends on stating where the method ends, how its application can fail, and what evidence would require a conclusion to change.

The record may never become complete

Some evidence no longer exists, was never created, cannot be authenticated, or remains outside the available process. The analyst must not replace it with a confident narrative. The report should identify the missing source, explain its possible significance, state what can still be concluded, and describe the remaining uncertainty.

Retrospective reconstruction has limits

Even a careful timeline cannot reproduce the full environment in which care occurred. Tone, workload, interruptions, competing patients, informal communication, evolving concern, and tacit clinical judgment may not be preserved. The method can reconstruct the available evidence and identify reasonable inferences. It cannot claim access to experience that the evidence did not capture.

Professional scope remains controlling

A disciplined model does not enlarge the user's license, education, or authority. Analysts must work within competence and refer questions that require specialty interpretation. Attorneys control legal judgment. Retained experts control their opinions. Treating professionals control care. Clear boundaries are not restrictions on Clinical Intelligence; they are part of its reliability.

Jurisdiction and purpose affect use

Legal standards, evidentiary rules, discovery obligations, privilege, admissibility, and expert requirements vary. A Clinical Intelligence finding should not be represented as a legal conclusion. Counsel determines how the analysis may be used in the relevant jurisdiction and matter.

Reproducibility does not require identical conclusions

Complex evidence can support more than one responsible interpretation. The method is reproducible when qualified reviewers can identify the same record universe, apply the same pillars, see the sources and assumptions, understand the treatment of contrary evidence, and locate the point at which interpretations diverge. Forced agreement would conceal judgment rather than improve it.

Validation occurs at several levels

Process validation asks whether the required controls were followed. Source validation asks whether material facts are traceable. Clinical validation asks whether the interpretation is coherent and within competence. Specialty validation tests questions requiring additional expertise. Outcome validation asks whether the work supported the decision it was intended to inform without overstating what the evidence could prove.

The discipline should also examine its own performance over time. Corrections, recurring quality findings, expert disagreement, client feedback, and changes produced by additional evidence can reveal where education or workflow must improve. These measures should not be used to reward conclusions favorable to a client. They should assess the integrity and usefulness of the process.

The model must remain open to challenge

The Lexcura Clinical Intelligence Model™ should be tested against difficult matters, competing professional perspectives, and new forms of evidence. A proprietary model can still be intellectually transparent. Its reasoning, limits, and quality expectations must be clear enough to examine. Protection of intellectual property should not become protection from scrutiny.

Education is not authorization

Reading this book may improve a professional's understanding of the discipline. It does not confer certification, licensure, expert status, commercial-use rights, or authority to teach, reproduce, or represent the model as an authorized system. Competency, certification, and licensing are separate matters governed through their own requirements.

The duty to correct

When new evidence changes a conclusion, the responsible response is correction. The updated work should identify what changed, why it mattered, and how the conclusion was affected. Professional credibility is not protected by defending an earlier statement after its foundation has changed. It is protected by making the correction traceable.

CHAPTER 18

Technology and Human Judgment

Technology can locate, sort, compare, and display information at a speed no individual reviewer can match. It can assist with document inventory, duplicate detection, date extraction, laboratory trending, terminology normalization, and identification of possible gaps. Used well, those functions give the analyst more time to examine relationships and test meaning.

Technology also creates risk. Extraction can detach a statement from its author or context. Automated chronology can confuse order time with administration time. A summary can repeat an inaccurate copied statement without recognizing that every occurrence came from the same source. Generative systems may produce fluent explanations that are unsupported by the record. Confidence in the wording must never be mistaken for confidence in the evidence.

The method therefore treats technology as an assistive layer. The human reviewer remains responsible for source verification, clinical interpretation, alternative-explanation testing, professional boundaries, and the final conclusion. Protected health information must be handled within approved systems and access controls. The organization should know what data entered the system, what output was produced, who reviewed it, and which version supported the final report.

The most useful question is not whether technology was used. It is whether the resulting work can be traced, tested, corrected, and defended. A tool that saves time but obscures reasoning weakens the discipline. A tool that makes evidence easier to verify can strengthen it.

Appropriate uses

Technology is well suited to mechanical tasks that can be checked against a source. It can inventory files, detect duplicate pages, extract dates, compare medication lists, flag missing intervals, and create preliminary laboratory trends. It can also help reviewers locate every occurrence of a term or identify records that require closer inspection.

These functions are valuable because they reduce the time spent searching without deciding what the evidence means.

Uses that require caution

Clinical interpretation, standard-of-care evaluation, and causation analysis require context that may not be present in the extracted data. A system may identify hypotension without understanding whether it was transient, expected, treated, or material to the outcome. It may summarize an imaging report without recognizing that later review disputed the original interpretation. It may assign importance to the frequency of a phrase even when every occurrence was copied forward from one note.

The reviewer should treat generated summaries as working material until each material point has been verified. A citation to the source page is useful only if the cited passage actually supports the statement being made.

Data protection and vendor governance

Organizations should know where protected information is processed, who can access it, how long it is retained, whether it is used to train another system, and what happens when the engagement ends. Technology vendors should not be selected solely on the quality of a demonstration. Security, contractual controls, audit capability, incident response, and the ability to retrieve or delete data are part of the professional decision.

Human accountability

The final report must belong to an accountable professional, not to a tool. The reviewer signs or approves the work because the reviewer has examined the material conclusion, tested it against the record, and accepted responsibility for its wording. Technology can extend professional capacity. It cannot assume professional responsibility.

A Controlled Role for Technology

Technology can make complex evidence easier to handle, but its use should be matched to the risk of the task. Inventory, duplicate detection, date extraction, optical character recognition, search, and preliminary trending can reduce mechanical effort. Those functions remain subject to verification because a missed page, incorrect date, or merged patient identity can distort everything that follows.

Automated chronology deserves particular caution. Systems may select note-entry time when event time is required, treat a copied history as a new event, or separate an order from the administration that gives it meaning. The output is a draft analytical aid until a reviewer connects each material event to its source and chooses the correct time.

Generative systems can produce coherent summaries that exceed the evidence. They may fill gaps, merge similar events, present inference as fact, or invent a source reference. Fluency is not reliability. Any generated material used in professional work must be tested against the record, and the accountable reviewer must approve the final wording.

Protected information requires approved systems, contractual controls, access limits, retention rules, incident response, and a clear understanding of whether data are used for another purpose. Convenience does not override confidentiality. The organization should know what entered the tool, what was produced, who reviewed it, and whether the material was retained.

Verification by consequence

Not every extracted item carries the same risk. A misspelled provider name may be corrected during ordinary review. A medication time, imaging finding, exposure date, or statement used in a causal conclusion requires direct source verification. The greater the consequence of the fact, the stronger the verification control should be.

The reviewer should also test negative findings. A system that reports no occurrence of a term may have failed because of image quality, handwriting, abbreviation, access limits, or document segmentation. Absence from a search result is not proof of absence from the record.

Audit trail and reproducibility

When technology materially contributes to the work, the matter file should identify the source set, tool or process used, output retained, verification performed, reviewer, and final disposition. This does not require preserving every experimental query. It requires enough information to understand how a material result entered the analysis and who accepted responsibility for it.

Vendor and change control

Technology should be assessed before use with protected or consequential information. Security, data location, retention, access, subcontractors, training use, export capability, deletion, and incident response belong in the decision. A tool may also change after selection. Model, feature, or extraction updates can alter output, which means organizations need change control rather than assuming yesterday's validation still applies.

Explainability at the point of decision

Counsel does not need a technical account of every software function. Counsel does need to see the evidence and reasoning supporting the conclusion. If the professional cannot explain why a system surfaced a pattern or cannot verify it against the record, that result should not carry a consequential decision.

The final decision remains human. Technology may identify a pattern, but a professional determines whether the pattern is clinically meaningful, whether an alternative explains it, whether the question exceeds scope, and how uncertainty should be communicated. The responsible person cannot transfer accountability to software.

Technology is useful when it makes the work more traceable, consistent, and reviewable. It weakens the discipline when it makes the reasoning faster but less visible.

PART IV

WORKED MATTERS

Applying the complete method from allegation to attorney decision

CHAPTER 19

Delayed Recognition of Sepsis

The following matter is an educational composite. It does not describe an actual patient and contains no identifying information. Its purpose is to show how the seven pillars change the analysis when the initial allegation is plausible but incomplete.

The intake account

A sixty-eight-year-old patient underwent elective abdominal surgery. The intake summary alleged that nurses failed to recognize sepsis during the first postoperative night, that antibiotics were delayed, and that the delay caused respiratory failure, kidney injury, and a prolonged intensive-care admission. The claimant reported having been healthy before surgery. The initial record set contained the operative report, several progress notes, selected nursing notes, laboratory results, and the discharge summary.

The allegation appeared straightforward. Temperature and heart rate increased overnight. Blood pressure later fell. Broad-spectrum antibiotics were started after transfer to intensive care. The patient required vasopressor and respiratory support. If review had begun with the allegation and the selected chronology alone, the file might have been described as a missed-deterioration case.

Pillar 1 Record Integrity

The first task was to determine whether the supplied records could support that conclusion. The operative report referred to an intraoperative anesthetic event that was not explained in the selected notes. The medication record showed two antibiotic administrations that did not appear in the narrative timeline. Laboratory timestamps reflected both collection time and result time, but the intake chronology used only the result time. A nursing note referenced repeated calls to the covering service, yet the communication log was absent. The record set also lacked the preoperative anesthesia assessment, post-anesthesia recovery record, complete intake-and-output data, imaging reports from the first postoperative day, and the electronic audit trail.

The integrity finding did not establish that care was appropriate or inappropriate. It established that the file was not ready for a causation conclusion. The next action was targeted rather than indiscriminate: request the missing perioperative record, full medication administration record, communication log, imaging, and the prior three months of relevant records.

Pillar 2 Baseline Profiling

The additional records changed the description of the patient. The preoperative history documented chronic kidney disease, diabetes, obesity, obstructive sleep apnea, limited mobility, and a recent admission for heart failure. Baseline creatinine was already elevated. Pulmonary function was reduced, and the anesthesia assessment described increased postoperative respiratory risk. The patient was stable enough for surgery, but was not clinically equivalent to a person without significant comorbidity.

This did not make the postoperative injury inevitable. It changed the counterfactual question. The analysis could no longer compare the outcome with an assumed healthy baseline. It had to distinguish new injury from pre-existing impairment and consider whether the baseline reduced the patient's ability to tolerate infection, hypotension, fluid shifts, and respiratory stress.

Pillar 3 Imaging Analysis

The first chest image was described in a brief note as showing postoperative change. The formal report identified low lung volumes and bibasilar atelectatic opacity without focal consolidation. A later image showed increasing bilateral opacity and vascular congestion. Abdominal imaging did not identify an obvious anastomotic leak at that time. The written record used infection, aspiration, atelectasis, and fluid overload at different points without clearly separating them.

Imaging did not prove the cause of deterioration, but it narrowed the responsible conclusions. It supported evolving respiratory compromise and raised more than one plausible mechanism. A specialty review was required before attributing respiratory failure entirely to sepsis.

Pillar 4 Timeline Reconstruction

The timeline was rebuilt using observation time rather than note-entry time. At 18:20, the patient became increasingly tachycardic after an episode of vomiting. Oxygen requirement rose gradually. At 20:05, the nurse documented reduced urine output and contacted the covering service. A fluid bolus was ordered. At 21:10, the patient remained tachycardic but blood pressure had improved. The first abnormal lactate was collected at 22:02 and resulted at 22:41. Blood cultures were collected at 22:18. Antibiotics were administered at 22:36, before the lactate result appeared in the chart. At 23:15, respiratory status worsened rapidly. The intensive-care team evaluated the patient at 23:28 and transfer began shortly afterward.

The corrected sequence exposed two errors in the intake account. Antibiotics had not begun only after intensive-care transfer, and the apparent delay created by using result time rather than collection time was inaccurate. The timeline also revealed a question that remained important: whether the response between the first sustained change in oxygen requirement and the later rapid deterioration was sufficiently proactive given the patient's baseline risk.

Pillar 5 Standard of Care Review

The review considered what information was available at each decision point. Early postoperative tachycardia had several plausible explanations. The patient had pain, recent anesthesia, vomiting, fluid shifts, and significant cardiopulmonary risk. The initial response included assessment, communication, laboratory testing, cultures, fluid administration, and antibiotics. Those actions could not be judged using the later diagnosis as though it had already been established.

The material issue was more specific than the original allegation. The record suggested that individual interventions occurred, but it was unclear whether the combination of increasing oxygen need, reduced urine output, persistent tachycardia, and baseline vulnerability should have triggered earlier bedside medical reassessment or a higher level of monitoring. That question required review by a qualified postoperative-care expert. The analyst could define the question and assemble the relevant evidence without deciding the expert opinion.

Pillar 6 Regulatory & Compliance Overlay

The hospital escalation policy required bedside reassessment within a stated period when specified deterioration criteria persisted. The nursing note documented calls, but the record did not clearly establish when the covering clinician attended. The rapid-response policy also required documentation of the criteria considered when activation was deferred. No such entry was located.

Policy variance does not automatically establish negligence or causation. The policy did, however, identify an organizational expectation relevant to communication and escalation. The audit trail and staffing record were therefore requested. They showed that the covering clinician entered orders remotely and was simultaneously responsible for another deteriorating patient. This information placed the individual decisions within the system in which they occurred.

Pillar 7 Causation Mapping

The causal analysis separated three questions. First, what caused the initial deterioration? Infection remained plausible, but aspiration, fluid-related pulmonary compromise, and limited cardiopulmonary reserve also contributed to the presentation. Second, did the response depart from what should reasonably have occurred? That required expert review focused on escalation and reassessment rather than the inaccurate claim that no antibiotics were given. Third, would an earlier escalation probably have changed the outcome? The answer depended on the speed and mechanism of deterioration, the patient's baseline vulnerability, and the degree to which earlier respiratory support or different fluid management could have altered the course.

The resulting map did not force the evidence into one cause. It showed a vulnerable baseline, an acute postoperative trigger, evolving respiratory and circulatory changes, actions that were taken, a possible escalation weakness, and more than one physiological pathway to the final injury. It also identified the evidence needed from critical-care and surgical experts.

The litigation-ready conclusion

The initial allegation was not supported as written. Antibiotics were not delayed until after intensive-care transfer, and the patient did not have a clinically uncomplicated baseline. The file nevertheless contained a potentially supportable issue involving the timing of bedside reassessment and escalation as respiratory needs and oliguria developed. Whether that issue represented a breach and whether earlier escalation would probably have prevented or reduced the injury required independent expert opinion.

For counsel, the value of the analysis was practical. It prevented investment in a demonstrably inaccurate theory, preserved a narrower concern that deserved expert review, identified the specialties required, and defined the records and questions that should be provided. The case became more defensible because the uncertainty was clarified rather than concealed.

CHAPTER 20

Anticoagulation and Intracranial Hemorrhage

This educational composite concerns an older adult who developed an intracranial hemorrhage while receiving anticoagulation. It demonstrates a matter in which the original allegation was partly inaccurate, yet the integrated analysis identified a narrower and more supportable concern.

The intake account and decision question

The patient was seventy-six years old and admitted after several days of weakness, poor intake, and intermittent confusion. The intake account alleged that a nurse administered an anticoagulant despite a physician order to hold it, causing a preventable intracranial hemorrhage. The family recalled being told that the medication should have been stopped. The supplied file contained an emergency department note, selected progress notes, a medication list, laboratory results, a head CT report, and the discharge summary.

Counsel needed to decide whether the medication-administration allegation was factually supported, whether the hemorrhage was plausibly related to anticoagulation, and which expert specialties would be required. The first review could not begin with the assumption that a medication error had occurred. It had to establish what medication was ordered, whether it was administered, what the patient's risk was, and when the neurological change developed.

Pillar 1 Record Integrity

The review first examined the medication evidence. The supplied medication list showed the anticoagulant as active, while a progress note stated that anticoagulation would be held if platelet count declined further. Neither source established an actual hold order or administration. The medication administration record was absent. The pharmacy verification history, order-discontinuation log, nursing handoff, and electronic audit detail were also missing.

The analyst identified another problem. Several laboratory values appeared twice under different interface timestamps. One set reflected specimen collection; the other reflected posting into the hospital record. The intake chronology used the later time, creating the impression that staff administered medication after the abnormal result was known.

The complete medication administration record and audit history showed that the scheduled dose was administered at 08:04. The platelet result was collected at 07:42 but did not become available until 08:31. A conditional plan to hold the medication appeared in a physician note entered at 09:18. The formal discontinuation order was entered at 09:26. There was no order to hold the 08:00 dose before it was given.

This pillar revealed that the allegation of administration in defiance of an existing hold order was not supported. That mattered because the original theory attributed both factual error and causation to a sequence that had not occurred. Record Integrity did not end the inquiry. It corrected the factual foundation and exposed a different question: whether the patient's evolving bleeding risk had been recognized and acted upon soon enough before the morning dose.

Pillar 2 Baseline Profiling

Baseline review extended beyond the recent admission. The patient had atrial fibrillation, a prior ischemic stroke, hypertension, chronic kidney disease, recurrent falls, and fluctuating adherence to anticoagulation. Earlier records documented a prior gastrointestinal bleed and a history of thrombocytopenia during acute illness. The patient also had mild cognitive impairment and required family assistance with medication management.

These facts revealed competing risks. Anticoagulation reduced thromboembolic risk but increased bleeding risk. Renal impairment could affect drug handling depending on the agent and clinical circumstances. Prior stroke and atrial fibrillation made abrupt interruption consequential. Baseline therefore prevented the medication decision from being framed as though continuation was obviously dangerous and withholding was risk-free.

The baseline also showed that intermittent confusion was not entirely new. The relevant change was not the existence of confusion but its character, persistence, and association with new focal findings. The difference mattered when reconstructing when a neurological event became reasonably apparent.

Pillar 3 Imaging Analysis

The initial head CT obtained in the emergency department showed no acute hemorrhage. It documented chronic small-vessel changes and an old infarct. A repeat CT approximately thirty hours later showed a new acute subdural collection with mild mass effect. A later study documented interval expansion before stabilization.

Imaging Analysis examined the documented findings, comparison language, acquisition times, and the clinical reason for each study. It did not attempt an independent radiological interpretation. The studies revealed that no hemorrhage was documented at admission and that the acute finding emerged later in the hospitalization. They also narrowed the period in which the event developed.

The imaging mattered because it prevented the analysis from assuming that the bleed was already present when the patient arrived. It also established an objective change corresponding with the later neurological deterioration. The question of the precise age and mechanism of the hemorrhage required neuroradiology or neurosurgical expertise.

Pillar 4 Timeline Reconstruction

The timeline separated collection, result, administration, observation, communication, and order times. On the first hospital day, platelet count declined but remained above the facility's automatic notification threshold. The patient received the scheduled morning anticoagulant before the updated result was available. During the afternoon, nursing documentation described increased restlessness but no focal deficit. Overnight, the patient attempted to get out of bed twice. A bed alarm was documented, and staff assisted the patient back to bed. No witnessed fall was recorded.

At 05:50 the next morning, the patient was described as difficult to arouse. At 06:07, the nurse contacted the covering clinician. A bedside assessment occurred at 06:24. The anticoagulant was held, urgent imaging was ordered, and transfer to a higher level of care followed the result. The repeat CT was performed at 06:58.

The timeline revealed that the original medication-order allegation was inaccurate. It also showed that the more important period began the previous afternoon, when platelet decline, renal dysfunction, restlessness, and fall risk were all present. The timeline could not establish an unwitnessed head impact. It did establish when the neurological change became clear and how quickly the team responded after that recognition.

Pillar 5 Standard of Care Review

The screening review focused on three decisions: continuation of anticoagulation as bleeding risk evolved, monitoring of a confused patient at risk of falling, and response to the acute neurological change. The morning dose could not fairly be judged as a violation of a hold order that did not yet exist. The later response after the patient became difficult to arouse appeared prompt in the available record.

The unresolved issue was whether the combined pattern before that deterioration required earlier reassessment of anticoagulation and safety precautions. The answer depended on the specific drug, renal function, platelet trend, stroke risk, indication, hospital protocol, and information available to the prescribing clinician. Those questions required an expert qualified in the relevant medical management. Nursing expertise was also required to evaluate surveillance and fall precautions in the actual unit context.

This pillar mattered because it separated three decisions that the intake account had collapsed into one accusation. One theory was not supported. One response appeared timely. A narrower monitoring and medication-risk question remained appropriate for expert review.

Pillar 6 Regulatory & Compliance Overlay

The hospital anticoagulation policy required review of renal function, platelet trends, active bleeding, and specified medication interactions. Its fall-prevention policy used a risk score and linked higher scores to defined precautions. The analysis verified that both policies were in effect and applicable to the unit.

The record showed completion of the fall-risk assessment, bed-alarm use, and assisted toileting. It was less clear whether the anticoagulation-risk review had been repeated after the renal and platelet changes. Pharmacy documentation showed verification of the original regimen but did not show a later intervention before the morning dose.

The overlay did not establish that a policy variance caused the hemorrhage. It identified an organizational control designed to bring changing laboratory and medication risk together. That mattered because the clinical question was not limited to one administration event. It included whether the system reliably prompted reassessment as the patient's risk changed.

Pillar 7 Causation Mapping

The causal map began with verified exposure: the medication had been administered before the hemorrhage was detected. It then incorporated the patient's age, hypertension, renal impairment, platelet decline, prior bleeding, fall risk, and competing need for stroke prevention. Possible pathways included spontaneous anticoagulant-associated bleeding, bleeding after an unwitnessed head impact, and a multifactorial event in a patient with increased vulnerability.

Temporal association supported further inquiry but did not determine the mechanism. The analysis could not establish that omission of the morning dose would probably have prevented the hemorrhage. The event may already have been developing, and the medication's effect did not begin and end with a single dose. The relevant counterfactual required pharmacological and clinical expertise: whether earlier reassessment or interruption, in light of the evolving risk, would probably have changed the occurrence or severity of the bleed without creating an unacceptable thromboembolic risk.

Supported outcome and clinical truth

The allegation that a nurse ignored an existing hold order was not supported. The chronology showed that the dose preceded both the result's availability and the formal discontinuation order. The record did, however, support a narrower question about whether changing renal function, platelet count, confusion, and fall risk should have triggered earlier multidisciplinary reassessment of anticoagulation.

The clinical truth was more complex than a single medication error. The patient carried serious risks on both sides of the decision. The hemorrhage occurred after verified anticoagulant exposure, but its precise mechanism and preventability were not established by temporal sequence alone. Counsel was given a corrected theory, the relevant specialty questions, and a clear account of what the evidence could not yet prove.

CHAPTER 21

Long Term Care Deterioration and Pressure Injury

This educational composite concerns a long-term-care resident transferred to hospital with sepsis and an advanced pressure injury. It demonstrates a matter in which clinical deterioration, documentation weakness, staffing, nutrition, mobility, and organizational response had to be examined together.

The intake account and decision question

The resident was an eighty-three-year-old woman with dementia who had lived in the facility for eighteen months. The intake account alleged that the facility allowed a sacral pressure injury to progress without treatment and failed to recognize infection until the resident became hypotensive. Photographs taken after hospital transfer showed extensive tissue damage. The family reported that the resident had been walking with assistance several weeks earlier and believed the wound developed because she was left in bed.

Counsel needed to determine whether the available evidence supported a preventable-injury theory, when the deterioration became recognizable, what role baseline decline played, and whether the matter required nursing, wound-care, medical, nutritional, or administrative expertise.

Pillar 1 Record Integrity

The supplied chart contained weekly skin assessments, selected treatment records, monthly summaries, and the hospital transfer packet. Several expected sources were missing: daily treatment administration records, certified nursing assistant flow sheets, repositioning documentation, dietary intake records, wound photographs referenced by the wound consultant, staffing assignments, and records from a recent hospital admission.

The weekly skin assessments created an apparent progression from intact skin to a small Stage 2 injury and then to an unstageable wound. Closer review showed that some entries had been completed after the stated assessment date. Measurements alternated between centimeters and an unlabeled format. The location was described inconsistently as sacral, coccygeal, and right buttock. A monthly summary copied the same wound dimensions across three weeks despite treatment notes referring to change.

The complete treatment records and photographs established that a wound had been identified earlier than the intake chronology suggested. They also revealed gaps in daily documentation and inconsistent measurement technique. Record Integrity therefore showed both that the injury was not entirely undocumented and that the available facility record could not be treated as a reliable continuous account of progression.

This mattered because the issue was not simply whether a wound appeared in the chart. Counsel needed to know whether care, response, and change could be reconstructed with enough confidence to evaluate preventability.

Pillar 2 Baseline Profiling

The resident's baseline had changed substantially during the three months before transfer. She had advanced dementia, diabetes, peripheral vascular disease, chronic anemia, urinary incontinence, and a history of weight loss. After pneumonia and hospitalization six weeks earlier, she returned with reduced mobility, increased assistance needs, poor appetite, and new dependence for transfers. Physical therapy notes documented limited participation and progressive fatigue.

The family account that she had previously walked with assistance was accurate but incomplete. That function described an earlier baseline, not the condition in the weeks immediately preceding the wound. The relevant baseline included a recent decline in mobility, nutrition, cognition, and physiological reserve.

Baseline Profiling revealed high vulnerability to skin breakdown and infection. It did not make the pressure injury inevitable. It identified the level of prevention, surveillance, nutrition, and response that required examination. It also prevented damages analysis from attributing every loss of function to the wound and infection when significant decline preceded them.

Pillar 3 Imaging Analysis

Imaging was not the primary evidence of early skin deterioration, but it became material after hospital transfer. Pelvic imaging documented soft-tissue abnormality without a definitive bony finding on the first study. A later magnetic resonance report described findings concerning for osteomyelitis. The studies were performed at different points and answered different clinical questions.

The analysis correlated the reports with wound depth, inflammatory markers, surgical findings, and treatment. It did not convert the first study into proof that deeper infection was absent or the later study into proof of when bone involvement began. That timing required specialty interpretation.

Imaging Analysis revealed that the injury's later severity was objectively supported while the onset and duration of deeper infection remained uncertain. This mattered to both causation and damages. It also defined the question for radiology, infectious-disease, and wound-care experts without asking the analyst to interpret the images independently.

Pillar 4 Timeline Reconstruction

The timeline was built around changes in mobility, intake, skin condition, vital signs, mental status, laboratory testing, treatment, and communication. After readmission to the facility, the resident spent more time in bed and began refusing meals. A reddened area was documented during the second week. Barrier treatment and pressure relief were initiated. Over the following ten days, entries described increasing skin breakdown, but measurements were inconsistent and two treatment days lacked administration confirmation.

During the fourth week, the resident became less interactive and consumed less fluid. A temperature elevation was documented one evening, followed by a lower reading after acetaminophen. The on-call service was notified of poor intake and lethargy the next morning. Laboratory testing was ordered but the mobile service did not collect the specimen until the following day. Before results were reported, the resident became hypotensive and was transferred.

The chronology identified two related but distinct turning points. The first was the change from redness to open skin injury in a resident whose mobility and nutrition had deteriorated. The second was the systemic change marked by lethargy, poor intake, temperature variation, and delayed laboratory collection. Treating the entire month as one undifferentiated failure would obscure the different decisions and professionals involved.

Pillar 5 Standard of Care Review

The screening analysis examined risk assessment, repositioning, support surfaces, incontinence management, nutrition, wound measurement, treatment response, medical notification, and escalation. The record showed that several preventive measures had been ordered. The central question was whether they were implemented consistently and adjusted as the resident's condition changed.

The wound documentation supported concern about measurement quality and response to progression. The systemic deterioration raised a separate question about recognition and transfer. A single transient temperature might reasonably be observed in some circumstances. In this resident, the combination of poor intake, lethargy, known wound, diabetes, and declining reserve could carry different significance.

Nursing and wound-care experts were required to evaluate prevention and treatment. A physician qualified in geriatric or long-term-care medicine was required to assess medical response and whether earlier evaluation would probably have changed the course. The analyst could identify the decision points and evidence without converting the screening review into those expert opinions.

Pillar 6 Regulatory & Compliance Overlay

Long-term care is deeply affected by facility systems. The analysis examined the applicable care plan, pressure-injury prevention policy, change-in-condition protocol, wound-consultation process, dietary escalation procedure, staffing assignments, and quality-assurance review. It also identified federal and state requirements for assessment, care planning, notification, and provision of necessary care, leaving their legal application to counsel.

The care plan still described the resident as requiring one-person assistance after therapy records documented a two-person transfer. The repositioning plan did not clearly change when she became largely bedbound. Weekend staffing records showed use of agency personnel unfamiliar with the resident, and treatment documentation gaps clustered during that period. The mobile laboratory delay exposed a further system dependency: ordering a test did not ensure timely collection or review.

These facts revealed that individual actions occurred within a care system that had not fully adapted to the resident's changed baseline. The overlay mattered because the case could not be understood solely by asking whether one nurse documented a turn or one clinician returned a call.

Pillar 7 Causation Mapping

The causal map included immobility, poor nutrition, diabetes, vascular disease, incontinence, tissue pressure, treatment consistency, wound progression, possible deeper infection, delayed systemic recognition, and limited reserve. The pressure injury was multifactorial. Baseline vulnerability increased risk, but it did not answer whether appropriate prevention and timely response could have reduced severity.

The map separated formation, progression, infection, and final decline. Evidence supporting preventable progression included the changing mobility baseline, inconsistent measurement, treatment gaps, and delayed plan revision. Evidence limiting certainty included incomplete daily records, serious comorbidity, family refusal of some interventions, and uncertainty about when deeper infection developed.

The counterfactual required careful framing. The question was not whether perfect care would have guaranteed intact skin and recovery. It was whether consistent prevention, earlier recognition of progression, and more timely medical escalation would probably have reduced the depth of injury, infection burden, or severity of systemic deterioration.

Supported outcome and clinical truth

The matter supported further expert investigation. The evidence did not justify the simple claim that the resident received no preventive care or that the wound alone caused every later loss. It did support concern that the care plan, documentation, treatment consistency, and escalation process did not reliably adapt to a materially changed baseline.

The clinical truth was that severe vulnerability and system performance interacted. The resident was at high risk, but risk did not make the outcome irrelevant or unavoidable. The strongest analysis distinguished the formation of the wound, its progression, the development of infection, and the timing of systemic decline. That structure gave counsel specific expert questions rather than one broad allegation of neglect.

CHAPTER 22

Contrast Exposure and Acute Kidney Injury

This educational composite concerns an allegation that radiographic contrast caused acute kidney injury after an emergency evaluation. It demonstrates a defense-oriented matter in which verified exposure was present, the temporal sequence initially appeared persuasive, and the complete clinical analysis substantially weakened a single-cause theory.

The intake account and decision question

The patient was a sixty-two-year-old man who underwent contrast-enhanced computed tomography in the emergency department and later required temporary dialysis. The intake account asserted that contrast was administered despite known kidney disease and that the exposure caused renal failure. The supplied materials included the imaging report, several laboratory results, an emergency note, and a nephrology consultation written after the injury was established.

Counsel needed to determine whether the exposure and risk were accurately described, whether kidney injury began after the study, what alternative pathways were present, and whether expert investment was warranted. The fact that renal failure followed contrast administration made the allegation plausible. It did not make it complete.

Pillar 1 Record Integrity

The initial file omitted the full emergency services record, medication administration record, fluid balance, intensive-care flow sheets, contrast administration detail, prior nephrology records, and several hours of laboratory data. The imaging report confirmed that contrast was used but did not state the full administration history or establish the dose shown in the intake summary.

Complete records verified the agent, dose, and administration time. They also showed that the patient received nonsteroidal anti-inflammatory medication before admission, had several days of vomiting and diarrhea, and arrived hypotensive. Blood cultures later grew an organism consistent with systemic infection. Urine output had already declined before the imaging study, although the first creatinine result posted afterward.

Record Integrity revealed that the intake chronology had used result time as though it marked the onset of kidney injury. It also showed that important competing evidence had been excluded from the initial packet. This mattered because the theory depended on contrast being the first significant renal insult.

Pillar 2 Baseline Profiling

Earlier records documented hypertension, diabetes, chronic kidney disease, intermittent proteinuria, and prior episodes of acute kidney injury during illness. Baseline creatinine was not a single stable number. It varied over the preceding year, with partial recovery after each episode. The patient also took medications affecting renal perfusion and reported reduced oral intake before presentation.

Baseline Profiling revealed limited renal reserve and susceptibility to several forms of injury. It also established that dialysis dependence was new and therefore clinically significant. The correct comparison was not between normal kidneys and post-contrast failure. It was between vulnerable kidneys already exposed to volume loss, hypotension, medication effects, and infection, and the condition that followed the full emergency course.

The difference mattered to both causation and damages. Pre-existing disease did not explain away the acute injury, but it materially changed the likelihood and severity of injury from competing insults.

Pillar 3 Imaging Analysis

The contrast-enhanced study was ordered to investigate severe abdominal pain, hypotension, and concern for a time-sensitive vascular or infectious process. The report identified inflammatory findings and no major vascular occlusion. A later ultrasound showed no obstructive cause of renal failure. Imaging therefore contributed to both the exposure question and the exclusion of another pathway.

The analysis verified the documented indication, timing, contrast administration, findings, and subsequent renal imaging. It did not independently judge whether the original study should have been performed. That decision required consideration of the emergency differential, diagnostic alternatives, urgency, renal risk, and information available at the time.

Imaging Analysis revealed that the study was not an incidental test performed without clinical purpose. It was part of an urgent evaluation in a patient already physiologically unstable. This mattered when screening the reasonableness of the decision and when constructing the counterfactual of what might have happened without the study.

Pillar 4 Timeline Reconstruction

The timeline separated symptom onset, arrival, hypotension, fluid administration, urine output, medication exposure, specimen collection, result availability, contrast administration, antimicrobial treatment, and renal progression. The patient reported three days of gastrointestinal loss before arrival. Blood pressure was low during triage and again before imaging. Intravenous fluids began before the scan. The first blood specimen was collected before contrast administration, although its creatinine result became available afterward. Urine output was already reduced.

During the next twelve hours, hypotension recurred, inflammatory markers rose, and antimicrobial therapy was broadened. Creatinine continued to increase over two days. Nephrology described the injury as likely multifactorial, citing volume depletion, sepsis-associated injury, hemodynamic change, medication exposure, baseline disease, and possible contrast contribution.

The timeline revealed that renal injury was clinically underway before the contrast exposure even though the confirming laboratory result appeared later. It also showed that the deterioration did not occur in isolation after an otherwise stable study. This was central to evaluating both mechanism and causation.

Pillar 5 Standard of Care Review

The screening review examined the indication for imaging, recognition of renal risk, available alternatives, hydration, medication management, monitoring, and response to deterioration. The record documented concern about renal function and discussion of the diagnostic need. Fluids were administered, and renal function was monitored. Whether another imaging approach would have provided adequate and timely information required radiology and emergency-medicine expertise.

The analysis also considered the risk of not performing the study. Retrospective review can make avoidance of exposure appear simple once the feared diagnosis is excluded. At the decision point, clinicians were evaluating potentially serious conditions in an unstable patient. The reasonableness of the choice depended on what had to be ruled out, how quickly, and with what alternatives.

The available evidence did not identify a clear screening concern that the study was ordered without appreciation of risk. It did support expert review if counsel wished to test dose, preventive measures, or imaging alternatives. The distinction mattered because a poor outcome alone could not establish an unreasonable diagnostic decision.

Pillar 6 Regulatory & Compliance Overlay

The hospital policy required assessment of renal risk, review of relevant laboratory information when available, documentation of urgent exceptions, and post-procedure monitoring for higher-risk patients. The analyst verified the policy version and its emergency provisions. The record documented risk recognition and the urgent clinical rationale, although one electronic field in the screening form was incomplete.

The incomplete field represented a documentation weakness. It did not prove that risk was ignored, because the emergency note and radiology communication documented the discussion. No evidence showed that a facility process prevented access to laboratory information or delayed treatment after the study.

The overlay therefore revealed a limited compliance issue without a corresponding clinical failure on the available evidence. This mattered because the intake theory treated an incomplete form as proof that no risk assessment occurred.

Pillar 7 Causation Mapping

The causal map began with verified contrast exposure and a biologically plausible contribution to renal injury in a vulnerable patient. It then incorporated kidney disease, prolonged volume loss, hypotension before and after imaging, systemic infection, medication effects, and reduced urine output before exposure. The map did not remove contrast from consideration. It tested whether contrast could reasonably be isolated as the principal cause.

The temporal relationship was less persuasive after event time was corrected. Kidney stress and reduced output preceded the study, and the first abnormal specimen had already been collected. The subsequent course fit several overlapping mechanisms. The nephrology record itself described the injury as multifactorial.

The counterfactual also contained risk. Avoiding contrast might have reduced one potential insult, but it might have delayed or weakened evaluation of a serious emergency condition. Whether non-contrast imaging would have been adequate and whether avoidance would probably have prevented dialysis required independent expert opinion. The existing record did not support certainty on either point.

Supported outcome and clinical truth

The analysis substantially weakened the allegation that contrast alone caused an otherwise unexplained renal failure. Verified exposure and vulnerability justified careful expert consideration, but the patient arrived with renal stress, hypotension, volume loss, infection, medication risk, and reduced output before the scan. The clinical course was more consistent with a multifactorial injury than a clean single-exposure sequence.

The clinical truth was not that contrast played no role. The evidence could not responsibly support that absolute conclusion. It was that the record did not establish contrast as the sole or clearly predominant cause, and it did not establish that avoiding the study would probably have prevented the outcome. Counsel could therefore decide against an overconfident defense claim while still challenging the unsupported simplicity of the opposing theory.

What the Four Matters Demonstrate Together

The four worked matters do not provide outcome formulas. They show how the same disciplined structure produces different decisions because the evidence is different.

In the delayed-recognition matter, the method corrected an inaccurate allegation while preserving a narrower escalation question. In the anticoagulation matter, it separated an unsupported administration accusation from a legitimate need to examine evolving risk and monitoring. In the long-term-care matter, it showed how baseline vulnerability and organizational adaptation had to be evaluated together. In the contrast matter, it weakened a single-cause theory without claiming that the exposure played no role.

The cases also show why every pillar must be considered even when its weight varies. Imaging was central to the hemorrhage and renal-injury matters, supportive in the long-term-care matter, and one part of the deterioration analysis in the first case. Regulatory and organizational evidence carried particular importance in long-term care but remained relevant to medication-risk controls and escalation. Causation could not be tested responsibly in any matter until the record, baseline, objective findings, sequence, decisions, and system context were understood.

Most importantly, the supported outcome was not predetermined. A disciplined method must be capable of strengthening, narrowing, weakening, or leaving unresolved the theory that arrived at intake. If the same conclusion emerges from every case regardless of the evidence, the method is not being applied. The result is being selected.

For counsel, the practical question is what changed. The review may change the records requested, expert specialty, deposition focus, damages theory, settlement posture, or decision to proceed. A useful analysis does not simply produce more information. It changes the quality of the next decision.

PART V

THE ATTORNEY REFERENCE DESK

Practical tools for building and testing the clinical investigation

CHAPTER 23

The Attorney Clinical Intelligence Toolkit

Intake questions

- What is the alleged event, and what evidence currently supports it?
- Who was the patient before the event, including function, comorbidities, and relevant prior treatment?
- What changed, when did it change, and when did that change become clinically recognizable?
- Which records or objective data would ordinarily exist but have not been provided?
- What alternative explanations remain clinically reasonable?
- What decision must counsel make now, and what unresolved fact could change that decision?

Record request framework

Evidence group	Examples	Question answered
Clinical narrative	Progress notes, consultation notes, handoffs, discharge material	What was understood and communicated?
Objective data	Laboratory results, waveforms, imaging, pathology, device data	What was physiologically occurring?
Treatment execution	Orders, administration records, procedure logs, therapy records	What was ordered, performed, delayed, or omitted?
Electronic evidence	Audit trail, access history, metadata, message routing	When was information entered, viewed, changed, or transmitted?
Organizational context	Policies, staffing records, escalation protocols, competency material	What system conditions shaped care?
Patient experience	Prior records, family communications, functional evidence	What existed outside the encounter-focused chart?

Expert referral questions

- What precise specialty judgment is required?
- Which facts have been verified, and which remain disputed or incomplete?
- What competing explanation should the expert specifically test?
- What material should the expert receive, and what should not be summarized for them in advance?
- Could the expert's answer alter intake, discovery, pleading, deposition, settlement, or trial strategy?
- What limits must be preserved if the evidence cannot support a definitive opinion?

Deposition preparation framework

Foundation: Establish what the witness knew, reviewed, observed, and relied upon.

Time: Separate event time, observation time, documentation time, notification time, and action time.

Meaning: Ask what the finding meant in the context of this patient's baseline and clinical course.

Alternatives: Identify reasonable competing explanations and the evidence that supports or weakens each one.

Opportunity: Define when a different action remained available and whether it probably could have changed the outcome.

Limits: Clarify what the witness cannot conclude from the available evidence.

Litigation-Ready Output quality check

- The patient is identifiable as a clinical person, not merely a collection of diagnoses.
- Every material conclusion can be traced to a source.
- Facts, interpretations, and professional opinions are clearly distinguished.
- Conflicts and missing evidence are visible rather than silently resolved.

- The chronology uses the time relevant to the question being answered.
- The standard-of-care discussion reflects what was reasonably knowable at the time.
- Causation addresses competing pathways and does not rely on timing alone.
- The limits of the analysis are stated in language proportionate to the evidence.
- The document answers the attorney's decision question and identifies the next useful action.
- The intended recipient, matter, version, and final document are confirmed before release.

CHAPTER 24

The Responsibility Created by Understanding

The Responsibility Created by Understanding

Clinical Intelligence began for me with a recurring discomfort. I could read a record, recognize the clinical language, and still feel that the patient's experience had not been fully understood. More information did not always resolve that concern. What helped was learning to ask the questions in a disciplined order and to remain honest about the point at which the evidence stopped.

The discipline has now been stated more formally, but its purpose remains practical. Can the records be trusted for the question being asked? Who was the patient before the event? What do the objective findings show? How did the journey unfold? Were the decisions reasonable in the circumstances? What influence did the surrounding system have? What explanation best accounts for the outcome?

Those questions do not belong to one profession. They create a common evidentiary foundation from which clinicians, attorneys, analysts, experts, and healthcare leaders can perform their own responsibilities more effectively. They also make disagreement more useful because the point of difference becomes visible.

Clinical Intelligence will continue to develop. The method should be tested against difficult cases, challenged by qualified professionals, and corrected when experience exposes a weakness. A discipline that cannot tolerate scrutiny is not mature enough to guide consequential decisions.

The final responsibility is simple to state and difficult to practice. Once we understand the patient's reality more clearly, we must allow that understanding to change the decisions that follow.

The discipline will be judged by what happens when the evidence is inconvenient. If the method is used only to strengthen a preferred position, it has failed. If it identifies a missing record before an expert is retained, corrects an inaccurate theory before years are invested, or reveals a supportable issue that routine intake missed, it has done useful work.

My purpose in writing this book is not to close the discussion. It is to state the discipline clearly enough that others can examine it. Clinical Intelligence should grow through careful use, challenge, education, and documented experience. Its future depends on professionals who are willing to ask better questions and remain answerable to the evidence.

A Discipline That Must Earn Its Place

Clinical Intelligence should not be accepted because it has been named. It should earn its place by improving the reliability of the decisions made from complex healthcare evidence. That requires more than persuasive language. It requires a stable method, visible reasoning, professional boundaries, quality controls, and the willingness to change when the evidence changes.

The seven pillars provide the analytical structure. Record Integrity asks whether the evidence can carry the weight placed upon it. Baseline Profiling identifies the patient who actually entered the event. Imaging Analysis contributes objective findings without exceeding the reviewer's qualifications. Timeline Reconstruction restores sequence and turning points. Standard of Care Review frames professional decisions in context. Regulatory & Compliance Overlay makes the surrounding system visible. Causation Mapping tests how the outcome developed. Litigation-Ready Output then gives the decision-maker a clear account of what is supported, what is limited, and what must happen next.

The model does not remove judgment. It makes judgment more accountable. It does not eliminate disagreement. It gives qualified professionals a common evidentiary foundation from which disagreement can be understood. It does not promise a favorable answer. It protects the decision from being built on an answer the evidence cannot support.

For the discipline to mature, its practitioners must remain open to scrutiny. Difficult cases should be examined, errors should be documented, education should respond to recurring weakness, and new evidence should be allowed to alter established assumptions. The method must never become more important than the patient or the truth it was created to pursue.

I began with a question that followed me from clinical practice into medical-legal analysis: have we really understood what happened? This book does not bring that question to an end. It gives us a more disciplined way to keep asking it.

Glossary

Baseline Profiling. The reconstruction of the patient's health, function, risks, treatment, and relevant circumstances before the event under review.

Causation Mapping. The structured examination of the pathways connecting baseline, events, decisions, biological processes, system factors, and outcome.

Clinical Intelligence. The disciplined process of converting fragmented healthcare evidence into a reliable account of the patient's clinical reality for consequential professional decision-making.

Counterfactual. A disciplined examination of what probably would have occurred without the alleged event or with the proposed alternative action.

Delivery control. The final confirmation of the intended recipient, correct matter, approved document, version, and secure delivery channel after substantive review is complete.

Documented fact. A statement directly established by a traceable source.

Event time. The time a clinical event occurred, distinguished from the time it was entered, signed, resulted, or filed.

Imaging Analysis. The review and correlation of diagnostic imaging findings with the clinical record, sequence, and issues under investigation.

Lexcura Clinical Intelligence Model™. Lexcura Summit's governed seven-pillar model for developing Clinical Intelligence.

Litigation-ready output. A report or analytical product that makes the evidence, reasoning, limits, and next questions sufficiently clear to support counsel's decision.

Record Integrity. The assessment of whether the available evidence is sufficiently complete, accurate, consistent, timely, and traceable for the question being asked.

Regulatory & Compliance Overlay. The examination of policies, regulations, organizational expectations, and operational systems relevant to the patient's journey.

Source traceability. The ability to connect a material factual statement or analytical conclusion to the evidence on which it relies.

Standard of Care Review. The contextual examination of professional decisions against what should reasonably have occurred with the information available at the time.

Supported inference. A conclusion that reasonably follows from connected facts but is not directly stated by a single source.

Timeline Reconstruction. The rebuilding of the patient's journey using clinically meaningful event time and sequence rather than relying only on document order.

Turning point. A point in the patient's journey at which the available information, risk, or required response materially changed.

Unresolved question. A material issue that the current evidence cannot responsibly answer.

Selected References

These sources support the broader clinical, evidentiary, patient-safety, expert-evidence, and technology-governance concepts discussed in this book. The doctrine, terminology, seven-pillar structure, and original figures are the intellectual work of Lexcura Summit.

Agency for Healthcare Research and Quality. TeamSTEPPS 3.0. U.S. Department of Health and Human Services.

American College of Radiology. ACR Appropriateness Criteria. Reston, Virginia: American College of Radiology.

American College of Radiology. ACR Manual on Contrast Media. Reston, Virginia: American College of Radiology.

Balogh, Erin P., Bryan T. Miller, and John R. Ball, editors. Improving Diagnosis in Health Care. Washington, DC: National Academies Press, 2015.

Croskerry, Pat. A Universal Model of Diagnostic Reasoning. Academic Medicine 84, no. 8 (2009): 1022-1028.

Federal Judicial Center and National Research Council. Reference Manual on Scientific Evidence. Third edition. Washington, DC: National Academies Press, 2011.

Institute of Medicine. To Err Is Human: Building a Safer Health System. Washington, DC: National Academies Press, 2000.

Institute for Safe Medication Practices. ISMP Guidelines and Medication Safety Resources. Horsham, Pennsylvania: Institute for Safe Medication Practices.

National Institute of Standards and Technology. Artificial Intelligence Risk Management Framework AI RMF 1.0. NIST AI 100-1. Gaithersburg, Maryland, 2023.

Office of the National Coordinator for Health Information Technology. SAFER Guides. U.S. Department of Health and Human Services.

Centers for Medicare & Medicaid Services. State Operations Manual, Appendix PP, Guidance to Surveyors for Long Term Care Facilities.

U.S. Department of Health and Human Services. Health Insurance Portability and Accountability Act Security Rule.

The Joint Commission. Sentinel Event Policy and Procedures. Oakbrook Terrace, Illinois: The Joint Commission.

United States Courts. Federal Rules of Evidence, Rule 702, Testimony by Expert Witnesses, including the 2023 amendment.

World Health Organization. Patient Safety Incident Reporting and Learning Systems. Geneva: World Health Organization, 2020.

Acknowledgments

No discipline develops through one person's experience alone. Clinical Intelligence grew from more than four decades of work in healthcare and from the people who allowed me to see difficult events through perspectives other than my own.

I am especially grateful to the patients and families whose experiences kept bringing me back to the same question: have we understood what actually happened? Their journeys taught me that the medical record matters enormously, but that it does not always contain the whole clinical reality.

I am also grateful to the nurses, physicians, allied health professionals, leaders, attorneys, paralegals, analysts, and experts whose questions sharpened this work. They showed me where disciplines connect, where they speak past one another, and why a shared method of inquiry is needed when the evidence is complex.

Finally, I thank my family and everyone who supported the long process of turning years of observation into a discipline that could be explained, taught, and tested. This book carries my name, but it rests on what many people have taught me. I remain sincerely grateful to each of them.

About the Author

Michelle Carroll is the Founder and CEO of Lexcura Summit and the originator of the Clinical Intelligence discipline.

Her work draws on more than four decades of healthcare experience and the analysis of complex clinical evidence. She developed the Lexcura Clinical Intelligence Model™ to help legal and healthcare professionals move beyond record accumulation toward clear, traceable reasoning that can withstand review.

Through Lexcura Summit, Michelle continues to develop the education, governance, and professional application of Clinical Intelligence in medically complex litigation.

About Lexcura Summit

Lexcura Summit is a medical-legal analysis company focused on helping attorneys understand complex healthcare evidence. Its work integrates record integrity, patient baseline, imaging, chronology, professional decision-making, organizational context, and causation through the Lexcura Clinical Intelligence Model™.

Lexcura Summit is not a law firm and does not provide legal advice. Its purpose is to provide Clinical Intelligence for Better Litigation Decisions.

www.ingramcontent.com/pod-product-compliance
Ingram Content Group UK Ltd.
Pitfield, Milton Keynes, MK11 3LW, UK
UKHW060022051026
15591UKWH00006B/335
* 9 7 9 8 9 9 7 2 2 9 7 1 9 *